GULLY DIRT

GULLY DIRT

On Exposing the Klan, Raising a Hog,
and Escaping the South

a memoir

Robert Coram

Gully Dirt
On Exposing the Klan, Raising a Hog, and Escaping the South

Cover Design by Jason Orr
Author Photo by Jeff Von Hoene

ISBN: 978-0-9983820-0-5

Library of Congress Control Number: 2016960081
Biography & Autobiography : Personal Memoirs

Published by:
Five Bridges Press
Atlanta, GA USA

My son, hear the instruction of

thy father, and forsake not the law

of thy mother.

PROVERBS 1:8

1

A lot of romantic claptrap has been written about the South. I was born in rural Georgia and grew up there during the 1950s, and I never saw the romance. All I ever saw were people who were as mean as uncovered cat shit, people who took pride in being on the losing side of just about everything, people who could quote the Bible one minute and go into a violent rage the next. My hometown of Edison is deep in the southwest part of the state, about twenty miles from Alabama and about fifty from Florida—a place that has always been separate from the rest of the world. This is farming country, and the dirt ... when turned by a plow ... is as red and angry as a gaping wound. Creeks and rivers run red.

This land, this place, this searing furnace, marks its children more indelibly and more visibly than does any other part of America. So I must begin by telling you about the place where I was born and grew up, and then I will tell you how the place affected me.

"Remote" is the first word that comes to mind when I think of southwest Georgia. This was the last part of Georgia to be settled. Elsewhere in the state, people were wearing suits and building cities while Southwest Georgians were still fighting Indians, fighting the red clay, and praying to a hard God. Even today, there are no roads going *to* Edison; they go *through* Edison on the way north to Atlanta or south to Florida. To the people in Edison, this is the natural order of things.

Once this land was sea bottom. But not even the ocean liked this place … and it receded, and now the unrelieved flatness of the land stretches into the haze. Beyond the haze is more red clay and more haze. The land is covered by pine trees and row crops, spavined houses and decrepit barns, broken windmills and old tractors rusting in the sun. Over it all, like the miasmic remnants of a biblical plague, is the feeling that this is the place where, when God finished making the world, He tossed all the leavings.

Even other Georgians consider this place terra incognita, a baffling and backward place where the people are as tough and unyielding as the land. The people born and raised here tend to stay. Those who go out into the world rarely leave a mark. But Edison standards are so low that if someone does leave, all he has to do to be considered a success is to get a job.

Then there is the heat. The blinding white heat of the South is like a great forest fire that sucks everything around it into its killing heart. The people who live here are tempered by the fire. They have their ways. Those who leave may bear the marks of the fire, but they have not been hardened by it. They are not part of those who stay.

I spent my childhood in one of the most remote corners of America. I came of age in the 1950s, America's last age of innocence, idyllic and protected years before the turmoil and anger of the 1960s. I grew up caught between a tough father and a gentle mother, between a man I considered a near devil and a woman I believed to be a saint.

All I ever wanted to do was leave. I knew I was *from* the South; I could not help that. But I was not *of* the South. My earliest thoughts and my oldest dreams were to escape the maelstrom, to move into that big world I sensed was somewhere out there. A man should be proud of his hometown; he should be able to look over his shoulder with a smile. The memories of his beginnings should be fond memories. But I do not smile when I look back. And as for my memories … well, let me tell you my story.

My story began when I was twelve years old and the new Baptist preacher came to town. Although the preacher would soon baptize me, I was not really born again until I was sixteen, the year I killed my daddy.

The preacher was important to my story because not long after he arrived, I experienced sex for the first time, joined the church, and learned that my daddy was the instrument of a vengeful God. The preacher was the ribbon that held together this box of glory and pain.

The preacher's name was Dunagan, and this being a Baptist church in rural Georgia, he was called Brother Dunagan. He was one of those long-faced, sweaty Christians, a heavy man with dark hair, a perpetual five o'clock shadow, and the hooded eyes of one who has harbored many un-Christian thoughts. When he smiled, it was the satisfied smile of a man who believed in his moral superiority, and when he talked, he looked up and paused as if he were reading words written across the sky. The preacher had three daughters, one of whom had a cleft palate. Everyone in town referred to her as "the preacher's harelipped daughter."

By the way, this girl was herself a bit strange. At the drugstore, she would gather her classmates around a table, pull the straw from her Coca-Cola, and demonstrate how far she could push it up into her head. There were times when I would lean back and look at the top of her head wondering what the hell had happened to that straw.

Brother Dunagan had lost three fingers on his right hand, and only the thumb and index finger remained, giving him a claw hand. When he preached, he always waved that claw hand in the air and pounded it on the pulpit. And whenever he met someone new, he would hold up that hand, splay the thumb and forefinger and wiggle them as if to prove they still worked, and say, "See that?

Yep. Lost 'em in a sawmill accident when I was working my way through seminary."

I think the point he was trying to make was that he had once been a workingman, that he had grown up poor and had had to work his way through seminary. But what I got out of his story was that here was a man studying to do God's work, and a ripsaw took off his fingers. What I got was that here was a preacher with a harelipped daughter. If these things happened to a preacher, what was in store for the rest of us?

The first time I met Brother Dunagan and we shook hands, I felt the stubs of his missing fingers press into my palm, and it was all I could do not to shriek and run.

The preacher liked to drop in on different Sunday school classes and have everyone stand in a circle and hold hands while he delivered the closing prayer. I guess this was something he learned in seminary. One Sunday morning I saw him coming and maneuvered to stand on his left side away from his claw hand. He smiled, gathered us in a big circle, looked through the ceiling up into the sky and got his instructions. "Today let's do something different," he said. "Let's cross our arms and hold hands."

His stomach was so big that when he crossed his claw hand over his body, it barely reached his belt buckle. He snugged me up under the shadow of his belly, where I smelled preacher sweat and felt as if I was squeezed under the overhang of a sagging barn. Brother Dunagan took off on the longest prayer in history. With every breath his stomach heaved, and the sharp nubs of his missing fingers bumped across my palm, and puffs of acrid preacher sweat belched from under his arms. Maybe that is why, from the beginning, preachers and religion frightened me.

Brother Dunagan liked to tell jokes about harelipped people. Even if he was a preacher, his humor, as was the case with almost everyone in Edison, was heavy-handed, revolving around the scatological, the coarse, and the crude. Subtlety was not part of the humor equation in Edison.

Brother Dunagan's favorite harelipped joke was about a young couple who decided to marry. "Well, now, both of them were hare-lipped," he would say as he rocked back on his heels and dazzled us with that expansive smile. "One day somebody asked them if they could kiss. 'Yeth, we can kith,'" the preacher would say in a pronounced lisp, tilting his head to one side and twisting his lips in a grotesque contortion. "But we don't get muth thuction." Then he would throw back his head and laugh. Of course, him being the preacher, we would all laugh with him. But his harelipped daughter would always cover her mouth and bow her head.

Brother Dunagan had a preacher Bible. It was big and black and had gold around the edges of the delicate pages. When he came out of his office behind the pulpit, he always carried the Bible in his left hand because it was too big and too heavy to hold in his claw hand. I thought that a preacher should be able to go through life saving souls and tending to the shut-ins and be able to wave the Bible with either hand.

Maybe it was because he was new in town or because he had a claw hand and a harelipped daughter, or maybe it was just the nature of preachers, but Brother Dunagan wanted to change things at the Edison Baptist Church. He had not been in Edison long enough even to learn the names of the deacons when he announced from the pulpit, "I been praying about something. I been praying hard. Now God has told me the new direction I ought to go."

Going in a new direction and doing things differently were not good things in Edison. Any preacher who said that God told him to change things at the Edison Baptist Church had not been praying very hard. And he sure had not listened for an answer.

Brother Dunagan smiled and paused. Preachers do great pauses. He banged his claw hand on the pulpit and said, "I think you oughta be able to come in the church and pray not just on Sunday morning and Wednesday night, but anytime you want. And I think you oughta be able to come into this sanctuary and pray and meditate not just on Sunday morning and Wednesday night, but anytime you want. God is here all the time."

He paused and looked up through the ceiling. "Starting tomorrow, the doors of the church will be open every morning. We're goan have a noonday meditation, and I want you to come in and pray with us, worship with us, have fellowship with us. You don't have to pray out loud. Just come in and listen to the piano playing the old hymns. Pray to God in your own way. Talk to God. Like the old spiritual says, I want you to 'have a little talk with Jesus.'"

My daddy worked for the telephone company, and about the only thing he had in common with the local farmers was that he believed Sunday was for church and weekdays were for working. His job as a telephone lineman took him to three counties, and he had neither the time nor the inclination to spend his lunch hour sitting and praying. He said that farmers weren't going to stop plowing to come to church, and he wasn't coming down off a telephone pole. But mother thought it was a fine idea and said she would go to the noon meetings as often as she could. "Brother Dunagan is a new preacher, and we ought to help him out," she said.

If I am going to tell you about my twelfth year, then early on you need to know some things about my daddy. Most mornings I was awakened by his voice — his angry voice — coming through the closed bedroom door.

I shared the bedroom next to the kitchen with my brothers, George, who was a year younger than I, and Butch, the baby. George and Butch slept in a double bed, and across the room was my single bed. On this particular morning my eyes popped open when daddy thundered, "I'll just be confounded."

I heard him crumple the newspaper as Mother said, "Your breakfast is almost ready."

Daddy was off on a tear about Ralph McGill, publisher of the *Atlanta Constitution*. This happened once or twice a week. I don't know why Daddy continued to read Ralph McGill's column if it upset him so much.

"He's always bellyaching about the South. I wonder where he's from. Why is he always telling us do this, do that?"

"Remember your blood pressure," Mother said.

"He gets up on his high horse, and you would think he is the Almighty."

"Ready for more coffee?"

"He wrote that column about what's going to be happening by the year two thousand. He wrote about jet planes going faster than a thousand miles an hour and about spaceships and people going to the moon. That man's crazy as a striped-ass ape."

He slid his cup across the table for a refill.

Mother was trying to silence Daddy, hoping that he would settle down and be part the family, not the romping, stomping retired Army sergeant that he was. Even when I was twelve, I sensed that my mother could not stand up to him. She tried, God knows she tried, every day she tried, but any man who spent thirty years in the Army and retired as a master sergeant was, by his very nature, the Big Dog who tried to dominate all around him. Life was one big boot camp, and he was in charge of whipping recruits into shape.

As usual Mother's efforts to start the day off quietly did not work. Daddy was wound up.

"And he's always writing about niggers and how we got to get along with them. He makes —."

"I don't think you should say that word around the children."

In Edison the word "nigger" was the only way I ever heard anyone refer to black people. It was a word used by teachers, by businesspeople, by my friends' parents, by people who worked in local stores. It was a word used so casually that I think the user would have been bewildered had anyone corrected him. We did not know that the word was humiliating and demeaning. We only knew our world.

Brother Dunagan said "nig-ras" but was excused because he was the preacher. Once a boy who was about ten years older than I came back to Edison and visited the barbershop. He was wearing sunglasses, an affectation that, in Edison, automatically made him "Mr. Hollywood" and caused a few knowing smirks to be exchanged among the customers. The boy was dressed in a suit and kept saying "Negroes," pulling the word into the conversation deliberately. When he left, there was a long silence, then one of the farmers, staring straight ahead, said, "Nice suit ol' Jim was wearing." A moment later the barber, whom everyone called "Judge," stopped clicking his scissors, turned toward the long church pew filled with farmers, and said, "You can put a silk handkerchief over a pile of cow manure, but it is still cow manure."

This was the culture in which I lived. Nevertheless, the word made my mother uncomfortable.

There was a moment of silence, and I knew that Daddy must have looked up from the paper in surprise. Rarely did Mother directly confront him. Daddy had retired more than ten years earlier, but he still expected Mother to be a good military wife, to agree with him — at least publicly — in all things.

"Niggers is niggers," he insisted, raising his voice as if volume made him right.

"JB, I asked you not to use that word."

He returned to the paper. "Says here two Navy destroyers docked in a place called Saigon and four thousand people demonstrated, waving the flag of some guy named Ho Chi Minh. What the hell kind of name is Ho Chi Minh? He must be a Chinaman. Who the hell does this chink think he is demonstrating against the U.S. Navy?"

"Any *good* news in the paper today?" Mother asked.

"Nope." I heard Daddy shift around and knew by the sound he was wearing his Army boots. I knew his field jacket, with the chevrons of a master sergeant and hash marks denoting thirty years of service, was hanging on the back of his chair. I knew Daddy was wearing old Army khaki pants and a khaki shirt. He beamed when people in Edison called him "Sarge." He liked "Pole Climber," too. Only mother and one or two close friends called him "JB"

"Sweetheart, can I get some more coffee? And where is my breakfast?" he asked.

"It's coming."

I had thought for a moment when Daddy said "nope" that he was about to enter one of his periods of pouting, when he did not talk for two or three days. But when he called Mother "Sweetheart," I sighed with relief.

Mother's name was Augusta, and everyone but Daddy called her Gussie. He called her Sweetheart not just at home, but all the time, no matter where they were or who was around. If he had realized what a tender and loving thing it was, he probably would have stopped.

I got out of bed, slipped on a pair of jeans, and stumbled through the doorway, wiping my eyes, still half-asleep.

Mother, still trying to change the subject, asked, "JB, where you working today?"

He snorted. "Somebody busted the Nelly Hoover curve again, and I have to replace the pole in Miss Nelly's yard."

"Again?"

"Miss Nelly is going to shoot somebody if they don't stop tearing up her yard."

Nelly Hoover lived on a sharp curve outside of town. Boys a few years older than I, boys with far more testosterone than good judgment, were always trying to see who could run the curve the fastest. Occasionally one of them lost control of his car, ripped up Miss Nelly's yard, uprooted her azaleas, and knocked down the telephone pole.

Daddy looked up. "Put on a shirt, young man. You know better than to come to the table without a shirt."

Daddy had the eyes of a man trained to find fault, and he practiced all of his advanced ideas about raising children, on me. I turned back toward the bedroom without speaking.

"I didn't hear you," he said.

"Yes, sir."

When I returned, Mother was pushing a plate of grits and eggs and bacon and biscuits toward Daddy. The grits were steaming, and the warm, comfortable odor of fried food filled the kitchen. Daddy sat at one end of the table, Mother at the other end near the stove. I sat next to Mother, as far down the table from Daddy as I could.

Mother was eighteen when I was born, so that winter she was thirty, and she was beautiful. She had dark hair and dark eyes, and there was a smoldering air about her. Born in Fayetteville, North Carolina, she was descended from raggedy-ass Scottish immigrants who traveled up the Cape Fear River in the 1700s and settled in the sand hills around Fayetteville. Her mother's people were Grahams and her father was a Buie, a branch of Clan Donald. Both sides of her family were born piss-poor and fighting: they were defiant, uneducated, proud, and bristly. She was one of ten children in a family that didn't have two nickels to rub together. They lived in an unpainted house with no electricity and cooked on a wood stove. For a bathroom they used an open field behind the house. When we visited and the wind blew over the shit toward the house, we sat around breathing through open mouths.

Somehow Mother learned to read even before she started the first grade, and in the early grades she often helped the teacher with other children who had difficulty reading. She went barefoot unless it was cold or the school was having some sort of event, in which case she borrowed a pair of shoes from one of her brothers, who then had to go barefoot.

She graduated from high school and went to work in a Fayetteville dime store. She was looking at a bleak life and wondering what piece of local white trash she would eventually marry when one day my daddy peered in the window. He had just been assigned to Fort Bragg after spending seven years in Alaska. He was so very different from the boys she knew. He had already spent more than twenty years in the Army and had wonderful stories to tell about all the places he had visited and the things he had done. As a young man he had been the second person ever to ride a motorcycle up Stone Mountain near Atlanta. Here was a man who could take her away from Fayetteville and show her the world. A year later they married, and the year after that I was born.

I knew vaguely that Daddy was much older than Mother, but I never thought much about it. To me the big difference between my parents and the parents of my friends was that my daddy was not a farmer and my mother was the prettiest mother in the county. The local farm wives were worn from too much work, too much food, and too much sun. I didn't know how old they were, but they all seemed older than dirt. But my mother was flat-out beautiful. When she walked down the street with her unself-conscious slink, the farmers' cold, dull eyes followed every step.

"Can I have some sugar toast?" I asked.

"Please," Daddy growled.

"Please."

Mother put two slices of light bread on the table, slathered them with butter, and sprinkled a tablespoon of sugar on each one. She raised her eyes and looked at me. "That enough?"

"No, ma'am. Some more....please."

She sprinkled another spoonful of sugar on each slice and slid them under the broiler.

I put my left elbow on the table and cupped my face in my left hand.

Daddy looked around the paper and said, "Sit up straight."

"Yes, sir."

"And get your elbows off the table."

"Yes, sir."

He retreated behind the paper. Mother smiled and patted my shoulder.

"Don't forget to feed Pal when you get through with breakfast," Daddy said. "That dog looks like he missed a few meals."

"I been feeding him."

"No excuses."

"Yes, sir."

"You working on your Second Class examination?"

A few years earlier Daddy had formed Boy Scout Troop 82 in Edison and he wanted two of his Scouts to go to the national jamboree in Valley Forge, Pennsylvania, that summer. A boy had to be a Second Class Scout to attend this international gathering. I was a Tenderfoot.

"A little bit."

"Little bit won't do it."

I shrugged.

The paper shifted, and I saw one eye. "You *do* want to go." It was not a question.

I waited as long as I thought was safe and said, "I think so."

He retreated behind the paper. "You getting older."

I looked at Mother. She raised her eyebrows, and almost imperceptibly, her head moved from side to side. She didn't know what this meant.

"Thought about what you wanna do when you grow up?"

"Leave Edison?"

"You smart-mouthing me?"

"No, sir."

"I might need a helper this summer," he said casually. "Somebody to ride in my truck with me every day. But I'd want a helper who was responsible enough to study and get his Second Class ranking and go to the jamboree."

Mother squeezed my shoulder and smiled as she stood up to get my sugar toast from the oven. The heavenly smell of caramelized sugar and steaming butter filled my nostrils, but I ignored it. I sat there staring at Daddy. His truck was a pickup, but rather than a simple bed in the back, it had high sides filled with compartments—mysterious compartments containing tools and parts and equipment. On top of the truck was a pipelike frame on which Daddy sometimes loaded telephone poles. Calhoun County had hundreds of pickup trucks, but Daddy's truck was the most distinctive. When people saw it, they smiled because they knew the telephone man was coming. In addition to installing poles, he installed telephones, and when the phones stopped working, he repaired them. Everyone loved the telephone man.

Daddy needed a helper, someone to go into the truck, retrieve a tool or piece of equipment, and throw it up to him when he was high up on a telephone pole. I would have done anything to ride backcountry roads with my daddy. It was the most exciting way imaginable to spend the summer. I would do anything to be my daddy's helper. I broke into a big smile, nodded vigorously, and said, "Yes, sir."

"Eat your breakfast." He turned back to the paper and stared at the picture of Ralph McGill. "Nobody gives a continental damn what Ralph McGill thinks."

I don't think Daddy realized he was retired. I think he became a Scoutmaster because it allowed him to give orders to people in uniform. I think he saw me as a recruit to be whipped into shape and taught the rules. I know that I considered my life an endless boot camp.

I had been in the Scouts only a few months when Daddy got the idea that two Scouts from his troop would go to the jamboree. The two would be selected after demonstrating their knowledge of Scouting. Night after night Daddy made sure I studied the *Handbook for Boys* and that I worked on the requirements for becoming a Second Class Scout. As soon as he got home from work and got out of the truck, he would point a finger at me and say, "Scout motto?"

"Be prepared."

"Scout oath?"

"OnmyhonorIwilldomybesttodomydutytoGodandmycoun-tryandto..." I would rattle it off so fast, all the words blurred together.

"Scout law?"

"Ascoutistrustworthyloyalhelpfulfriendly..." Machinegun fire.

"Knife sharp?"

I would pat the pocket where I kept my Boy Scout knife. "Like a razor."

That winter and spring I learned how to perform first aid, to dig a one-man latrine in the woods, find my way with a compass, read a map, cook a meal over a campfire, and track someone through the woods. I did a good deed every day, and I learned that if I was wearing my Boy Scout uniform when a parade passed by, I should salute the flag. If I was not in uniform, I was to put my hand over my heart. Daddy's rules about what he called "Old Glory" were sacrosanct, and time after time he said, "People have died for that flag. You will show respect when you see it."

"Yes, sir," I'd reply, not really understanding but knowing that agreeing with him was one way to keep my ass out of trouble.

Four Scouts from Troop 82 became Second Class Scouts. The Edison Lions Club, which was sponsoring the two Scouts' trip to the jamboree, appointed a committee to test the eligible Scouts and pick the best two. The test was in the school cafeteria where the Lions Club met. Daddy had the open Scout handbook on his lap. As he flipped through the pages, he went down the line of boys, asking detailed questions about every phase of Scouting. The committee sat behind him, watching and listening.

Each time a question was directed at me, I fired back the answer before Daddy could complete the question. I quoted long passages from the handbook. I took off on soaring flights of exposition and was absolutely obnoxious on my way to making a perfect score. I was the first pick. Two of the other boys were tied, so they drew straws to see who would go. James Brooks won.

That night as we drove home, Daddy said, "Son, you have a big responsibility. Remember what the handbook says about the Scout badge."

"Yes, sir." I knew he was going to remind me anyway.

"It says the badge can be recalled any time a Scout is deemed unworthy to wear it."

He paused.

"So you make sure you behave yourself up there in Valley Forge, Pennsylvania," he continued. (In Edison we often identified places by both the city and state, or the city and country, as in London, England. We did this even if we were talking about a nearby town that we visited every week. I don't know whether this was to help others understand what we were talking about or a way to keep things straight in our own minds.) "Remember who you are and all your Mother and I have tried to teach you. You going up to Valley Forge, Pennsylvania is like a soldier going overseas. You represent the people of Edison. Don't do anything that will make your leaders want to take away your scout's badge."

"Yes, sir."

I didn't give a rat's ass about the Scouts or the jamboree or the Scout badge. All that mattered to me was that going to the jamboree meant I could ride with my daddy when I returned. I would be his helper. He and I would roam southwest Georgia, and I would help him replace broken insulators and watch him as he repaired telephones. I would cut briars and heavy brush away from telephone poles, help Daddy install new phones, and show him that I was a good son. I would be his helper, and we would become close. And on the days when we were too far away to come home for dinner, we would carry sandwiches in brown paper bags and stop at a country store for two 6-ounce bottles of ice-cold Coca Cola and maybe a Baby Ruth candy bar for dessert. I looked forward to riding with my daddy far more than I did to being one of the first Scouts from Edison to attend the national jamboree.

2

ONE Saturday in May a group of us were playing hide-and-seek on the grounds of the Baptist church. The church was a big, square, brick structure, one of the biggest buildings in Edison, and the spacious corner lot on which it stood was a popular place for children to gather. Parents didn't worry about their children hanging out at the church because nothing bad ever happened there.

Gail, a little blonde eleven-year-old, was in the game. Gail lived only a few houses away from us and was often at our house. Mother said that Gail had "lots of grown-up ideas."

In our version of the game, the person who was "it" covered his eyes and counted out loud while the rest of us scattered like a covey of quail as we looked for places to hide. As Gail and I ran around the corner of the church, I said, "Come on. I know a great place to hide. Nobody will ever find us."

I ran up the back steps of the church, through the door, and across the rear of the sanctuary. I unconsciously slowed down as I turned onto the long, sloping, carpeted aisle toward the pulpit. I jumped the single step to the pulpit, pushed open a door, turned right, and went behind the heavy green velvet curtain that screened the empty baptismal pool from the congregation. Breathless, Gail and I sat in the cool concrete pool, our backs against the wall.

"Nobody will ever think of this place," I whispered in her ear. Because we were playing hide-and-seek and because we were in church, it seemed natural to whisper. Gail tilted her head, and my lips brushed her ear. Her sweet, soapy smell filled my nostrils and rattled what little reason I had. I racked my brain to find something else to say so that I could inhale Gail's sweet girl smell again. "Later on, everybody will want to know where we hid. Don't tell them."

She turned and this time her lips brushed my ear as she murmured, "I won't tell anybody."

I leaned toward her and repeated, "Don't tell anyone."

"I won't."

"Not ever."

"Not ever."

We sat there in the semidarkness, shoulders touching, occasionally looking at each other and whispering, as we imagined how everyone else had been found and no one could figure out where we were hiding. Then Gail put her hand over her mouth and shook with silent laughter.

"What you laughing about?" I whispered.

She leaned toward me. "Nobody will *ever* find us." She stared at me. Our faces were inches apart. My eyes still locked on hers, I wiggled around, reached into my pocket, pulled out my Boy Scout knife, and held it toward her. She cradled it, her fingers touching mine, staring and waiting.

"I'll give you my Boy Scout knife if you'll let me get on top of you," I said.

I've often wondered why that line was never used in a movie.

She took the knife and placed it on the floor. Her eyes never left mine as she lay back on the concrete, unbuttoned her jeans, and calmly pushed them off. She waited, a half-smile on her face, as I took off my jeans.

Moments later I looked down. I had to see what was going on that felt so good. I recoiled in horror. A few drops of bright red blood oozed from her body. If a person can scream silently, I did. "Aaaaaaaggghhhhhh!" I thought she was about to bleed to death. A naked corpse would be found in the baptismal pool, and everyone would remember having seen Gail and me run around the corner. I would be charged with murder. My head was filled with all those Baptist hymns about blood, none of which mentioned blood in a baptismal pool, the most sacrosanct and symbolism-ridden part of the Baptist church. I knew that sitting up there on the spire atop the church was an Old Testament God, an eye-for-an-eye God, a God of wrath and retribution. If God knew when a sparrow fell, there was no way that doing it in the baptismal pool would escape his notice.

I was panic stricken. The walls were closing in, giving me a foretaste of what a jail cell would be like. Gail lay there smiling beatifically, as if she did this every day. I nodded toward the drops of blood and said, "I thought you had done this before."

"Nobody ever asked me."

I had no response for that. Then I heard something, turned my head, and raised a cautionary finger.

Someone was in the sanctuary.

We heard whispers and shuffles as people sauntered down the aisles. At first we thought our friends were searching for us. I looked over my shoulder. If someone opened the curtains concealing the baptismal pool, the first thing they would see was my shiny ass. I pulled on my jeans and motioned for Gail to do the same. She smiled and ignored me, stretching like a cat in the sunshine.

We heard more noise, more moving about, and then someone began playing the piano. I heard more people coming down the aisle, the soft murmur of conversation, and I remembered Brother

Dunagan and his noontime meditations. Mother was sitting out there just a few feet away.

I was frantic. Again I motioned for Gail to pull up her jeans, and again she ignored me. We couldn't leave now. I was terrified, but Gail just lay there, one arm under her head, smiling and looking at me as if I were not too bright. A few feet away, several dozen people were in the pews staring at the green velvet curtain that hid us.

I was stricken with remorse and contrition and silently making promises to God about all the things I would do to rectify my great sin. As I begged for forgiveness, Gail sat up and moved closer. She picked up my Boy Scout knife, placed it in my hand, and with her lips against my ear whispered ten little words that doomed me: "You can have it back if we do it again."

I was only twelve and not yet fully responsible for my actions. God would forgive me for doing it once in the baptismal pool. But twice?

Still, I had to have my Boy Scout knife for the jamboree. Gail folded my hand around the knife and lay back on the concrete.

She seemed to be in good health. If death came, it would not be in the next few minutes. So I slid off my jeans, and there in the baptismal pool, accompanied by the silent prayers and meditations of those in the congregation and by the soft sounds of old Baptist hymns, I discovered what Brother Dunagan meant when he talked about achieving a state of grace.

A half hour later I heard Brother Dunagan's claw hand thumping the lectern as he began a long prayer. The tempo of the music picked up, and I heard people moving up the aisles, filing out of the church. I peeped through a crack in the curtains and watched the last person leave. The piano player folded up her sheet music and said goodbye to Brother Dunagan. A moment later the preacher walked up the aisle and out the side door. I turned to Gail and whispered, "I'll go out the back door. You wait five minutes and go out the front door." Within seconds I was bounding down the front steps.

No one could figure out where Gail and I had hidden. And we never told them.

She and I visited the baptismal pool two or three times a week during May and June. We always met early in the morning or in midafternoon, when there was no one in the sanctuary. When you are twelve years old and live in a small town, the Baptist church is one of the few places where you can screw without fear of being discovered.

Every Sunday when I came upstairs from Sunday School to meet Mother and Daddy and sit through Brother Dunagan's sermon, there was Gail, sitting across the church with her parents, smiling and rolling her eyes toward the baptismal pool. After about five seconds I would reach forward and pick up a Broadman Hymnal from the rack on the back of the pew in front of me. I'd put it on my lap and slowly leaf through it, studying the hymns. The first time I did this, Mother pointed toward me, looked at Daddy, and raised her eyebrows in surprise. "He's learning all the hymns," she whispered.

Daddy nodded and said, "That's because he's been studying the Boy Scout handbook."

Not really. I was using the hymnal to hide an erection.

A lot of sermons seemed directed at me during those two months. Brother Dunagan liked the story about Jesus driving money changers out of the Temple when all they were doing was transacting a little business. I wondered what was in store for me.

Those sermons taught me there was a name for people like me. At twelve I had already become one of those weak and pitiful people who were slaves to the flesh. Brother Dunagan put more loathing in the phrase "slave to the flesh" than most people can summon in a lifetime. He drew out the word "slaaaaaaave." His lips fluttered, and bubbles of saliva glistened at the corners of his mouth. His claw hand grappled with the air and he stared through the ceiling, his eyes glinting with revulsion. And when he said "flesh," it sounded like an ax falling on a chopping block. Then he dropped his gaze and stared around the church. His eyes seemed to be focused on me.

During that May and June, Gail showed me what heaven was like, and Brother Dunagan gave me a foretaste of hell. I was a Baptist, and I knew a day of accounting would come.

Toward the end of June, Gail and I met in the baptismal pool for the last time before I left for the jamboree. Usually we talked very little. We just slid down our jeans, went at it, got dressed, and went our separate ways. But in a day or so I was leaving for my first long trip away from home by myself, and I wanted to talk. "Maybe when I come back from Valley Forge, Pennsylvania … " I began.

Gail looked away and nodded. She did not want to talk.

My eyes were drawn, as they were every time we met in the baptismal pool, to the spot of blood on the floor. No baptizing had been done for months, so the pool remained empty. By now the blood had soaked into the concrete and could never be washed away. The spot was not big enough for anyone to notice, but to me it was a scarlet billboard and a reminder that one day God would have his revenge.

I wanted to go to Valley Forge, but I also wanted to stay home. I knew that one day I would leave Edison, but I was still young, and things were safe and secure and predictable there. Gail was waiting in the Edison Baptist Church baptismal pool. George Washington froze his ass off in Valley Forge.

A few days later James and I, dressed in our Scout uniforms, boarded the train in Albany. On the way to Atlanta the Scouts from around southwest Georgia talked a lot about "the War for Southern Independence" and argued about who had the most ancestors in that war. I must have been the only Scout on the train who did not know whether he had a relative who had given his life for the Glorious Cause. I must have been the only Scout who did not have a Confederate flag in his pack. And I must have been the only Scout who did not let loose with a rebel yell every five minutes.

In Atlanta we joined Scouts from all over Georgia, and some six hundred of us boarded a special train to Philadelphia. The talk about Confederate credentials increased, and soon the reigning philosophy of double-barreled simplicity was, "Yankees don't know squat" and "Yankees are et up with the dumb ass."

The closer we got to Valley Forge, the more frequent were the rebel yells. It sounded as if Johnny Reb was invading Pennsylvania.

The Scouts from Georgia camped together there and a Confederate flag waved from almost every tent. Rebel yells echoed endlessly across the green swales of Valley Forge. I heard a Scoutmaster say that we were meeting in a place that had made America a nation and that here was a group of Scouts emulating the people who had wanted to split America into several nations.

The first night some 47,000 scouts gathered in a valley that formed a natural amphitheater to listen to President Harry Truman speak. During the days that followed we were pretty much on our own. I wandered alone throughout the encampment and all across Valley Forge, meeting Scouts from around the world.

James and I had been assigned to different tents, and I never saw him except in the evening. On the third evening when I came in from my roaming, I asked him where he went every day. "Stick around tomorrow and see for yourself," he said.

After breakfast the next day I walked over to James's tent and threw back the flap. It was like flinging open the door of a bar in the Wild West. The half dozen Scouts inside the tent looked at me as if I were a stranger in town.

"He's okay," James said. He closed the flap, and we were enveloped in soft shadows. Sitting on ground cloths, we formed a circle, our feet on the grass in the center of the tent. After a moment James said, "We wrote a poem."

"Yeah?" I said. "Ain't no merit badge for that."

"Want to hear it?"

I looked around. Apparently the poem was part of whatever was going on here.

"Okay."

James looked at the others, then lifted his hand and began nodding his head. On the count of three, the boys recited the poem together:

> *Pussy is good.*
> *The clap is worse.*
> *So jack your fist*
> *For safety first.*

I nodded as if I understood. But then I asked, "What does it mean?"

"What do you mean, what does it mean?" James said.

The other Scouts smiled.

"You mean to tell me you never beat off?" James said.

"Beat off what?"

The other boys laughed.

"Well, I don't guess you have."

I got the feeling that a lot was going on that I didn't know about. James was a year older than I and knew things I didn't. The other Scouts were older. Whatever it was they were talking about, I wanted to know.

"Tell me how you do it," I said.

"You just take that ol' thing out and beat it."

I thought about that. "Why?"

James stared. Then he looked at the others and shrugged. He was probably wondering why he had invited me into the tent when I was so damn stupid.

I tried again. "With what?"

"What?"

"Beat it with what?"

"Your hand." He looked at the others. "Want us to show you?"

"Yeah."

James stood up, unzipped his Boy Scout pants, and released his erect "thing." That's what we called it: a "thing" or a "rod" or a "dick." I saw nothing unusual in his thing being hard. At twelve or thirteen years old, a boy's thing could become hard if he looked at a passing truck. Or a tree.

James slapped his thing with the back of his hand, grinned, and said, "Harder than Chinese arithmetic."

The other Scouts seemed glad we were getting down to business and simultaneously unzipped their pants and grabbed their dicks.

One boy bent his knees slightly, grabbed his dick, waved it, and said, "I could drive a tent peg with this ol' thing."

"Mine's so hard a cat can't scratch it," said another.

They waited, staring at me.

"You gonna do it?" James asked.

Failure to do something an older boy wanted would, when we returned to Edison, excommunicate me from any group before I even belonged. So I unzipped, grabbed, and waited.

James went into a crouch and began moving his hand rapidly. His eyes went glassy. Like an orchestra that had watched the maestro pick up his baton, the others joined in, faces equally intent.

"You like this?" James asked. His voice was strained, his head was tilted to the side, and his eyes were rolling back in his head.

I nodded and wondered how I got to be twelve years old without knowing about this. I had found the promised land.

I had never had an orgasm in the baptismal pool, maybe because I knew God was looking over my shoulder and I was afraid of a lightning bolt. Now I had discovered the secret of the Sphinx, the riddle of the ages, the ninth wonder of the world, and I knew I was about to go into a catch-up frenzy.

Within seconds we all ejaculated onto the grass, and the cloying smell of semen permeated the air. We stuffed ourselves back into our Boy Scout uniforms.

"So what do you think?" James asked. His voice had returned to normal.

"Better'n getting jobbed in the eye with a sharp stick," I said.

I had a lop-sided grin on my face.

"I liked it."

"That the first time you ever did that?"

I shrugged.

He nodded toward a boy across the tent. "He's got him some of the real stuff before. He says it's better than jacking off."

I shrugged again. Dimly I realized that there was supposed to be a progression here. Masturbation until that blessed day arrived when a boy had sex. I didn't know anyone else my age who had experienced sex. There was a senior who was widely reputed to have had sex, but most of us didn't believe it. And if I told them about Gail, no one would believe me either. Besides, if Daddy found out about it, I could imagine how it would go. "Hey, Sarge, I heard that oldest boy of yours got baptized when there wudn't any water in the pool." Heh, heh, heh.

James pointed at the blob of semen at my feet. "That could have been a president," he said.

"A what?"

"A president of the United States."

"The hell you talking about?"

"My daddy told me if I saved this until I was married and put it inside my wife, I might have a boy who could grow up to be president. My daddy told me that."

26

"Your daddy knows you do this?" I was astonished.

"Nah. He was just telling me a bunch of stuff to keep me from doing it. He told me I'd go blind. He said it would make warts grow on my hand." James grinned. "It don't bother me if we are squirting out presidents." He nodded at his grinning friends. "That's what we call this, squirting presidents."

I looked down. Damn. Twelve years old and I had just altered the future of America.

"Let's do it again," James said. Before I could blink, pants were unzipped, erect rods were in hand, and eyes were beginning to glaze over.

In a moment there would be a blob on the grass that could have been another George Washington, or Thomas Jefferson, or Abraham Lincoln, or even the revered Franklin Delano Roosevelt. The horror of what we were doing overwhelmed me. But not enough to make me stop.

Maybe every other one could be a president. Maybe every third one. Maybe mine would be another Rutherford B. Hayes or Ulysses S. Grant or that Johnson guy from Tennessee, the ones our teachers said were lousy presidents. Maybe I was too young to spill a real president. Maybe all I could manage were congressmen. Or county commissioners.

For the rest of the week, while Scouts from all over the world were walking around Valley Forge and trading patches and collecting souvenirs, I was with James and his band of history-changing fiends. We were having our own jamboree, and for me it was almost as much fun as being with Gail in the baptismal pool, but without the guilt. I believed that business about going blind was just another way for our parents to keep us from having fun. At least I hoped so.

On the last night of the jamboree, the Scouts again gathered in the natural amphitheater, this time to listen to General Dwight David Eisenhower, who was running for president. As his motorcade entered the grounds, he waved from an open car, and 47,000 Scouts stood up and waved and clapped and cheered. Then General Eisenhower gave a speech, and after the speech a Scout official said we were going to have a special treat. The general came back onstage and said, "Let 'er rip," the same words he had used to launch the D-Day invasion, and the biggest display of fireworks I had ever seen exploded overhead for about half an hour.

Daddy saved the newspaper stories about General Eisenhower and showed them to me when I returned home. The papers said that he had spoken about the history of Valley Forge, the momentous events that had taken place there, and how George Washington's greatness had emerged under the cold and bitter winter he had spent there so long ago. Daddy almost choked up when he read the clippings. "I never served under General Eisenhower," he said. "But I know he will make a great president."

All I could think of was how General Eisenhower was one lucky man. His daddy had obviously not gone around squirting presidents when he was a boy.

3

AFTER I regained my strength, I called Gail. But in the past two weeks she had found someone else. He had a horse, and he and Gail rode together through the pine forests. There was no regret in her voice, no sadness, no nostalgia. She just thought pine straw was better than concrete.

Since Gail and I would not be returning to the baptismal pool, I was no longer a slave to the flesh. This was a chance to repent of my screwing and probably my masturbation. There might be something to all the shadowy talk about how harmful masturbation was. Out of fear and desperation more than out of a theological epiphany, I made a deal with God: I would join the church if He would not zap me with a lightning bolt. I would be baptized in the pool where Gail and I had been doing it. The bloodstain was still on the concrete. Once the pool was filled, the blood would be diluted, and when I was baptized, I would be swimming in blood.

While God and I had a deal, it was a deal *I* had worked out — a one-sided deal with no comment from the other side. What if God still had to have his vengeance? I was only twelve, but that was old enough to know that when blood and fornication and church marinated for months and were then set to fermenting with the bitter yeast of guilt, only hell could bubble up.

Nevertheless, the next Sunday morning, after Brother Dunagan preached his sermon and stepped off the pulpit and faced the congregation for the altar call, as the choir softly began singing "I Need Thee Every Hour," I stepped out of the pew. Showing firmness and resolve, I strode down the aisle toward a beaming Brother Dunagan. He and I shook hands, and I turned to face the congregation who were smiling upon me as they continued singing.

During the last verse, Brother Dunagan lifted his face and moved his lips in a silent prayer. I guess he was praying for one more miserable little sinner to march down the aisle. He must have had a quota. Standing in front of the congregation with every eye on me made me nervous, so I kept my eyes on Mother. She smiled and her eyes were teary. Daddy was trying to smile but didn't know how. He attributed my joining the church to the fact that I had heard a speech by General Eisenhower.

The preacher put his claw hand on my shoulder, smiled, and leaned toward me. I thought for a moment he was going to whisper the harelip joke in my ear. Instead he squeezed my shoulder and nodded to reassure me. When the hymn was over, he told the congregation that my parents were proud of me and my classmates were proud and Edison was proud. He said that it was only through the grace of God that a boy so young was led to take this step toward becoming a member of the church and Edison's spiritual community and that I would be baptized in the fall.

In my innocence I thought my deal with God was working, especially after I saw Daddy lean toward Mother and say, "I think he's getting straightened out."

I was too young to understand what joining the church meant, too young to have the theological understanding, much less the conviction, that should accompany such a significant event. For me this was strictly a business deal. I wanted God off my ass.

DADDY liked lemon drops, a hard candy, and always kept a bowlful atop what we called "the chifferrobe" in the front bedroom where he and Mother slept. Sometimes, when he was not around, I ate a couple. Daddy must have been counting them because one day he stalked into the kitchen and said, "Who's been eating my candy?"

Daddy thought he could be able to put out a bowl of lemon drops and leave the house for five years and when he returned, every piece of candy would still be in the bowl. He had a sense of place and order that was unshakeable.

I almost said, "Not me, Papa Bear." The thought made me smile, which was a big mistake, because now Daddy was certain I was the thief.

I did not confess to this major felony because if I did, Daddy would whip my ass. He always called it a "spanking," but in reality it was an old-fashioned ass whipping. I mean, he got down on it and got serious. Sometimes he used his big leather Army garrison belt, sometimes a branch — he called it a switch — from a peach tree in the backyard. When he used the belt, my ass had purple stripes. When he used the switch, he usually hit me on my bare legs until blood ran down them. On the rare occasions when Mother was provoked enough to spank me, she held my left hand with her left hand while she swung a switch with her right hand. I danced like a wild Indian and screamed and yelped, and she usually started laughing and forgot about the spanking. Not Daddy. He didn't hold my hand. He just pointed to a spot on the ground, and I became rooted to that spot. No dancing allowed. No crying allowed. Stand there and take it like a man. It was only when I wandered off into the field of broom sedge (we called it "broom sage") that surrounded our house that I could sit down and sob.

My brother George did not confess to taking the candy because he was not guilty. Mother didn't like lemon drops. My sister,

Susie—who was born between George and Butch—said she didn't do it, and since she was a girl, everything she said was written on stone tablets. And Butch was too young to be a thief.

During my childhood, this was the usual dynamic among the children. I was usually guilty whatever the crime of the moment might be. George was rarely a suspect. And Susie and Butch were remote from it all. They were so much younger than George and me, that we had little interaction with them.

In this instance, Daddy knew the only possible felon was me. It couldn't be George. As a baby, George had been sick for several years—so sick he had almost died. George still had occasional stomach pains that left him curled up in a ball and crying. They were more than a the usual green-apple stomachache. Something was wrong with him. Daddy was very protective of George and made only a token effort to hide the fact George was his favorite son. Daddy shifted his stare to me, the smiling one. "I find out who ate my lemon drops and he's going to get a good spanking. Now get out of here."

The next morning Mother said that she was going shopping in Albany and that George and I were going with her. Trips to Albany usually began early in the morning and ended by early afternoon, but on that day Mother dawdled. It was 4 p.m. when we got home. She turned on the record player and put on one of the big band records she and Daddy liked to play. They normally did this at night in the bedroom, but that afternoon we could hear "Be Happy" and "Tuxedo Junction" all through the house. I wondered if something was wrong, if the music was to get Daddy into a good mood.

Mother went to the kitchen. She had seemed preoccupied all day and kept cutting her eyes at me as if she wanted to tell me something. I followed her and asked "Mother, is everything okay?"

She paused. She did not look at me when she said, "Well, Miss Bobby Lou has been sick for the past few days, and I made a cake for her. I was hoping to take it up there today, but I guess I'll go tomorrow."

Mother was always making cakes or pies and visiting with people who were sick, so I didn't think anything else of it.

George and I went into the living room, and scattered on the mantel were the contents of what appeared to be a box of Chiklets, a candy-covered chewing gum, in plain sight. Daddy never left candy in the living room. Something was wrong. Suddenly the candy on the mantel and Mother's preoccupation came together for me and I was like a feral animal circling a baited trap.

"Hey, George," I said. "Look at that. Want some chewing gum?"

He looked at me in surprise. I was thirteen months older than he and usually demanded the rights of the firstborn, which means I got first crack at everything and he got seconds.

"Go ahead," I said. "Tell me what you think."

"Ah-ite," he said. That's how everyone in Edison pronounced "all right."

He grabbed a handful, chewing, swallowing, and gulping it down as if he was afraid I might change my mind. "This is not chewing gum," he said. "It's candy. What kind of candy is this?"

"Is it good?"

"Yeah, real good."

"Eat some more."

"I will."

He chewed, his cheeks as full as those of a squirrel eating acorns, and looked at me. "You don't want any?"

"Nah, you eat it."

"Ah-ite."

He pointed at the few pieces remaining. "Don't you want these?"

"Nah, we ought to leave some."

About a half hour later Daddy came home. When he walked through the door, his eyes locked on the mantel, and then his parade ground voice bellowed through the house. "Okay, young men. Front and center."

George and I came running. We stood at attention in front of Daddy, eyes straight ahead.

He looked us over. "Stand up straighter."

George and I threw our shoulders back.

He would have gone through the whole routine with "Eyes straight ahead" and "Shine those shoes" and half a dozen other orders, but he was in a hurry.

"Who ate the stuff I left on the mantelpiece?"

Now my alarm bells were really going off. Daddy didn't say "candy;" he said "stuff."

George and I stood mute.

"One of you got it," he said. He was really working himself up. He kept his eyes on me, and I knew he was looking forward to whipping my ass. "When I find out who did it, I'm goan give him a good spanking. Not for eating it, but for not being man enough to stand up and confess. I want my boys to have integrity, to be truthful. One of you is lying and I'm goan find out who it is. I just can't stand a liar."

When George and I said nothing, he bellowed, "Sweetheart!"

"Yes," said Mother from the kitchen. She came to the door, scratching her head, and I knew her dandruff was acting up again. Mother had a bad problem with dandruff.

"What time you get home?"

"Four o'clock, like you told me."

Daddy looked at his watch. He smiled and nodded in satisfaction. "Sometime in the next few minutes, I 'spec somebody is goan have to go to the bathroom."

Daddy paced up and down in front of George and me. He was pleased with himself. "That wasn't chewing gum you took off the mantelpiece," he said. He stopped and looked straight at me.

"I didn't do it, Daddy."

"We'll see, young man, we'll see."

Daddy thought he had me nailed. Even when I was only twelve, it seemed he sensed that his firstborn was an alien, someone whose main desire in life was to get out of this place to which he had retired. He was determined to whip me into shape, to make me understand the verities of life. He *wanted* to punish me.

Daddy resumed pacing, hands behind his back. "That was Feen-a-mint. It's a laxative like castor oil. Makes you doo-doo. So whoever goes to the bathroom is the one who's been stealing my lemon drops." He fingered his leather belt and looked at me. "And I'm goan give him a good one." He pointed to the sofa. "You two sit down. We goan wait."

Daddy had planned this thing like a military exercise. This was Operation Crap Attack. Making children crap was one of the common lesser punishments around Edison. Many parents made their children drink castor oil or take a dose of Epsom salts. "That'll teach you," Daddy would say as he ladled out two tablespoons of castor oil. Teach me what? So I had the squirts for a while, and then I was supposed to be pure or something?

Daddy sat across the room, eyes locked on me. I leaned back and waited. A few minutes later George began fidgeting. His fidgeting increased. He jumped up and said, "I gotta go," then ran for the bathroom.

Daddy looked down the hall in disbelief. Then he turned and looked at me. "Don't you have to go?"

"No, sir."

"Your belly doesn't hurt?"

"No, sir. I'm okay."

George returned and sat down, but he didn't stay long. A moment later he jumped up and again ran down the hall.

Daddy's brow wrinkled. He stared at me.

"No, sir. I don't have to go."

George was pale when he returned. Before he could sit down again, he twirled, and ran down the hall. When he came back, he leaned on the door for support. "I did it," he moaned.

His confession was not exactly a revelation. He had about crapped himself to death.

Daddy's face was filled with concern. "You okay, son?"

"No, sir. I don't feel good. My stomach hurts."

Daddy was angry that he had made George sick and disappointed that he didn't get to whip my ass. If it had been me making those trips to the bathroom, he would have been spanking me every time I came back into the living room. "We're just goan have to see what we do about this," he said.

He never did anything.

If Daddy wasn't shouting about Ralph McGill, the early-morning hours seemed calm and peaceful to me. In those half-waking moments when I heard Mother in the kitchen but before I crawled out of bed, I sensed the continuity of our family life. Three hundred and sixty-five days a year, Daddy's morning ritual was the same. Without an alarm clock he arose at 5:30 a.m., took a bath, shaved, and was sitting at the table less than twenty minutes later.

Sometimes, on the faint and distant edges of consciousness, I heard him shut our bedroom door after he walked through on his way to the kitchen. Mother always walked through the living room, but Daddy was used to tramping through a barracks filled with recruits, so he clumped through not caring about the noise his boots made.

By the time Daddy arrived in the kitchen, Mother had picked up the newspaper from the front porch, prepared coffee, and had Daddy's breakfast under way. She poured a cup of steaming coffee, put it in front of him, and turned back to the stove. Daddy liked his eggs right out of the pan, his grits steaming, and his biscuits too hot to touch.

Getting hot food to the troops is a sacred thing in the Army, and it remained so with Daddy. I never saw anyone who could eat such hot food or drink such hot coffee.

I wondered when I would start riding with Daddy. It was the end of July, and school began in little more than a month. Daddy said he would let me know soon.

One day George was sitting at the kitchen table blowing spit bubbles while I made a mayonnaise sandwich. I smoothed a thick layer of mayonnaise on a slice of light bread, put a slice of bread on top, slathered on another layer of mayonnaise and another slice of bread, more mayonnaise and still another slice of bread. I looked approvingly at the four slices of bread with mayonnaise oozing out; then I sat down as Mother poured me a big glass of sweet tea.

Daddy suddenly appeared in the front door and hiked into the kitchen. He was holding Butch's hand. We all looked at Daddy in surprise. It was 3 p.m., and we didn't expect him home until 4:58 p.m., which would give him just enough time to wash his hands and sit down to a hot supper at exactly five o'clock.

He looked at Mother and said, "Somebody is not looking after Butch." Then we noticed that Butch's mouth was covered with turpentine. Mother grabbed him, took him to the sink, and began washing his mouth.

A few months earlier Butch had decided that he liked to eat wood. He was the perfect height to walk up to a windowsill and start chewing. He would start at one end and gnaw his way to the other, nibbling on the sill like it was an ear of corn. Then he discovered the young pine trees in the front yard. He had girdled several, and we knew they were going to die. He was worse than the pine blight. The turpentine in the trees blistered his lips but didn't slow him down. He just liked to eat pine trees.

The doctor said that Butch had a mineral deficiency and gave Mother a list of foods she should be sure he ate. Some of our meals were prepared around Butch's need for minerals. It didn't matter; he still ate window sills and pine trees.

So the plan was to keep a close eye on him. Somehow he had gotten out the door, slid down the steps, and teetered off to chew on the trees. And Daddy was not happy.

"It's a good thing I came home early today," he said.

"JB, I don't know how he got outside," Mother said. "I thought he was napping."

I was smiling. I couldn't help it. Having a brother who ate pine trees was as funny as hell to me.

"Wipe that smile off your face, young man," Daddy said.

"Yes, sir."

"I just got the word and came home to tell you that the Lions Club wants you and James to tell them about your trip to Valley Forge, Pennsylvania," he said. "They want to know everything you did from the time you left Edison until you got back. The meeting is next Tuesday. I want you to prepare a good speech. The men in the Lions Club financed your trip. They are the men who run Edison."

I called James and told him what Daddy said. "Yeah, I heard about that," he said.

"Think we ought to tell them everything?"

"Don't spec so."

Daddy had a plan. I would speak first and talk about the train ride from Albany to Atlanta and then on to Philadelphia and the tour of the historical sites there. My speech would end at the gates of Valley Forge. James would take over and talk about the jamboree, about trading patches, visiting Scouts from other countries, and hearing President Truman and General Eisenhower.

I had never given a speech and was terrified at the thought of appearing before the Big Possums of Edison. But to Daddy it was all very simple: "Stand up straight. Speak loudly and clearly. Start when you get on the train in Albany, Georgia and stop when the train reaches Valley Forge, Pennsylvania."

I wrote a speech and practiced it for hours. To get away from the snickers of my younger siblings, I went into the front bedroom and closed the door. Mother sat on the edge of the bed while I stood across the room and began reading the speech. "Put that speech up on the chifferrobe," she said. "Just talk to me about your trip." She said I should put in a few gestures, so I practiced those. I didn't know how to use appropriate gestures and occasionally flopped an arm or waved a hand.

Mother hugged me and said, "Son, you are going to do just fine. Don't you worry."

Tuesday morning Mother washed my Scout uniform. Daddy told her to starch the pants and shirt so they would hold a sharp crease. When Daddy came home, he told me to put on my uniform. "And don't sit down after you put it on. It will ruin the creases. I want you looking sharp." The summer Scout uniform called for shorts, and there was not enough material to wrinkle, but daddy wanted razor creases.

I stood around practicing nonchalance until Daddy was ready to go. Mother started to kiss me, but Daddy stopped her. "You will do okay, son," Mother said.

When we got to the car, Daddy told me not to sit down, but rather to stand behind the front seat. "We have to keep those creases sharp," he said.

"Yes, sir," I mumbled. My feet were spread wide, and I leaned over the front seat feeling as if I was pressed into a box. I was glad it was only two miles to town.

The Lions Club met in the cafeteria at Edison High School. James and I strutted around in our uniforms, and all the Lions shook our hands and told us how proud they were that two boys from little ol' Edison, Georgia, made it to a Boy Scout jamboree way up in Valley Forge, Pennsylvania, and how they bet we showed the Yankees how young men should conduct themselves. "I bet you showed them how Georgia boys do it," they said over and over. "I know you made us proud."

I could be wrong, but I don't think people from New York said to their Scouts, "I bet you showed them how New York boys do it" or "I know you made us proud." But that night I agreed with the Lions. We had indeed made them proud. We had left enough semen on the ground to float George Washington's boat.

After dinner the head Lion looked out over the twenty-five or thirty men present and said, "You all know the Sarge. He will take over from here."

My bony knees were banging together. This was the most frightening moment of my childhood. I was about to make a speech to grown-ups.

Daddy thanked the Lions for sponsoring our trip. Then he called on me, and I stood up. As I looked out over those impassive, sun-browned, wrinkled faces, my fear made me a talking machine. I told about the train trip and Philadelphia and the Betsy Ross House and the Liberty Bell and Valley Forge and Scouts from all over the world and trading patches and souvenirs and President Truman and General Eisenhower and the fireworks and how much we learned and thank you for making it all possible. The realization of what I was doing made me talk even more. Not only was I leaving parched earth for James, but I was plowing up that earth and sowing salt over it. Out of the corner of my eye I saw his stricken face. Still I rattled on for half an hour, occasionally wiggling a shoulder, waving a hand, or jerking my arm up in the air like a spaz. I vomited up details that shouldn't have been in any speech. I even talked about how nice the Scout leaders were to us. Then I sat down, exhausted.

After enthusiastic applause, James stood up and slowly walked to the lectern. I could almost hear the gears grinding as he clawed for something, for anything, for any scrap, any shred, any detail I might have left out. He sighed, cracked an embarrassed smile, said we'd had a good time and thanks for sending us, and then sat down. His speech lasted about ten seconds. After a moment of silence came a few surprised grunts and a polite sprinkling of applause.

Afterward the old men of Edison came up and shook my hand and congratulated me. "I spec yo daddy is proud of you," they said.

James and his daddy left quickly. My daddy kept me around until the last Lion had gone home.

Daddy was smiling as we walked to the car, smiling like I had never seen him smile before. There was a bounce in his step. He kept turning to look at me, trying to say something, but it wouldn't come out. I was mortified, humiliated beyond description. This was the most embarrassing night of my life, and the ripples would last into the school year. When school started, James would remember what I had done, and he would tell everyone how I had stabbed him in the back. There would be talk that Daddy had set it up for me to be the star of the evening. They would say that Daddy had had me speak first because he knew I was going to talk about the entire trip.

"Get in the front seat with me," Daddy said. I stared at the floor, saying nothing. We passed the city limits and were almost home when Daddy cleared his throat three or four times, gripped the steering wheel tightly, looked straight ahead, and blurted, "Son, I'm proud of you."

It was the only time in my life he ever said that to me.

THE next day the Sarge came in from work, washed his face and hands, and walked into the kitchen. He looked at me and was about to speak when Mother said, "What did you do today, honey?"

He shrugged. "Some young rascal busted the Nelly Hoover curve again. Cracked my pole, but I braced it and I think it will be okay. They ripped up Miss Nelly's front yard. Shame on them if she catches them."

"Know who it was?"

"No. Some kid." Daddy turned to me, pointed his finger and said, "You're spending the rest of the summer up on the farm with your aunt Grace and uncle Felix and your daddy's mama." "Daddy's Mama" was what we called my paternal grandmother.

I looked at Daddy in disbelief. He ignored me as he sat down and Mother began bringing steaming platters of food to the table. I had studied for the jamboree so that I could ride with him. I had made a speech to the Lions Club, and Daddy had said he was proud of me.

I stood behind my chair, fighting the tears. "You said I was going to be your helper this summer," I said.

"Sit down so I can say the blessing and we can eat while the food is hot. You can be my helper next summer."

"I want to be your helper *this* summer," I said, moving from one foot to the other. Why couldn't Daddy understand?

He looked at Mother in exasperation. "Your son needs to learn to do what he is told."

Mother sat down and put her hand on my arm. She smiled and tried to pull me into my chair. I resisted. "It will be okay, son," she said. "You can ride with your uncle Felix and help out around the house and the farm."

I didn't care about farms. I didn't care about being isolated way out in the country with relatives who were older than dirt. I wanted to be Daddy's helper.

A twelve-year old boy needs the affection of his daddy. I was the first born and at some level I believed it was my right to be first in my daddy's affection. If I was not first, the least Daddy could do was to space his affection equally between George and me. But Daddy never tried to hide that George was his favorite.

I believed if I could ride with Daddy, if I could spend all day every day with him, that I would be such a good helper that I would be elevated in his eyes; I would be equal to George.

Plus, riding in the back of an open truck and traveling the dirt roads of three counties was just plain fun.

But now Daddy was sending me off to the farm.

George came in, pulled out his chair, and sat down. He was grinning like a mule eating briars, and I knew then that he was going to be Daddy's helper.

"Daddy," I implored.

Usually, if I did not obey Daddy immediately, he either barked or threatened a spanking. That he did not do so now told me he knew he was wrong.

"You told me…"

He pointed to the chair. "Sit down. I just said you could be my helper next summer. Now stop whining and let me say the blessing."

4

It was the summer of a rooster and a rolling store, of an outhouse and a mule, but most of all it was the summer of Edgar Allan Poe.

For as long as I could remember, one Sunday each month my family visited Daddy's Mama and Aunt Grace and Uncle Felix. We went up after church and sat down to a big dinner and a long lazy afternoon. But this was the first time I had been there longer than a few hours. I knew very little about Daddy's Mama except that she turned seventy-nine that summer. She had a bun of white hair tied at the nape of her neck and she was stooped and quiet. When she spoke, she used old-fashioned expressions such as "He commenced to talk to me" or "She wore a blue frock." Her only expletive was "I swan," a polite way of saying "I swear."

When people talked, Daddy's Mama always leaned forward in her chair and rocked back and forth as she listened intently. I was struck by her susceptibility to summer colds. Every afternoon she developed a delicate cough. "I need my medicine," she said. Whereupon Aunt Grace poured an ice tea glass half full of bourbon and then stirred in four or five tablespoons of sugar. Daddy's Mama nursed this concoction through the evening, and by bedtime her cough was gone and she was smiling beatifically.

My grandfather died years before I was born, and I knew only two things about him. The first was that he had been a schoolteacher and a successful farmer until his oldest son, my Uncle Byron, came back from World War I and squandered everything but the family home and about thirty acres of land. "You know he was gassed in the war?" people said as a way of explaining his failure. Why didn't they just come out and say he couldn't pour piss out of a boot if the directions were on the heel. My Uncle Byron was so dumb he always looked as if he were half asleep.

The other thing I knew about my grandfather was that he had worked in several presidential campaigns of William Jennings Bryan and was so enamored of him that he named my daddy Jennings Bryan Coram. Daddy, for reasons I never knew, passed along the Bryan as my middle name. George's middle name was William, and Butch's first name was Jennings. This meant that each of the Coram boys was saddled with the name of a three-time presidential loser, a Bible-thumping whack job who had been the prosecutor in the famous Scopes "monkey trial" in Tennessee. But we were from Edison, Georgia, and there was little to brag about, so we bragged that we were named for a man who had run for president.

Aunt Grace, Daddy's older sister, was a wiry woman whose eyes were as sad as they were steady. I think she sensed early on that her life would be a long, grinding road covered with the dust of poverty. She was the salt of the earth, one of those women who, even though life was indifferent to her, managed to keep on keeping on. A sweet smile often played around the corners of her mouth.

There was another sister named Beatrice—we emphasized the second syllable—whom we called "Aunt Bat." She was a school teacher over in Fort Gaines about twenty miles away.

Uncle Felix was a jovial, roly-poly man who, enormous stomach notwithstanding, could outwalk any man in southwest Georgia. Maybe he was trying to walk off his lot in life. He loved to hunt quail, but he usually hunted alone. Although other men admired his ability to find birds, they came home complaining that Uncle Felix had walked them half to death.

Uncle Felix had a bird dog that many hunters in southwest Georgia had tried to buy from him at one time or another. It was not that the dog could sniff a covey of quail from a great distance; many dogs could do that. But sooner or later those dogs would get excited and flush the covey before the hunters could move into position. Flushing a covey is the worst thing a bird dog can do, and Uncle Felix had trained his dog to have an iron discipline. He trained his dog the same way everyone else in southwest Georgia did: the first few times the dog flushed a covey, Uncle Felix held the dog by the neck and beat the hell out of him. The next time Uncle Felix shot him. Well, he shot near him, close enough that the dog got enough bird shot in his ass to get his attention.

Now that dog would hold a point until the cows came home. When he was on point, his body quivered with excitement, and he rolled his eyes as if urging the hunters to walk forward, there, exactly where his nose pointed.

Uncle Felix loved Dog. That was his name, Dog. Uncle Felix pronounced it "dawg." So did Aunt Grace and Daddy's Mama.

Uncle Felix and Aunt Grace moved in with Daddy's Mama after Granddaddy died. The house they lived in was the old home place, the only place Uncle Bryon did not lose while demonstrating what a great farmer he was. It also was where I was born. Daddy was stationed up at Fort Benning near Columbus, Georgia, at the time, and Mother wanted to be with his family when she delivered me.

The house was an unpainted wooden structure that sat well back off a dirt road. The sandy front yard was planted with a few crape myrtle bushes, and on the north side of the house were two large pecan trees. The house was L-shaped, with the inside of the L facing the road. It sat on rock pillars and was about three feet off the ground. Visitors had to climb a flight of steps to reach the porch that ran around the inside of the L.

At the top of the steps, the first room on the left belonged to Daddy's Mama. It was the biggest room in the house and a room I never entered. From the steps the front door was straight ahead and opened into the dining room. A table that could seat ten people took up much of the space. A pie safe where Aunt Grace kept cooked food sat against the wall to the right. Another sat on the opposite wall, and a small icebox sat in the corner. From the ceiling over the dining room table hung long strips of flypaper. When flies landed on the papers they stuck to the surface and sat there buzzing for a while until they died. It was my job to throw out the old flypaper every day or so. No one thought it unusual to sit at a table laden with food, with curly brown fly-covered stalactites hanging eighteen inches above the table.

If there was a persistent fly that would not land on the flypaper, we had a Flit Gun. It had a barrel-shaped container for a liquid spray and a handle about a foot long. Inside the handle was a piston. Point that thing at a fly, pump the handle a few times, and a cloud of fly-killing spray filled the air, and often settled over the table.

The kitchen was to the right and almost filled by a six-burner woodstove. On that stove aunt Grace wreaked culinary magic, both in quality and quantity. For dinner—served in the middle of the day—there were always at least two meats, usually chicken along with ham, beef, or quail; a half dozen vegetables, fresh or canned; biscuits and corn bread; and two big desserts, all washed down with an endless supply of ice tea so sweet it was syrupy. Supper always consisted of leftovers, and they were even better after a few hours in the pie safe.

There was no air-conditioning and no fan, only a screen door that opened onto the back porch. When Aunt Grace was cooking, the temperature in the room was above one-hundred degrees.

To the left of the dining room was a big room that served both as a living room and a bedroom. The room had two double beds—the mattresses were large sacks filled with corn shucks—one for Aunt Grace and Uncle Felix and the other for whatever family member was visiting. When you lay on one of these beds, the corn shucks got pushed to the side, and you awakened thinking you had fallen asleep in a ditch. There was a sofa, which we called a daybed, against one wall. The room had a fireplace, around which the family gathered both winter and summer.

There was no bathroom. Aunt Grace and Uncle Felix kept a chamber pot under their bed. So did Daddy's Mama. As soon as I got up in the morning it was my job to take the chamber pots to the outhouse and dump them. I had thought I would be spending the summer riding with Daddy, and here I was toting old people's crap.

About twenty feet from the outhouse was the well, and on beyond the outhouse was the smokehouse, where meat was stored, and beyond that was a small barn.

On the back porch was a shelf that held chipped galvanized blue buckets filled with cool water from the well. There was a washbasin, a dipper, and a dingy towel for cleaning up. On Saturdays, one by one, Daddy's Mama, Aunt Grace, and Uncle Felix would go to the back porch, close the door behind them, and sponge off using water from the washbasin.

A long flight of steps descended from the back porch to the sandy yard. Uncle Felix was always building and repairing, so there was usually lumber of various sizes strewn about the backyard. Off to the right was an enormous fig tree, maybe twelve feet tall, that, when greened out, seemed to cover half the yard. Near the fig tree was a stump where every Sunday morning before church Aunt Grace performed a ritual.

After breakfast she would walk into the yard, scattering corn to attract the free-running chickens. The chickens were watched over by a rooster, who wouldn't hesitate to attack anyone coming into the yard. Corn was the only thing that would divert his attention.

"Robert, get around behind them chickens and grab the first one you can," Aunt Grace would say. But while I stood there looking around and wondering which chicken I would consign to the dinner table, she would lean down, grab a chicken by the legs, and, with a deftness born of long experience, wring the chicken's neck with her other hand. When the head came off in her hand, she would toss it away and let the chicken go, keeping her eye on it as it darted erratically about the yard, blood spurting from the long, shiny stalk of its neck. After what seemed a long time, the chicken would collapse. Aunt Grace would hold the chicken by its legs and dip it into a pot of boiling water, which made the feathers easy to pluck. Finally, she would wad up a piece of paper, set it afire, and, holding the chicken in one hand and the burning paper in the other, move the flame back and forth around the carcass to remove the pinfeathers. If everyone had to smell burning pinfeathers before they ate chicken, there would be fewer chicken eaters.

Aunt Grace always dissected the chicken there on the stump, the top of which was covered with the blood of a hundred predecessors. She would throw the drumsticks, thighs, breast, wings, and back into a bowl, then scrape the viscera off the stump onto the sand. Finally, she would carry the bowl inside and put the chicken pieces in the icebox.

As soon as she walked into the house after church, she would place her Bible by her bed and put on an apron. She'd poke at the stove a few times—she could start a fire faster than any Boy Scout who ever lived—and cook the chicken in a large, blackened cast-iron skillet. It was a measure of her wiry strength that she could carry the heavy skillet, filled to capacity with chicken, to the table with one hand. She always served Uncle Felix first, and he always said the same thing: "That chicken is so hot you must have cooked it twice."

Then he'd look at me and say, "Boy, you hungry?"

I knew what he wanted to hear, so I would grin and bounce on the cane-bottomed chair and say, "I'm so hungry my stomach thinks my throat has been cut."

He'd chuckle and with dancing eyes say, "Then I guess we better feed you. Don't want yo mama and daddy thinking we let you get puny."

After dinner we would move to the front porch to talk, knowing that soon Uncle Felix would stand up and announce, "Well, I got to go do my bidness," then amble off through the house and out the back door to the outhouse.

Uncle Felix had a two-holer. Why, I do not know. It must have been a status thing, because going to the outhouse is not something you do with anyone else. A two-holer is as good as it gets. You don't see them any bigger except at church picnics.

The outhouse was located about fifty feet from the back porch. In the winter, when the wind was howling, fifty feet seemed like a long way to go, and a person may have wished it was located closer to the house. But in the summer, even at fifty feet, the odor was a physical blow that made it seem as though the outhouse was right under the back porch.

The construction of the outhouse was simple. Uncle Felix had dug a trench about three feet deep and over it put a frame structure made of rough planks. The structure was just big enough to cover the trench, with maybe a foot or so of space near the front. Once inside, there was no room to do anything but turn around and sit.

The bench inside was built from two boards. On one board Uncle Felix sawed a six-inch cut at about a 45-degree angle. Down the board, maybe a foot away, he made another six-inch cut at a 45-degree angle, this one angled toward the first. With a hammer he knocked out the piece of wood between the cuts, giving him a rough semicircle. He moved down the board about two feet and did the same thing. He used that board as a template for the second board, mating them so the semicircles formed two big holes. A Sears, Roebuck catalog, which was used for toilet paper, hung by a string from a nail. I sat there many times, thumbing through the catalog, and breathing through my mouth because of the odor. I'm convinced that is where I developed the habit of reading in the bathroom.

Even though a breeze could blow through the rough planks, inside the outhouse the odor was almost intolerable. In addition, I had a heart-stopping fear of falling through the hole and into the trench filled with God only knows how many years of old people's shit and piss. I always braced myself with both hands when I sat down. That was a hot summer—there is no other kind in southwest Georgia—and I hated that tiny oven like structure.

On the south side of the house, maybe fifty feet from the outhouse, was the well from which Aunt Grace drew water. The well was surrounded by a framework of boards that stood about waist high. A short piece of log, smooth and worn by countless revolutions of the rope wrapped around it, sat inside a V-shaped support that cradled it and straddled the gaping maw of the well. There was a handle on one end of the log, and the rope around the log was attached to a galvanized bucket.

When I timidly approached the waist-high wall and peeked over the side, the well seemed bottomless: smooth, dank walls narrowing into green darkness. Aunt Grace didn't like when I dropped things into the well, but one day I dropped in a rock and it seemed like an hour before I heard a soft splash somewhere down around the middle of the earth.

"What would happen if I fell down the well?" I asked Aunt Grace. My fear of falling into the well was almost as great as my fear of falling through the hole in the outhouse.

"Well, I don't know how we'd get you out, Robert. So you'd best not fall in."

"But what if I did and you weren't here or you couldn't hear me hollering?"

"I guess you'd stay there until somebody heard you."

Fresh water and a place to do your business, two of the fundamental needs of life, and to me that summer both were scary business.

Aunt Grace and Uncle Felix had cows for milk and butter and the chickens to provide eggs and meat. Years later I learned that the chickens were of a breed properly known as Dominique, but we called them Dominickers. As mentioned earlier, they were ruled by the meanest and most aggressive rooster God ever made. He had bright yellow legs and gray barred feathers. His high comb and dangling beard made his head a bright red mass punctuated by yellow-rimmed eyes and a saberlike beak. He was big, maybe eight pounds, and he held his head high, neck arched, with his tail feathers curved in an arrogant plume. He owned the backyard, and, almost every time Uncle Felix walked across the yard, the rooster attacked him. Uncle Felix would laugh and kick at the rooster, then threaten to have him for Sunday dinner. Aunt Grace kept a broom by the back door to fend off his attacks. For some reason the rooster never bothered Daddy's Mama. I asked her why, and she dismissed the question with a wave of her hand. "Pshaw, I ain't studying that rooster."

Every time the rooster saw me come out the back door, he dropped his wings to the ground, puffed out the feathers on his body, making him look as big as a turkey, and pulled his head pulled back into a striking position. He sounded an angry, drawn-out "eeerrrppp," a noise that began like a shriek and ended with the crack of a black-snake whip. He began walking in circles, wings dragging furrows in the sand, eyes never leaving me, just waiting to make his move.

I was terrified of the rooster, in part because the first time he chased me, I was carrying a half-full chamber pot, the contents of which were sloshing over my bare legs as I made a mad dash for the outhouse. I barely made it inside before he skidded to a stop, blocked by the door. I stayed there, my legs covered with piss, while the rooster circled the outhouse for what seemed like an eternity. Eventually he wandered away, no doubt thinking in his little peabrain that I had fallen down the hole.

The rooster, like most predators, learned from his mistakes. The next morning I looked out back and, not seeing him, eased open the screen door. I crept across the porch, eyes scanning the yard, then walked down several steps and looked up under the house, one of his hiding places. I did not see the rooster or his flock.

"Hey, Mr. Rooster, you out there?" I called, loud enough to get his attention if he was close but not loud enough for him to hear if he was down near the barn. I took a final look around and bolted for the outhouse.

In the middle of the yard, far from any tree I could climb, I crossed the point of no return, and in that split second I heard his triumphant "eeerrrppp." I looked over my shoulder as he charged from behind the fig tree, a feathered juggernaut, head pulled back, neck cocked, and eyes gleaming. Loping in a stiff-legged gait, he lurched toward me like a top-heavy truck, yawping, bouncing along, neck cocked, and eyes gleaming.

Knowing I could not make the outhouse, I fell to the ground, wrapped my arms around my head, and screamed for Aunt Grace. The rooster jumped on me, roweled my back with his spurs, pecked me with his beak, and hammered me with his wings. Aunt Grace came running, broom in hand, shouting "Shoo! Shoo! Get away!" She was laughing so hard she did not sound as stern as she might have. But with a final beakstab on my bare leg and an angry screech, the rooster stalked out of the broom's reach, angry eyes wide, poised to dart in again if he saw an opening.

"Robert, you all right?"

"Yes, ma'am. I think so."

"I don't know what I'm going to do with that rooster."

"I like Uncle Felix's idea."

"Eat that stringy old thing?" She looked at me as if I had taken leave of my senses.

When Uncle Felix saw the gashes on my back and the beak marks and bruises, he laughed and said, "Boy, you either got to quit going to the bathroom or you got to learn to run faster." He paused and looked away. After a moment a thoughtful look settled on his face, and he spoke from a place of the deepest conviction. "A man ought to be able to do his bidness in peace."

After that I always carried the broom when I went to the outhouse. And I began swinging it wildly the moment I saw the rooster. He would dance out of reach, yawping, then get in a few pecks on my legs. But my skills at rooster defense grew, and so did my confidence. Soon the Dominicker no longer terrorized me. I'd walk, not run, to the outhouse. The rooster would drag his wings and make a few false charges, but he knew and I knew that his day was past. And during the last weeks of August I was able to do my business in peace.

I didn't want to be at the farm, but I was stuck there and decided to make the best of it. I do not recall a single moment of boredom that summer. I was as free as any child has ever been, and most mornings, barefoot and clad in nothing but a pair of short pants, I exploded through the screen door and was halfway to somewhere before the door slammed shut. I was off to explore the farm, running alone through deep gullies and across open fields. Stopping to fill my pockets with black walnuts, I'd eat some but always save enough for Aunt Grace to make ice cream.

Uncle Felix would shake his head, laugh, and say, "Boy, you so fast you get to where you going before you leave."

Aunt Grace would add, "We're going to have to replace that screen door if you don't put some brakes on in the house."

Sometimes I returned to the house for dinner, sometimes not until supper. Aunt Grace never worried and never told me to stay close to home.

Two days a week Uncle Felix drove a rolling store, a big enclosed truck that was a small grocery store on wheels. The door was like that of a school bus and was opened and closed with a long bar that he operated. The dark interior was filled with shelves loaded with boxes of fruit, bread, snuff, chewing tobacco, candy, and canned vegetables. On the floor were several barrels of salted beef and pork. Because the interior was so jammed with goods, only two people could shop at any given time.

One morning Uncle Felix and I rolled out of the yard before daylight, his right elbow flapping as he pushed and pulled on the long, floor-mounted gear stick. We went two miles to Mr. Ben Butler's store and gassed up, then headed for the back roads. I stood up, holding on to the back of Uncle Felix's seat. In the large rearview mirror I saw a thick cloud of red dust billowing out behind us and settling onto the fields beside the road.

Occasionally a car or pickup truck came up behind us, but the roads were so narrow there was no room for passing. The drivers never dropped back beyond the dust; they stayed snuggled almost under the rolling store, eating dust as if it was their lot in life, until we stopped at a house. As the drivers moved on, they wiped red grit from their faces.

The rolling store had an air horn, and Uncle Felix was a maestro at playing it. When we were maybe a halfmile from a house, he would reach up and pull on the string, making the horn moan and wail and hold a high note for a sweet forever. The houses were all on dirt roads. All were unpainted and built of wood and most had tin roofs. Children and grown-ups alike would pour out of those houses in a mad rush, all drawn by the sound of the air horn.

No one could resist that horn. By the time we arrived at a house, people were standing by the side of the road, bouncing from one foot to the other as they waited their turn to enter the dim confines. And when Uncle Felix opened the door, someone always asked, "Whatcha got in that there rolling store?"

The answer was always the same: "We got everything but amazing grace and a floating opportunity." I don't know what that meant, but Uncle Felix thought it was funny. Every time he said it, he chortled and his big stomach, cantilevered like stacked waterfalls, quivered and bounced.

Our arrival was a big event along those dusty roads, a matter of amazement to children and gratification to adults. Most of them had no car, and we were the only alternative to a long walk into a small town. Grown-ups and children alike would mosey through the store, buying food for dinner or candy for a treat, all staring with wide-eyed wonder at the rows of bounty.

Those people didn't need much, and Uncle Felix and I brought them most of what they did need.

One afternoon we passed a patch of plum bushes, a few ripe plums still on the limbs, causing Uncle Felix to grunt in surprise. "They came in late," he said. We stopped and stuffed ourselves on warm, sweet plums and then picked more, wrapping them in a handkerchief to take home. "Yo grandmama likes plums," Uncle Felix said. "Keeps her loosened up."

It was almost dark when he said, "Well, boy, let's go home."

"How many houses did we stop at?"

"More than you can shake a stick at."

We passed a silo, and Uncle Felix nodded and solemnly said, "Man died in there last week."

I was standing up, holding on to the bar that opened the door. Wide-eyed, I turned to him and said, "He did? How'd he do that?"

"Ran himself to death looking for a corner to do his bidness in." Uncle Felix chortled and shook and said "Lord, God" in approval of his humor.

As we approached his house, Uncle Felix geared down and slowed his speed so we would not pull a cloud of dust into the yard. He pointed toward the long, grimy string over his head and said, "Let 'em know we're home, boy."

I grinned, pulled the string, and sent a long toot through the quiet of the evening. I could not make the sound move up and down the scale the way Uncle Felix did. All I could do was send out a rude, sustained blast.

Uncle Felix turned off the ignition and said, "Bet you supper is on the table."

"How does Aunt Grace know what time we'll get home?"

"She just does, boy. She just does."

By 1950 only the smallest and poorest farms in southwest Georgia were without a tractor. Uncle Felix had no tractor for his thirty acres, and when he harvested his peanuts early that year, it was from behind a plow pulled by a sway-backed old mule.

At breakfast on the morning he began plowing up his peanuts, Uncle Felix looked at me and said, "Boy, you want to go with me and look up a mule's backside all day long?"

He didn't have to ask twice. I watched as he hooked up the weary mule to the plow, then looped the reins about his neck. The black leather of the reins was so old and so worn, it was as soft as a glove. I don't think I ever saw that mule with his head high in the air. In the barn, in the pasture, and out plowing a field, that mule's head was always down. If a mule can be sad, that was a sad mule.

Once in the field I followed Uncle Felix, jumping from row to row in the hot red dirt as he muscled the turning plow, rolling peanuts atop the ground to dry in the sun. I was barefoot and ran on tiptoes to a nearby terrace covered with blackberry bushes. I put my feet in the shade, keeping an eye out for rattlesnakes as I reached through the briars and plucked tight sun-warmed blackberries, stuffing myself until Uncle Felix reached the end of the row and returned. I followed him for a while, dancing through the freshly turned dirt, and then again dashed to the terrace, my feet and ankles red from the clay and my hands purple with blackberry juice.

Later that morning Uncle Felix shouted, "Whoa," and took the traces from around his neck and tied them to the back of the plow. He motioned for me to follow, and we walked to the edge of the woods where a gully, maybe twenty feet deep, stretched from the top of the hill, across his pasture, and down to the creek.

He unzipped his overalls and said, "Boy, you need to pee?"

"Yes, sir." So we stood on the edge of the gully, our urine arcing over and falling on the pale sandy dust at the bottom, man and boy united in the male ritual of peeing out-of-doors, both of us leaning back, going for distance.

"What made this gully?" I asked.

"Boy, half my farm has gone down this gully. The good dirt washes down to the creek, then to the Chattahoochee, and I guess on to the ocean."

"Why doesn't anything grow down there on the bottom?"

"Boy, that's gully dirt. Gully dirt ain't good for nothing. Only thing you can do with gully dirt is what we doing."

AUNT Grace and Uncle Felix were not readers. The Bible and *Leatherneck* magazine, sent home monthly by their son, Bubba, who was in the Marine Corps, were the only two publications I had ever seen in their house. But that summer on a table in the living room was a row of four blue books: the complete works of Edgar Allan Poe. The first time I opened the door, I saw the books looming like dark angels. I walked across the room and picked them up one by one, thumbing through them slowly.

From as far back as I can remember, I've loved to read. If such things can be transferred, my affection for books came from Mother. My earliest memory of her is being awakened by something late one night—I must have been five or six—and stumbling toward a light in the living room. Mother sat on the sofa reading. When she looked up and saw me, she put a finger to her lips, signifying that I should be quiet. She motioned for me to sit next to her. I did and put my head on her shoulder. I sat there with her for hours as she slowly turned the pages of a magazine.

My reading was undisciplined. I had not developed a taste for good books so much as a taste for all books. And I knew that these books by Edgar Allan Poe, a writer I had never heard of, would occupy my evenings that summer.

Every night after supper, if the mosquitoes were not bad, we gathered on the front porch to let our meal settle, to look across the open fields, watch the occasional passing car, and talk. We ate around 5 p.m. , so there was plenty of daylight after the meal.

One afternoon, as she did once or twice a week, Daddy's Mama, perhaps influenced by her cough medicine, suddenly stopped her rocking chair, pointed toward the yard, and said, "Robert, go sweep that yard."

From under the house I pulled the yard broom, a leg-thick gathering of limbs from bushes wrapped tightly together with string. Then I looked up and asked, "All the way out to the road?"

"Yes. Start at the road and work your way back so you don't track it up. And make sure you sweep it all in the same direction."

"Yes, ma'am."

I never understood the idea of sweeping a dirt yard. And I did not understand why the tracks left by the sweeping had to be in the same direction, all lined up. Maybe it was in the hope that when people drove by, they would look over and say, "The people that live here have a mighty nice yard. They keep it swept."

Whatever the reason, I walked up to the road and began making long, smooth motions with the stick broom until the yard looked like a sheet of corrugated tin. Then I joined the grown-ups on the porch. Aunt Grace and Uncle Felix might not have had much, but they had clean dirt.

Daddy's Mama went to bed early. But there was always a half-hour or so of talk in the living room while Uncle Felix took off his shoes, pulled at his toes, and chuckled at the jokes in his head. It was then that I picked up Poe. Uncle Felix and Aunt Grace never understood why a boy wanted to read, and if I drifted too far into Poe's brooding, death-haunted landscape, Uncle Felix would reach out with a toe as big as a banana, press it against the flesh of my leg, and squeeze hard. We always said that Uncle Felix had toes like a pair of pliers, and that August he put many bruises on my legs. When I'd yelped with pain, he would say, "What you doing with your nose stuck in that book, boy?"

After a while I'd turn my back while Aunt Grace and Uncle Felix undressed and put on their nightshirts—billowing, floor-length gowns made from feed sacks and soft from a hundred washes. They'd turn on the radio and listened to *Amos 'n' Andy*, *Mr. And Mrs. North*, or *The FBI in Peace and War*. Uncle Felix always went to sleep quickly, but Aunt Grace would listen for a while. Then, as she grew drowsy, she would ask me to turn off the radio.

I would move into the dining room and read Poe by the light of a bare bulb. A few flies were still buzzing around, and occasionally one would become stuck on the flypaper. Wings buzzing frantically in a fruitless effort to free itself, it soon grew still and joined the dozens of other dead and desiccated carcasses on the long strip of paper.

One night, several hours later, I heard someone using the slop jar. The door opened, and Aunt Grace stood there, small and frail in her billowing nightshirt, a bewildered smile on her face. "Robert, what are you doing out here this time of night?"

"Reading."

"Reading? What are you reading?"

"'The Pit and the Pendulum.'"

"Well, it must be good. Your eyes are big as saucers."

"Aunt Grace, where did you get these books? I've never seen them before."

"I don't know. Somewhere."

I was bewildered. How could someone not know where her books came from? "You don't know?"

She shrugged. "They just showed up."

"I like them."

"I guess you can't get into trouble reading books."

"No, ma'am."

"Turn out the light when you go to bed." She paused. "How late were you up last night?"

"About four o'clock," I said, afraid that she would tell me to go to bed now.

"Reading all that time?"

"Yes, ma'am."

She shook her head. The idea of someone staying up far into the night to read was a strange thing to Aunt Grace. Day was for working, and night was for sleeping. She smiled and said, "You better either finish those books or stop reading them. I don't know if we can afford the electric bill."

The books were illustrated, and even today I can close my eyes and see the dark drawings. For "The Pit and the Pendulum" there was a picture of a man tied to the edge of a black well as dozens of big rats poured out of the pit, crawling over his body. Overhead a pendulum with a curved blade swung toward him. The drawing for "Descent into the Malestrom" was even scarier. For years afterward I was frightened every time I lifted the plug in a bathtub.

I had always liked to read, to learn about the wonders of the outside world. It was a way for me to plan for the day when I would leave southwest Georgia. But that August I discovered the *magic* of books, how words on a page could bring tears to my eyes or fill my heart to overflowing. In reading Poe, I discovered emotions and feelings I did not know I possessed. That summer I learned that the contents of a book could resonate in the heart and linger in the memory. The sounds and the internal rhythms of "Annabel Lee" were forever etched in my soul.

Poe instilled in me an attraction to the midnight side of human nature, and by the end of August I sensed that something in me had changed. I was very young and did not quite know what it was, but something had changed.

On the last Sunday in August my family drove the fifteen miles from Edison to have dinner and take me home. School was about to begin.

After dinner, while the grown-ups were rocking and talking on the front porch, George and I roamed out in the backyard. "What you been doing all summer?" he asked.

"Helping Uncle Felix farm. Riding in the rolling store."

"I been doing some riding, too."

I was hoping this topic would not come up.

"Yeah?"

"Been riding with Daddy every day. Helping him out. He says I'm a good helper and maybe next summer he can pay me. I know the names of every one of his tools, and I helped him put in a telephone."

"He told *me* I could be his helper next summer."

"Daddy says you can't keep your mind on what you doing. He says you not very grown- up."

"Yeah. Well, I'm grown-up enough to whip your ass."

"You better not. I will call Daddy. I'm going to be his helper next summer, and you'll be back up here stepping in chicken doo-doo."

He wouldn't say the word "shit." He had to say "doo-doo." Ever since, I have never trusted anyone who, could not once in a while say "shit."

I was tempted to throw him into a pile of chicken shit and drag him around. But if I touched him, he would start bleating, and Daddy would come running.

"I made a seesaw," I said, throwing him off balance.

He looked around. "Where?"

I kicked at a two-by-four on the ground. "I just put this over a sawhorse, and that's it. Want to ride?"

"Okay."

I moved Uncle Felix's sawhorse closer to the well and balanced the two-by-four over it. George and I seesawed for a minute. Then I said I needed to fix the seesaw. We stopped, and I slid the two-by-four a few feet in my direction, giving me control. The minute George straddled the two-by-four, I hunkered down so that he was high in the air and crabbed sideways until he was dangling over the well. He looked down into the bottomless hole, and his eyes got very big.

"You shit ass," I said. "You make one sound, and I'll drop you in the well."

George started crying. He was terrified. "Daddy's goan spank you good."

"Yeah, but you'll be down there with the snakes. It's so dark down there, nobody can see you. You'll be dead from snakebite before they get you out. You will be covered with slime and your tongue will be green and you will be all puffed up and big rats will eat your ass."

Poe was having an influence on me.

George gripped the two-by-four tightly, head bent forward. He was shaking with fear and whimpering.

"I may not be as grown-up as Daddy thinks you are," I said. "But you the one crying."

"I'm goan tell on you."

I straightened my knees, allowing the board to drop a few inches. George yelped and curled around the two-by-four like a possum curled around a sapling. "I won't tell. I won't tell. Just don't drop me." I couldn't have pried him off that board with a crowbar.

I wiggled the seesaw from side to side.

"Robert, what in the world are you doing?" Aunt Grace was standing at the corners of the house. For a moment I was frightened. Then I saw the little smile at the corner of her mouth. "You swing that seesaw around right now and let George get off. You hear me?"

"Yes, ma'am."

"You better do it this minute before your daddy comes out the back door."

Aunt Grace was smart enough to know that had she come running across the yard in a panic, I might have been frightened enough to jump off the board and drop George down the well. She had stayed at the corner of the house, kept her voice down, and told me what she expected me to do. And I did it.

Of course the minute George was on the ground, he began squealing like a stuck pig. "I'm goan tell on you. I'm goan to tell on you." He ran a few steps, then turned and said, "I got to ride with Daddy, and you didn't. I'm Daddy's helper, and you're not." Then he scampered away.

I watched him run and mumbled, "Yeah, but you just wet your britches."

Aunt Grace chuckled. "Robert, what in the world got into you to make you do something like that?"

"I don't know."

I heard Daddy bellowing, and I looked around the yard. It was time to get my ass whipping and then go home. My first extended time away from home was over. I had defeated a Dominicker rooster, ridden in a rolling store, and looked at a mule's backside. George knew the names of all of Daddy's tools, but I knew the titles of just about everything Poe had ever written, and I was overflowing with the magic of words on a page. Even saying the words "Annabel Lee" raised goose bumps on my arms. George had the promise of being Daddy's helper again next summer. I had a hunger for words that would never leave me.

But I wasn't aware of all that at the time. All I knew was that George had Daddy.

5

AFTER Daddy whipped my ass, he said I needed a haircut. The barbershop was full of boys and their daddies, all sitting on the old church pew that ran the length of the shop. Judge was a one-man operation, but he had two barber chairs. I guess it was a matter of pride, sort of like having a two-hole outhouse. Customers sat in the chair near the window, and no one ever dared to sit in the second chair. Waiting customers sat on the pew as close to the door as they could get, both to watch who was walking up and down the sidewalk and to be close enough to hear every comment by the Judge. That part of the pew directly in front of the Judge's chair was the center of gravity in the barbershop. I've seen men come in the door, take a look at the crowded pew, and turn around and leave rather than sit in purgatory down at the far end.

"Hey, Sarge," Judge said when we walked in. He paused, scissors and comb in midair, and said, "You and your boy have a seat."

The radio was on, and Frankie Laine was singing "Mule Train." In one part of the song there is a series of whip cracks. I jerked my head back and forth with the sound until Daddy scowled. The only music he liked was military music and big band music, and his only reaction to music was either standing at attention or saying,

"They just don't make music like that anymore." Head jerking was not allowed.

As Daddy and I sat down, Judge said, "Sarge, we been talking about Korea." He pronounced it "KO-rea."

"The Army is there. The Marines are there," Judge said. "What's gonna happen, Sarge?"

People in Edison always deferred to Daddy on anything to do with the military. Given that he had retired as a master sergeant—as far as I know the highest rank anyone from Edison had ever reached—everyone assumed that he knew what the generals were thinking and that he had been consulted on the details of the invasion plans. Daddy never let them down. He leaned forward and looked up and down the pew as he talked so that everyone could hear him. They could have heard him anyway.

"Won't take us long to do the job over there in Korea," he said. "The U.S. Army is the best in the world. General MacArthur is in command, and he will settle that mess in a hurry. I served under General MacArthur."

Yeah, and so did four or five million other GIs.

"I don't know," Judge said. "Radio said the Russians might get into this thing. They got them an A-bomb, and they are out to take over the whole world. That's the way the Communists are."

"Got to watch them Communists," one farmer said.

"They out to do us in," said another. "They don't understand but one thing and that's power. We got to show them we stronger than they are."

"How'd they get an A-bomb?" another farmer asked. From his tone it was clear he thought nobody but America had the right to build A-bombs.

"I don't know, but they did," Judge said. "Got them an A-bomb. Sure did."

"We got us a whole bunch of them A-bombs," said another farmer. "We used 'em on the Japs, and we ain't afraid to use 'em on the Russians."

Everyone nodded in agreement and I did not doubt for a minute that had it been left up to these foreign policy wizards, we would be scattering A-bombs all over Korea.

The man in the chair spoke up. "I read the other day that it's so cold over there in KO-rea that our boys are crying and the tears are freezing on their faces. Sarge, you been around. You ever seen a place that cold?"

"Spent seven years driving a dogsled up in Alaska. Pretty cold up there."

Judge nodded and grinned. "Guess you don't miss that, do you?"

"Didn't see my commanding officer but once every six months. That was good duty."

"What was you doing driving a dogsled if you was in the Army?" someone asked.

"I was in the Signal Corps. Dogsled was the only way to reach some of our remote posts up there. I delivered mail and supplies."

A grizzled old farmer shook his head. "Drove a dogsled in Alaska. Don't that beat all."

Daddy would have gone on and on about Alaska, but Brother Dunagan came in, smiling and greeting everyone on the pew, even the Methodists. He shook hands all the way down, then sat next to me and offered me his claw hand. He leaned over and whispered, "You ready for your baptizing?"

"Got my new white shirt," I said.

"Then you ready."

Brother Dunagan looked around the barbershop and, as is the way of preachers when they see any group larger than two people, felt compelled to make a speech. "This is a fine town I moved into," he began. "Been here coming up on a year now, and that's long enough for me to say Edison is a mighty fine town."

He took a copy of the local newspaper from under his arm and waved it in the air. "Everyone seen this week's *Calhoun County News*?"

"Preacher, nothing in that paper," Judge said with a grin.

"Well, there's one story in here I'm fixin' to read out loud if y'all don't mind." Brother Dunagan opened the paper. "It says here that Edison High School has graduated an exceptionally large"—he paused and then repeated the last two words, bearing down hard—"*exceptionally large* number of students who entered college and the professions in the last ten years."

"That so?" Judge asked. He uncoiled a steaming white towel from the tanned face of a farmer, stirred a big brush around in a cup of soap, and smoothed the lather on the man's face and neck. Then he pulled out his straight razor, stropped it a few times, wiped off part of the lather with his thumb, and went to work. First he neatened up the sideburns, and then he trimmed the hairline all the way to the back of the farmer's neck. Then he did the same thing on the other side. The boys on the bench watched in envy. You had to be grown to get your sideburns and neck trimmed by the Judge's straight razor. He knew the names of the high school seniors—I think there were eight that year—and trimmed their necks. It was a big deal for a boy, one of the rites of passage, when the Judge trimmed his sideburns and the back of his neck with a straight- edge razor.

"Says here that in the last ten years Edison High School has produced two ministers, five teachers, twenty-five clerical workers, three nurses, one lab technician, one dentist, and ten boys for the military." Brother Dunagan put down the paper and looked at Judge. "I think that's pretty good for a little town like Edison. We ought to be proud of our young people and how well we prepare them for the outside world."

All up and down the pew the men nodded in agreement.

"They got to get them high-paying jobs these days just to make a living, to pay for what they gotta have," Judge said.

"That's the truth," echoed someone down the pew.

I asked Brother Dunagan if I could read one of his newspapers. He handed me the *Atlanta Constitution*. It was several days old, but I didn't mind. Ralph McGill's column was about going from New York to a town near Jerusalem in only thirty-one hours. He said the trip was "exciting" and "fantastic," and I believed him. It was inconceivable to me that an airplane could take a person so far in only thirty-one hours.

Mr. McGill had an exciting job. Plus, he could piss off Daddy in about ten seconds. I don't know which appealed to me more.

Daddy glanced my way, and I quickly turned the page so he would not notice I was reading Mr. McGill's column.

Down at the end of the pew a man spoke up. "I heard when Mr. Bill Israel finishes building his new picture show that he's going to charge a quarter to get in."

"They been charging fifteen cents at the old picture show," someone said.

"Yeah, but that's a fine new picture show Mr. Bill is building across the street," said a farmer.

Judge wiped shaving cream from his straight razor and nodded. "Read it's costing him forty thousand dollars. Got three hundred seats downstairs, another two hundred upstairs for the niggers, and a cry room where the ladies can take their babies."

No one raised an eyebrow at the word "niggers."

Brother Dunagan chimed in and said. "Cry room is a fine idea. Edison is right progressive on things like that. We don't take a backseat to nobody."

Daddy had been silent for a bit after the conversation moved away from Korea, but now he joined in. "Talking about niggers, that college over in Looseeanna might be letting one of them in law school this year. Law school! You believe that?"

"No more'n I believe a pig can fly," someone said.

Judge waved his razor, and his voice was hard. "That's going on over at LSU. The federal courts are all mixed up in that mess."

For a moment there was silence. Brother Dunagan stared up through the ceiling. Judge powdered the farmer's face, snapped the sheet from around his neck, and said, "That will never happen in Edison." His voice was flat.

Another farmer moved toward the chair. He and Judge locked eyes and exchanged some secret signal. "You mighty right," he said.

Everyone on the pew agreed. That would never happen in Edison.

As I feared, James told everyone at school that I was a snake in the grass and had embarrassed him at the Lions Club. I got lots of snotty comments about my wanting to be a famous orator. People in Edison had a real knack for pounding on a person's vulnerabilities. It was part of the propensity to thrive on the misery of others. People in Edison did not care about anyone's success; they cared only about a person's misfortune. Someone from Edison could win the Nobel Prize, and people would say, "Well, I hear tell he's doing okay." And that would be the end of that conversation.

Many people in Edison were uncomfortable with success and good fortune. It just wasn't part of our lives. But if someone got snakebit, or had a heart attack, a stroke, or surgery, or if a building fell on him, the old men in the barbershop would chew on it for hours, reliving every detail, playing out every moment of agony. If a plague of biblical proportions fell upon Edison and killed everyone in town, people in the cemeteries would be so happy, they would rise up and talk about it.

People in Edison learned that misery-loving behavior at a young age. So when James said I was a back-stabber, he set me up for a lot of grief. But the big baptismal event coming up in the Edison Baptist Church soon eclipsed any talk about me. The Baptist Church was the biggest church in Edison, and religion was only *slightly* more important than sports (I emphasize the "slightly") so I was glad when it was time to be baptized.

Brother Dunagan had done some powerful preaching the past few months . About a dozen boys and girls were to be baptized, and it was shaping up to be the religious event of the year. Never mind that among our dozen there was not enough religious conviction to fill a teaspoon. We were getting baptized, and it was the *appearance* of being a Christian that was important.

The night of the baptism the boys wore blue jeans and white shirts, and the girls wore blue jeans and white blouses. We arrived at the church early, and Brother Dunagan explained that when we stepped down into the baptismal pool and moved out from behind the green velvet curtains, only our white-clad upper bodies would be visible to the congregation. We would be young and sweetfaced and saintly.

The preacher lined us sinners up just outside the baptismal pool and out of sight of the congregation. I was third in line. When the person in front of me moved from the edge of the pool out into the middle, where Brother Dunagan waited, I was to step down into the water and wait behind the curtain. After the person in front of me was dunked and walked out the other side, I was to step forward into view. It was an assembly line: heathen sinners walked in one side of the pool, and Christians came out the other.

I turned to the boy behind me and said, "Brother Dunagan got himself a system. He's moving us through pretty quick."

"Like a dose of salts through a widow woman," he whispered.

The lights in the church were dimmed, and the pool was lighted by a soft spotlight from the rear of the church. It was like the painting that shows the beam of light from heaven descending on Jesus after he was baptized by John.

My eyes searched the pool, looking for the reddish tint I knew was there. I remembered the old Baptist hymn with the chorus that asks, "Are you washed in the blood of the Lamb?" I shook off those thoughts. God had accepted the deal I'd made with him. My summer had been good, and Daddy had not spanked me since that day I threatened to dump George in the well.

The organ was playing softly as Brother Dunagan baptized the first person. As that person walked out of the pool, the girl in front of me moved out to the center, and I eased down into the waist-deep water. The cold water took my breath away. As Brother Dunagan raised his claw hand in a moment of silent prayer, I involuntarily gasped and said, "Good God A-mighty! This water is cold."

I thought I had whispered, but in the silence of the sanctuary my words blasted out like Joshua's trumpet. Everyone in the church heard me.

I stepped forward and was bathed in the soft beam of the spotlight. I almost expected the clouds to part and a heavenly choir to sing and a voice to say, "This is my beloved son in whom I am well pleased."

The preacher raised his claw hand in silent prayer and placed the other hand behind my neck. Then the claw hand closed over my nose and the nubs gouged my cheek and I was lowered underwater, held half a second, and pulled upright. In Baptist theology I had been born again. I was a new person.

Afterwards I stood in line with the others. We were dripping wet as the congregation came by to shake hands. The church was packed — the biggest crowd I had ever seen, as relatives cooed over sons and daughters and nieces and nephews. Neighbors shook our hands and said they were proud of us. Everyone was smiling and laughing and having a good time.

I was feeling downright proud of myself and how well things were going until I saw Daddy steaming down on me like an out-of-control locomotive. His nostrils were flared, and his face was twisted in anger. He ignored everything and everyone as he marched in my direction. His right hand was fingering his belt buckle. What had I done?

Daddy grabbed my shoulder, spun me out of line, and marched me up the aisle and out the door, ignoring expressions of amazement on the faces of those we passed. He pushed me down the steps, and I suddenly realized this was the moment I had feared for so long. My deal with God had fallen through, and Daddy was about to be the instrument of God's vengeance. I didn't know what had caused Daddy's anger. But I knew that whatever it was, the real reason for the beating I was about to receive was what Gail and I had done in the baptismal pool.

"What'd I do?" I said in anguish as I reached the bottom of the steps and looked over my shoulder at Daddy. He pushed me across the lawn.

"You cussed in church," he said, jerking his belt from his pants. I heard the fusillade as the belt popped through his belt loops. He doubled the belt and held it tightly. "You embarrassed me and your mother in front of the whole town. Dammit, you will never amount to anything. You will always be sorry. But when I'm through with you, you won't ever cuss in church again."

He pushed me and adjusted his grip on the belt.

"I didn't cuss in church," I said. "What'd I say?"

"You know what you said. You said, 'Good God A-mighty.'" He was so angry his face was rigid and contorted.

"The preacher says that all the time. That's not cussing."

"Don't sass me, boy."

He pointed toward the ground. His body was taut and his eyes were as hard as I had ever seen them. There was nothing I could do when he was like that, so I gave up and stood on the spot. It was time to be a man.

Mother went to the car. It was parked under an oak tree only a few feet away. As I rooted my feet to the spot, my eyes met those of my mother. We held each other's gaze for a long moment. Her eyes glistened, and I knew that she would have helped me if she could. Then she looked down; she could not watch what was about to happen. My friends and classmates and members of the congregation stood on the steps or passed with averted eyes. Everyone knew about the Sarge.

The wet jeans clung to my legs, and each lash of the belt snapped and burned. For Daddy, only the two of us were there. He was oblivious to the presence of dozens of people coming out of the church.

A public ass whipping is mortifying beyond description. I was terribly and painfully aware of those people as they stared in horror and walked in a wide circle around us. As my friends and the parents of my friends and all the Baptists in Edison walked by, filled with the happy afterglow of seeing family members join the church, filled with the joy that accompanies one of the most sacred events in the church, they watched and heard my beating. Somehow it just didn't fit in with the prayers and soft music and young people being dunked.

Daddy beat me until he was exhausted. Then, leaning over and gasping for breath, he said, "Dammit. That … will … teach you … not to cuss … in church … ever again."

He straightened up, wove his belt through the loops of his pants, buckled it, pointed toward the car, and said, "Get in."

It was a moment before I could move. My legs were stiff with pain, and my back was bent in humiliation. But my eyes were dry. I cried so little as a boy that I knew a lot of tears had backed up.

I limped toward the car knowing that God had won.

In November I turned thirteen. I looked back and thought that my year of being twelve had been a real bitch kitty. Maybe my first year as a teenager would be better.

6

WHERE in the hell is all this going? Where is my high school experience, my life, going? What can I do to get the Sarge off my ass? Is there anything I can do that will make me fit in with my classmates? Who is going to show me the way? Not a Baptist God. I didn't have a guardian angel, and there was no teacher who had singled me out. There was only my mother, and often there was little she could do. How could I prove to the Sarge that I was responsible, that I had promise, that one day I might make something of myself? How could I become a good son?

I had no role model. Not one single person from Edison had ever done anything of note. Most of those who went away to college returned to Edison. A few went into the military, almost every one of them in the enlisted ranks like Daddy. Those who did go away were rarely heard from again. How the hell could anyone from southwest Georgia do something important?

You might think these unusual thoughts for a boy who had just turned thirteen. But my interior life was rich, even at an early age. I thought long and hard about things that boys my age usually did not think about. It was just one more way that I was different from my friends.

I set myself the task of resolving these thoughts. It would be a few months before the answer came, and you could say it came in a shocking fashion.

ONE day in 1951 I read in the *Calhoun County News* that "Old Butthead," the only passenger train that went through Edison, was being discontinued. From the talk around town, you would have thought the world had ended. People talked about how much they liked to hear the wail of the whistle as Old Butthead came into town, how the train linked Edison to the outside world and how—except for the Trailways bus that stopped on Tuesdays at the service station—we had no other link to civilization.

This bewildered me because I didn't know anyone in Edison who *wanted* contact with the outside world. Except for shopping trips to Columbus or Albany, people in Edison liked to stay close to home. The City Limits sign was no different from the wall around a medieval city. That was where the known world ended, and all beyond the gates were presumed hostile to our way of life.

Nevertheless, the city fathers were perturbed about the train. They had a meeting and announced that in the past ten years, Edison had gone from a population of 1,241 to 1,247, a 0.5 percent population gain, proving that, the demise of Old Butthead notwithstanding, Edison was on the move. We were going into the 1950s full speed ahead.

The utility company sponsored their Better Hometown Contest, and Edison won with the slogan "Pull For Edison or Pull Out." Imagine that: a contest about having a bigger and better hometown, and the winning slogan tells people to support Edison or get out.

Mr. Bill Israel built a big, rambling concrete-block building across the road from our house—a textile mill that would make what the newspaper called "juvenile clothing." We found out that meant underwear for children, and the place thereafter was known as "the seat cover factory."

A local boy was awarded the Silver Star for heroism in Korea, and the people of Edison could talk of little else for weeks.

But the big event for my family began one morning in early February. When I sat down for breakfast, I noticed Daddy was not reading the paper. George was a few steps behind me, holding his stomach, his face in a slight grimace.

"George, you feeling okay?" Daddy asked. "Your stomach hurting?"

"Yes, sir. A little bit. But I'm okay."

"Next time you have a bad stomachache, I'm taking you to Cuthbert to the hospital. We got to find out what's wrong with you once and for all."

"Yes, sir."

Daddy looked at both of us, his face solemn. "Speaking of hospitals, I'm going down to the VA hospital in Cross City, Florida. Got to have an operation. I'll be gone about six weeks." He stared hard at me. "Robert, you will be the man of the house, and I want you to act like it. Be a man. Help your mother." He paused. "I don't want to hear any reports about any shenanigans while I'm gone. If I do, I'll take my belt to you when I get back. You understand?"

"Yes, sir," George and I said in unison.

I don't know why George chimed in. Recorded history did not go back far enough to cover his last ass whipping.

"Six weeks. That's a long time," I said. "What kind of operation you having?"

Daddy hesitated. "I got to get reamed out. Sometimes that happens with men. Now eat your breakfast." He turned sideways in his chair so he could read the paper and eat at the same time.

For the past week Daddy had been particularly upset at Ralph McGill's columns. The Georgia legislature, a collection of freewheeling rascals, had introduced three pieces of legislation aimed at crippling the Atlanta newspapers. McGill said that the state legislators were petty and unworthy, that the legislature would not control the newspapers, and that the newspapers would be there long after the legislators were dead and gone. He called on the people of Georgia to repudiate their pettiness and the prejudice of the legislator, and said that if any of the bills passed, "Then indeed are we close to dangerous days."

Daddy did not sanction anyone flying in the face of authority. As McGill wrote column after column excoriating the legislature, Daddy chortled, "What a crybaby. Newspapers can't go against the law."

But that morning the paper had a front-page story saying that all three bills had been tabled. McGill and the *Atlanta Constitution* had beaten the general assembly.

Daddy shook his head in disgust. "I'll be confounded," he said.

DADDY was in the hospital more than two months recovering from his operation. What he called a "reaming out" was a radical prostatectomy. This was more than a major operation. It was, in 1951 at a VA hospital, a primitive procedure with lasting and damaging effects.

Mother drove back and forth to Cross City, a six-hour trip across the wilds of southwest Georgia and into Florida. Aunt Grace stayed with us while Mother was gone and made sure that in the mornings we were fed, dressed, ready to go when the school bus arrived and that we spent our afternoons studying or working around the house. The only latitude I had was the afternoon when I went to the barbershop, for the first time, without being accompanied by Daddy.

"Come in, Coram, and have a seat," the Judge said when I walked in. Like many people in Edison, he couldn't distinguish between George and me, so he called us both Coram.

The sheriff, a long-legged, taciturn fellow with the flat and impassive eyes of a shark, was sitting in the prime spot across from Judge's chair. He nodded and said, "Coram." The sheriff knew just about everyone in the county. He rarely had to go out and arrest anyone. When someone broke the law, he simply got on the telephone and said, "You better come on down here."

I was afraid of the sheriff and was glad the barbershop was full. I walked all the way to the far end of the pew, in the shadows at the back of the shop, as far away from the sheriff as possible.

I was going to have a long wait, so I picked up a newspaper and began skimming through it. The farmers resumed their conversation about a local woman who was beaten by her husband every time he came home drunk, which was often.

Sometimes I grew impatient with the never-ending cycle of stories at the barbershop. I thought if people had something to say, they should say it. Answer a direct question with a direct answer. But getting a straight answer out of someone in Edison was like trying to nail Jell-O to a tree. If the farmer at the end of the pew by the door did not recognize someone who walked by on the sidewalk, he would look around and ask, "Who was that?" Rather than simply stating the person's name, someone would say, "That's Claude Wilson's oldest boy. His people came from down near Camilla. His mama was a Jones before she got married. He's got two older brothers. One of 'em broke his nose a few years ago. The other spends all his time fishing. He's sorry, just sorry. I hear tell his wife is a good cook, especially fish. She fries 'em up good. People go a long way to eat her fried fish. They got a cousin somewhere up north of Columbus, maybe Manchester, comes through here once in a while. I think he works up at Lockheed. Went to school at the University of Georgia. Notice he was limping? That came when a bull gored him a few years ago. Woulda killed him, but his daddy heard the commotion and came running with his shotgun. Killed the bull. He never had much use for the boy after that though. That bull was special. His sister is ah-ite, married a tractor mechanic from Jakin. Don't see much of them."

I thought this was another of those wandering conversations and was only half listening to what the old men said. "I saw her yesterday," the Judge said, very solemn. "She walked by here, and she was black-and-blue. He really worked her over good."

Now I was listening.

One man started to say something, then there was silence, and I knew he was leaning forward and looking down the bench toward me. I became very intent on the newspaper. The man leaned back and said, "What somebody ought to do is catch that fellow out by himself and beat the ever living dog shit out of him."

The sheriff stared straight ahead. But the other men on the pew nodded in agreement. One said, "I know a bunch of folks who would be glad to do it. They don't hold with men beating up on women."

Then I heard a few whispering noises that sounded like "Shhhhhhhh." Again I sensed the men looking at me. I was holding the newspaper high so that it covered my face. I didn't move.

"It's all right," Judge said softly.

The men were silent for a few minutes, almost as if one of them had said more than he should have in front of me. The Judge flicked the sheet off his customer and said, "Next."

The sheriff climbed into the chair and settled in, and the men in the barbershop began a desultory conversation. Then one of them asked, "Any of y'all heard about this Liberace fellow?"

The men on the pew chuckled. By now they had decided I was lost in the newspaper. They figured that as long as they kept their voices low, I would not hear their conversation.

"I heard tell he's a morphydite," said one farmer.

The click of the Judge's scissors stopped. "Now what in the world is a morphydite?" he asked.

This was getting interesting. Judge was privy to the distilled wisdom of every man in Calhoun County. He knew it all, and he knew it first. It wasn't often that a customer could tell Judge something he didn't already know.

The man who had made the statement now had the floor. Every head turned toward him as he said, "Well, now. A morphydite is one what has it all. It's a woman, but it's got an old thing just like a man."

Silence. A man down my way got up, walked around me, and spit into the spittoon at the end of the pew. Then he sat down and said, "So that's a morphydite?"

"Yessireebobtail," said the font of wisdom. "I'll tell you something else, too."

He waited until someone said, "What's that?" Then he said, "A morphydite can do it to its own self. It can get that old thing hard, stick it in its own self, and flat go to town." He held up a bony Baptist finger, an admonishing finger, looked up and down the pew and said, "Now it can't have babies. But it can screw its own self." He nodded and said, "And that's a fact."

Men nodded. "A known fact," one of them agreed.

For a while they considered this startling information then one of them said, "If that's right, if one of these morphydites can screw its own self, then it can decide that anytime it wants a little, it's going to be the best it ever had."

The men on the pew chuckled appreciatively. The first man held up his finger again and said, "Well, if it ain't, he sure can't complain about it."

As the chuckles died down the sheriff spoke for the first time. "You ever actually seen one of these — what you call them? — morphydites?"

"I spec we've all seen them," said the man doing most of the talking.

I sensed that every man on the pew was shaking his head. It was unanimous. No one had ever seen a morphydite.

"I just don't believe we got any of them in Edison," said one.

"Where you catch 'em is at meetings," said the first man. He voice shifted to a conspiratorial whisper. "When they set down, that old thing starts rubbing against the woman's part, and the morphydite gets itself all excited." He looked up and down the pew. "I been to church and seen the way some people squirm around, and I have my suspicions."

Not a sound came from the pew. The man doing the talking was a Methodist and everyone else on the pew went to the Baptist church. The Methodist baptized people by sprinkling them rather than dunking them, and we always looked on Methodists as never having really washed their sins away. There was no explaining what Methodists did in church.

"Give us a name," said the sheriff in his soft voice. "Tell us the name of somebody you think is one of these here morphydites."

I knew that if the sheriff had a name he would put that person in jail. The sheriff of Calhoun County, Georgia, would not allow morphydites in his county. Nosirree.

"I can't give you a name. But I ain't never seen a real queer either. Not one that I could tell you for sure was a queer. But I know they're out there."

"Not in Edison," said Judge.

Everyone nodded in agreement. "Ain't no queers in Edison," someone said.

"What about Liberace?" someone asked.

Wide grins all around. "Now that there is a real queer. No doubt about it."

"Yeah, but he ain't from Edison."

"That's a fact."

"A known fact."

The consensus that afternoon was that Edison had no queers and no morphydites.

I left the barbershop with eyes wide at all I had heard.

My youth was filled with afternoons like that — long, shimmering afternoons where I sat in the barbershop or around the service station or at a little country stores and learned things that people who grew up in other parts of the country never knew.

DADDY came home weak and wan from his operation. He stayed at home ten days, then began working half days on easy things like installing or repairing telephones. He could not climb telephone poles for another month. He seemed unusually quiet, withdrawn, and preoccupied. I figured he was just tired from his operation.

ONE Saturday afternoon in late April two boys from my class, Joe and Ollie, drove up into the yard. Mother looked out the window, recognized Joe's truck, and said, "Robert, go answer the door."

When I opened the door, there was Joe's smiling face. "Ain't seen you since the hogs ate Granny," he said. "Ollie and me was riding around, and we thought we'd pick you up and ride out to Cordray's Mill." Cordray's Mill was a big pond and favored fishing spot about five miles away.

Both boys were the sons of big farmers and had been driving a tractor or a truck since they were ten years old. Daddy didn't hold with breaking the law and had made it clear that I would not be driving until I was of legal age.

If there was anyone in my class I looked up to and admired, it was Joe. He was a lanky and laconic boy, always smiling, a quip always on his lips. Joe had the most beautiful voice of any boy in school and often sang at school assembly. His favorite was a Stephen Foster song called "Jeanie with the Light Brown Hair." Almost everyone agreed that Joe could sing the birds out of the trees. Once Joe raised his hand and told our history teacher that he wished he had lived a thousand years ago. When the teacher asked him why, he said, "Think of all the history I wouldn't have to learn." Teachers in Edison did not favor smart-mouthed boys, but they all loved Joe. On top of everything else, he was a gifted athlete, on the first string of the track and basketball teams.

Ollie … well, Ollie had the bluest eyes of any person who ever walked. And you could see the devil dancing in those eyes. He was zany; there is no other way to describe him.

Mother and Daddy and all the children were lingering over the dinner table when I brought Joe and Ollie back to the kitchen. Daddy didn't look up. Mother scratched her head and smiled. I knew her dandruff must be acting up. What a family this was. Mother had a severe dandruff problem. Daddy had a chronic case of the red ass. George had stomach aches. Susie was a princess who lived in her own world. Butch ate pine trees. I was the only normal person in the family. Well, maybe. Daddy said I had a bad case of insubordination. I think he was afraid it might be contagious.

When I asked Daddy if I could go riding, he said, "Who all's going?"

"Just me and Ollie," Joe said.

Daddy lifted his head and stared at Joe and Ollie in turn. Daddy's stare could wilt the grass, and both of them were plainly uncomfortable. Then Daddy said, "I know y'all's people." He turned to me and said, "You can go," and I knew then for sure he had not fully recovered from his operation.

As I climbed into the truck between Joe and Ollie, Joe turned to me, held out a clenched fist, and said, "Pick up my thumb."

"I ain't picking up your thumb."

"I'll fart anyway." He said. And he did.

Then we went through the obligatory fart ritual. "Something crawled up your ass and died," I said.

Ollie grimaced, fanned the air, lowered the window, and leaned out and made retching noises.

Joe laughed with pride.

Growing up in southwest Georgia, we were crude and crass and offensive to everyone but ourselves. We gloried in our farts.

The county was paving the road to Cordray's Mill and in the process had changed the course of the road. The 90-degree turn about a mile from the pond was no more. The new road cut through a patch of woods. We knew the construction crews would not be working on Saturday, so we drove around the barriers and down the dirt road. About a half mile later, in what had been a clearing surrounded by thick woods, was a small, unpainted building.

"I didn't know that house was there," said Joe. He slowed down and then stopped. The three of us stared at the house.

"First house I ever saw with the windows painted over," I said.

"That ain't no house," said Ollie.

"If it ain't a house, what is it?" Joe asked. He opened his door. "Let's go see."

We were violating the most sacred taboo of southwest Georgia: trespassing on private property. Respect for other people's property was so strong that if a person was driving down the road and wanted to turn around, he would wait until he came to a wide place in the road or to a side road. He would not drive even ten feet into someone's driveway to make the turn. Poking around somebody's house when no one was at home ... well, you could get shot doing that.

The pine straw under the trees was packed, indicating a number of cars had parked there recently. "Look at that," Joe said, pointing to the eaves of the little house. "No power lines. They don't even have electricity."

"Or a phone," I said.

We walked to the door. "No front door lock either," Ollie said. "They must not be worried about anybody breaking in."

With his toe Ollie pushed open the door, and the three of us stared into a single room. Very little light came through the painted windows, and even with the door open, the room was in twilight. At the far end of the room was a small table, and behind it was a chair. Two kerosene lanterns sat atop the table. Behind the table, propped up against the wall, was a wooden cross. Several dozen folding chairs filled most of the room; more lined the walls. There was a big chest in the far left corner.

"Where's the bathroom?" Ollie asked.

"Ain't no bathroom," Joe said. "They pee in the woods."

"Who's they?" I asked. "What kind of place is this?"

"Nothing in here but that big chest," Ollie said. "Let's see what's in it."

"What if somebody comes up?" Joe asked.

"The road's blocked, and it's Saturday," I said. "Nobody's coming."

"Robert, you crazy as a sprayed roach," Ollie said. "Anybody could come up on us and we wouldn't know it until they walked in the door."

We stared at the chest. Trespassing on private property was bad enough. Walking in and searching a house was worse. But messing with someone's personal items was sacrilegious.

"What's the matter with you two?" Joe said. He walked across the room and flipped open the top of the chest. It was filled with neatly folded white robes covered with symbols and decorated with brightly colored stripes and piping. We dug deeper and found other robes that were plain white. To the side, folded neatly, were high peaked hats and masks with slits for the eyes.

"Oh, shit," Joe said.

"Oh, shit," I said.

"Oh, shit," Ollie said.

What we knew about the Ku Klux Klan we knew only from whispers. We didn't know anyone who would admit to being in the Klan, but there were some who were mean enough that we suspected they were members. Of all the dark secrets in Edison, and God knows there were plenty, the Klan was the darkest. No one wanted to get crossways with the Klan. No one wanted what we called "the guys in bed sheets" coming after them. Sometimes as a warning they burned a cross on the lawn of whoever had crossed them. But they did not always send a warning. Sometimes people just disappeared from the face of the earth and everyone took for granted the Klan had killed them, wrapped chains around them, and tossed them into a swamp.

And now we had walked into whatever it was the Klan members called their meeting place. We were in deep shit.

But being boys, we could not admit that. At least, not for a while.

I picked up one of the decorated robes and held it up. It was far too big for me, but I slipped it over my head and found the matching mask. As I put on the mask, I noticed a name tag sewn inside the headband. The mask belonged to one of the most prominent farmers in the county.

"Look at this," I said, holding the name tag so Joe could see it. He groaned.

We raced through the robes and masks, groping for nametags, never reading them aloud but holding them so the others could read them. We knew every name: bankers, farmers, businessmen, teachers, and county commissioners. I kept digging, wanting to know if my daddy's name was inside one of the robes. Somehow I knew it was. But the chest was deep and there were more robes and Joe and Ollie were too frightened to continue. We were looking at what no non-Klan member had ever seen. We saw names we knew and names no one suspected.

Joe backed away from the chest, eyes wide and arms outstretched as if to fend off demons. "I'm leaving," he said.

"Before we leave, let's get us a robe," Ollie said.

"What the hell for?" I asked.

" 'Cause we can," Joe said with irrefutable logic.

We each grabbed a robe and a mask, folded them tightly under our arms, and ran for the truck. We departed in a cloud of dust and raced for the paved road back to Edison.

"What we goan to do with these?" Ollie asked. "I can't take 'em home."

"Anybody find out we got these, they gonna come looking for us," Joe said. "They goan beat the every-loving dog shit out of us. Hell, they might burn a cross in our front yard."

"Next time one of them comes out here, he will know somebody has been poking around," I said. "They goan look for us."

Joe shook his head. "I don't know whether to shit or go blind."

We drove around for several hours, not knowing what to do with our booty.

It was dusk when Joe said, "We got to get rid of these things." He grinned his don't-give-a-damn grin and said, "Before we do, let's have some fun."

He pulled off the road into the woods, stopped, and stepped out of the truck. He reached for one of the rubes then turned to Ollie and me and said, "Put on the robe and the hat and lie down in the bed of the truck. When I stop, get out in a hurry and follow me."

"What…?" I said.

"Just do it," Joe said. "I'll explain when we get there."

Ollie and I lay on the bed of the pickup, looking up at trees and roofs, having only a vague idea of where we were. Then the truck eased to a stop.

Joe was a ghostly figure when he opened the door, slipped on a robe and mask, and whispered, "Come on, get out. Move fast before somebody comes by and sees us." He pointed at Ollie and me and said, "Put on those hoods."

I jumped to the ground and saw we were in front of the principal's house. Ollie and I giggled nervously and looked at Joe.

"We gonna scare hell out of Mr. Baxter," he said.

Robert Baxter was the principal for grades one through twelve. To the school children of Edison, he was the nearest thing to God.

Ollie turned to Joe and said, "I didn't see his name in a robe. Did you? What are we doing this for?"

"We doing it because his name was *not* in one of the robes. We gonna scare his ass off."

"I don't know about this," I said, hanging back.

"Get your ass on up here," Joe said as he stepped onto the low porch of Mr. Baxter's house. Through the screen door we could see into the living room. "We just stand here and look mean. He's goan shit in his britches." He pointed to the door and said, "Knock on it."

I did, tentatively.

"Harder, shit heel. We supposed to scare him. Make him think it's Judgment Day."

I pounded on the door, grabbed the handle and rattled it, and then, for good measure, kicked it twice. It sounded as if someone was breaking into the house.

The principal's wife came around the corner, head cocked in a quizzical manner. Who in Edison could be making such a racket? She took one look and began backing up, eyes wide in fright. "Bob! Bob!," she shouted. "There are men on the front porch with masks on."

Joe looked at Ollie and me, and I could tell by the sparkle in his eyes that he was smiling. Damn, this was fun. We were going to scare hell out of the principal.

From far back in the house we heard a seismic thump. It was as if the earth had been jarred from its foundations. And then came the sound of someone running, and I remembered that Mr. Baxter had been a halfback on a college football team. He wasn't very tall, but he was muscular. The three of us backed up a half step.

Mr. Baxter never slowed down when he came through the living room. He stiff-armed the screen door, knocked it off its hinges, and kept coming, eyes blazing. He was wearing only a pair of white boxer shorts. I had no idea that his chest was so massive, his arms so big, his legs so muscular. Adding to all this was the thick black hair that covered his chest and shoulders. The man looked like King Kong.

"What the hell are you doing on my porch?" he said, drawing back a fist the size of a ham.

I backed up and ripped the mask from my head. "It's just me, Mr. Baxter. It's just me. Robert Coram. It's just me."

Joe and Ollie ripped off their masks at the same time, and for a moment the three of us stared at Mr. Baxter, fully expecting him to beat the hell out of us. He was breathing hard and his face was contorted, and he kept clenching and unclenching his fists.

"It's just me," I repeated weakly.

No one spoke for a long moment. Mr. Baxter stared at each of us, pointed to the chairs on the front porch, and said, "Take off those things. Sit down." He let out a long breath.

We pulled the robes over our heads, rolled them up, sat down, and placed the robes on our laps. For a long moment Mr. Baxter said nothing. Then he began talking, and he talked for almost an hour. He told us about the history of the Ku Klux Klan and how its members had tortured and hanged and terrorized black people. He told us that Klansmen had exalted titles such as Grand Dragon and Imperial Wizard, but that only cowards wear masks and make mischief by night. When he stopped talking, Joe and Ollie and I were staring at the floor.

"We sorry," Joe said weakly.

"Sorry is not enough," Mr. Baxter said. And then, after a long pause, "You boys go on home." He waited a moment then added, "And get rid of those robes before you get into real trouble."

We gathered our now repulsive white robes and walked to the truck. Mr. Baxter watched us in silence. Joe waved goodbye, but Mr. Baxter did not respond.

About a hundred yards down the road Ollie said with a giggle, "I guess we messed up."

The thoughts of youth are not always long thoughts. All I could think of was how embarrassed I was and what Daddy was going to do when he heard what had happened.

"I didn't know Mr. Baxter was so big," I said. "I didn't know he had such a temper. He's a mean son of a bitch. He was about to kill us." After a moment I added, "What if he had had a gun?"

"I'da taken it away from him and whipped his ass," Joe said. The three of us broke out in uncontrollable laughter.

"Damn, that man has got some muscles," Ollie said. After a moment he added, "And he is getting on up there, too. What is he? About forty?"

"*Big* son of a bitch," Joe said.

"Were you scared?" I asked him.

"I ain't goan lie about it. I was shaking like a fox shitting peach pits."

We laughed again. Then Joe said, "That man don't wear many clothes around the house, does he?"

"It's hot," I said.

I didn't think that was so funny, but it set us off again. We knew we had barely escaped something big, something serious. We sensed that we had walked the edge of a bottomless chasm and, had it not been for Mr. Baxter, would have fallen to a place from which few returned.

No one spoke for a moment. "What we going to do with these robes?" I asked.

"Well, it's for damn sure we can't take them back where we got them," Joe said. "I would pack hot butter up a wildcat's ass before I would go back out there."

"I don't want mine," Ollie said.

"Me neither."

"Me neither."

"Well, shit," Joe said. "Let's don't wear a blister on it. We got to get rid of the things."

At the bottom of the hill we stopped on the bridge that crossed Bay Branch. We rolled the robes tighter, checked to make sure no cars were coming, and stepped outside the truck.

"We need a rock to weigh them down," I said.

"I ain't hanging around looking for no rock," Ollie said. "I got to get home."

"Me, too," Joe said.

We leaned over and threw the robes under the bridge. Bay Branch was shallow and sluggish, but we hoped the robes would be carried downstream and never be seen again. If someone did find them, the Ku Klux Klan would discover who stole the robes and would wreak a terrible vengeance.

EVEN though I was still in bed and more asleep than awake, on this morning in April 1951, I knew Daddy had a scowl on his face. He was consistent: he always had a scowl on his face. I didn't know if he got up with that sour expression or if he put it on in the bathroom. Maybe it came when he opened the newspaper and looked at the picture of Ralph McGill.

I heard a coffee cup slide across the table, and I heard Daddy shake open the paper. I opened my eyes and raised my head so I could better hear what was coming. Yesterday on the radio we heard that President Harry Truman had fired General Douglas MacArthur. Daddy was upset by the news and wanted to see what the paper had to say.

Any minute I expected the usual rant against Ralph McGill, but there was silence. More silence. And then in a voice so soft that I barely heard him, Daddy said, "Sweetheart, I served under General MacArthur."

"I know you did, JB," Mother said, her voice sympathetic.

The way Daddy said this you would have thought he served on the general's personal staff. But I knew that Daddy's last job before retiring was to supervise the training of a battalion that then went straight into combat in World War II. That battalion was under MacArthur's command, and that was the closest Daddy ever got to the general. Daddy had retired with numerous rows of ribbons on his chest, but when people in the barbershop asked him what he was most proud of about his career, he always answered, "Serving under General MacArthur." And if anyone said anything about "Dugout Doug" — one of the general's less flattering nicknames that he acquired in World War II — Daddy got his dander up.

He was also a big fan of President Truman and often said that Truman's decision to drop the A-bomb on Japan showed he was a true leader, a man who could make hard decisions. Daddy liked Truman's no-nonsense manner and appreciated that he had commanded an artillery battery in World War I.

"What does it say about the president firing him?" Mother asked.

For a long moment Daddy did not answer. And then I heard him mumble, "I don't know about this. I just don't know. They both are such good men."

This was a terrible trauma for Daddy. MacArthur was fired for violating the chain of command, for insubordination, for taking a public position contrary to America's official position, and for failing to obey orders. All these things were inviolate to Daddy.

He put the paper aside and quietly ate his breakfast. When he finished, he kissed Mother, picked up his cap, and was gone.

I walked into the kitchen, looked around, and said, "Well, I liked MacArthur's corncob pipe."

"Robert." Mother's voice was sharp.

A few weeks later the general made his farewell address to Congress and then he spoke to the cadets at West Point, where he ended with a line from what he called "a barracks ballad," a line saying that old soldiers never die; they just fade away.

I didn't think MacArthur exactly faded away. He had about the noisiest retirement I had ever seen. He was running for president.

In the coming weeks Daddy searched the paper every morning, eyes narrowed as he looked for news of the general. I wanted to ask him if there was any news about the Klan but I didn't think that was a good idea.

One morning I sat down for breakfast just as Daddy brought up the subject of the general abandoning his presidential campaign. He couldn't understand why MacArthur had withdrawn from the race.

"I guess the country had enough of Mac," I said.

Daddy's head snapped toward me and said, "It is General MacArthur to you, young man. And for your information, the country will *never* turn against him. You don't know what you are talking about. Get up from this table."

"JB, let him eat his breakfast," Mother said.

"He doesn't need breakfast if he thinks like that."

Mealtime conversations at our house were usually about local people or what was going on around Edison. Gossip. We rarely talked about national events. That morning I learned that in our house we did not raise questions about Army generals.

NOT long after I briefly shared membership in the Ku Klux Klan with some of the most prominent people in Calhoun County, something happened that revealed even more about the men whom everyone in Edison looked up to.

In Edison we had people who were "slow," people who were "peculiar," and people who were "not right." Those who were slow were simply not very bright and there was compassion toward them and a gentle sympathy toward their families. Most people who were slow were able to function and to perform the everyday chores of life, but at a, ... well, slower pace.

Peculiar was different. Anyone who did not fit into the tight framework of acceptable behavior in manners, beliefs, conduct, or speech was peculiar. There was a slight edge to the word. This category covered a wide range of behavior, everything from a person who would not respond to "Good morning" all the way to the high school teacher who flew the French flag on Bastille Day. Now she was *really* peculiar.

Finally there were those who were not right. These were people who, had they not lived in a remote section of the rural South, would have been committed to mental institutions. Some of them were as crazy as shit-house rats—we had a surprising number of them running loose in Calhoun County—but most of them were sweet and harmless people who lived in their own little worlds.

Will Dill was not right.

Nobody called him Will; he was always Will Dill. A round-faced, heavyset man of about thirty-five or forty, he always wore the same jeans, same khaki shirt, and same heavy brogans. His lopsided smile never left his face. At dawn every day he appeared at the main intersection in Edison and began waving at cars. As each car passed, Will Dill stepped off the curb and made a loud guttural sound that was supposed to be "Hello" but came out something like "Rrroooaahhh!"

Anyone passing through Edison for the first time got the hell scared out of him when Will Dill jumped off the curb and roared.

But most local passersby waved back and said, "Hey, Will Dill, how you doing?" And that was all Will Dill wanted.

When no cars were in sight, he leaned against a utility pole, muttered to himself, counted his fingers, and smiled sweetly, occasionally looking up and down the road for an approaching car.

Will Dill was a pivotal figure in a drama that played out that year in Edison, a drama that involved a girl who rode the school bus with me every day, a drama that showed how the less fortunate were sometimes treated in Edison, a drama that showed me how heartless and how mean grown-ups could be.

Thelma was sixteen, a big girl, maybe five foot ten, plain of face with stringy blond hair, and a bit on the slow side. She needed a lot of extra help in school. But she had a body of heart-stopping perfection. It is a measure of God's sense of irony that such a homely girl, such a slow girl, had a body that caused people to stare in utter disbelief. From the neck down she was the most perfect female ever to come out of Edison, Georgia. With a pretty face, she could have won the Miss America Pageant. She could have been a movie star.

When she walked to the refreshment stand during a basketball game, the referees stared. People from the visitors' section stared. Out-of-town players stared. The wealthy farmers and businessmen of Edison stared. When she strolled down the street in Edison, cars slowed as farmers watched Thelma slink like a lioness. She was unaware of all this. There was always a faraway smile on her face, so I think she lived in a world where she heard whispers and sweet music and where the sun was always shining and a gentle breeze always blew.

On the school bus she always sat in the same seat, two rows behind the driver. She sat slightly stooped over, elbows resting on her books, staring straight ahead, smiling, unblinking. I don't think I ever heard Thelma speak to anyone on the bus. And if you asked her a question, she tilted her head and smiled a little wider but she never answered. Sometimes when the bus stopped in front of her house, the driver had to say, "Thelma, this is where you get off." She would slowly stand, look out the window as if to confirm we had stopped at her house, and then saunter off the bus, never changing her expression. The driver always watched as she walked in front of the bus, walked across her front yard, passed the old pickup truck her daddy drove and the fenced-in area where a dozen chickens roamed, climbed the steps to her unpainted house, opened the door, and disappeared into the dark interior. Then the driver sighed and slowly drove away. Sometimes he would say, "Mighty pretty chickens they got." He wasn't looking at the chickens.

One morning when the bus stopped at Thelma's house, the screen door was sagging open, the chickens were running loose, the pickup truck was not in the yard, and Thelma was not waiting on the porch. The driver blew the horn, but no one appeared.

"House looks empty to me," the driver said. He looked over his shoulder. "Y'all kids stay on the bus." He climbed out of his seat, walked to the door, and knocked. No one answered. He walked to the edge of the porch and looked out back. Nothing, no sign of life, only that feeling you have when you know you are looking at an empty house.

"That beats all," the driver said as he sat back down in his seat. Then he cranked up the bus and drove away, occasionally looking back over his shoulder.

"Would you do that for me?" I asked the driver.

"Would I do what?"

"Come knock on my front door if I wasn't by the road waiting for you?"

He didn't answer for a moment. Then he snapped a look over his shoulder, glared, and said, "Boy, your daddy ever tell you that you got a smart mouth on you?"

"Just about every day."

"Well, he's right."

A few days later I heard Mother and Daddy whispering about Thelma, but I didn't catch enough to understand what they were talking about. I knew something big was going on when Mother shook her head, pursed her lips, and said, "They oughta be *ashamed* of themselves. That is just not right."

It was a week before word slowly spread through school, and the story was a real doozy.

Turns out that for a year or so, Thelma had been having sex on a regular basis with three or four men in Edison. I don't know any details — how she got away from home, whether all this happened during the day or at night. I don't know anything except that she was said to have been having sex with men older than her daddy, and it had been going on for some time. They were paying her. I suspect it wasn't much. Then she got pregnant.

Such things did not happen in Edison in 1951. This was a time when touching a girl's breast was daring behavior for a boy and allowing her breast to be touched was even more daring behavior for a girl. This was a time when most girls were virgins when they married. This was a time when Thelma found herself in the worst possible situation a girl could find herself in, a situation with only one solution: she had to get married.

When each of the men she had been having sex with denied that he was the father, Thelma showed she might not be slow in all things. She knew enough to say to them that that she was going to tell her daddy what had been going on and that he was going to come after somebody with a shotgun. The men told her not to worry, that they would work things out. One of them would marry her. They would get back to her in a few, days and everything would be okay.

Then these men sat down with Will Dill and told him he was the daddy of Thelma's baby and that he should marry her. At the same time, these men began dropping word in the barbershop and service station. "You hear what old Will Dill has been doing with that girl that lives out there behind the American Legion Hall? I think her name is Thelma. Young girl looks like a grown woman. Yeah, her and old Will Dill. Hard to believe." The man would give a sorrowful shake of his head, stare off into the distance, and say, "You just never know, do you?"

Will Dill began jumping off the curb with that lopsided grin, waving, and shouting, "Ahfuhthel," which several old men were kind enough to translate as "I fucked Thelma."

Overnight Thelma and her mama and daddy packed everything they owned into that old pickup truck and left town. No one seemed to know where they went, only that they were gone. Poof! Disappeared. Never seen or heard from again.

People in Edison knew that Will Dill was not guilty of anything except being a few bricks shy of a load. They tried to get him to stop shouting, "Ahfuhthel," but he sensed people were reacting to him in a different way, and he kept shouting.

The Big Possums shook hands with one another, congratulated themselves on how they had handled a potentially bad situation, and allowed as to how they were going to miss Thelma. Life went on.

That sorry episode taught me much about grown-ups, about those who keep their silence rather than revealing what they know to be the truth. I learned something about the vulnerability of those who are slow, too. But most of all I learned a lot about the Big Possums of Edison. They were mean enough to be in the Klan. And many of them were.

7

In Edison we were primitive in our profanity, having neither the eloquence of Arab countries nor the bite of young military men. We were scatological amateurs, "shit ass" being the most common pejorative description of someone, "morphydite" being next on the list. Occasionally someone would throw in a new word heard on a trip to Atlanta, but usually we stuck with the old standbys.

The one word we never used was what we called "the GD word" or "taking the Lord's name in vain." In all my years in Edison, I never heard "goddamn." Well, maybe a couple of times from Edison boys who had joined the Army and were home on leave. But this phrase truly shocked people. It halted the conversation. It simply was not done.

The closest I ever came to using profanity in front of Daddy was the morning of my electrifying epiphany. Before I tell you the details, you need to know that my daddy was a Mason. He went to all the meetings, did all the secret squirrel stuff, and was proud of being a member of such an ancient organization. Often at night he had his head stuck in some Masonic book, studying for various tests, and eventually he did whatever a Mason has to do to become a member of the Ancient Arabic Order of the Nobles of the Mystic Shrine—a Shriner. These are the aging party boys of the Masons. After Daddy became a Shriner, he bought a cattle prod to use in initiation rites.

A secret religious order with cattle prods. You figure it out.

A cattle prod has to be pretty powerful to force a big steer through the chute on the way to being slaughtered. Daddy bought the most powerful prod he could find. It had five batteries and was covered in shiny chrome. In my memory it was about two feet long and had prongs on the working end and a rubber handle on the other. The handle had a button that, when pressed, caused the prod to emit a high-pitched, sizzling buzz. Daddy was very proud of this thing and would pull it out at the least provocation, wave it around, and boast, "You don't see many this big."

Here I saw a philosophical disconnect between Mother and Daddy. She went to garden club meetings, made cakes for shut-ins, drove people to visit the doctor up in Cuthbert, and listened to anyone with a sad story. Daddy, well he poked people with a cattle prod.

One morning my questions about where I was going with my life came together with the cattle prod and brought a clarity about my future I never dreamed possible. About 6 a.m. one Saturday the Sarge tiptoed into our bedroom, slid the cattle prod under the covers on my bed, jammed the prongs against my leg, and pressed the button. I thought I had been struck by lightning. The pain was more a burning sensation than an electrical shock, and I was instantly standing up in bed and screaming in anguish.

Daddy laughed and jabbed at me, looking for an opening. He was holding his thumb down on the button, causing a constant sizzling sound, and I knew that if the two prongs even grazed my legs, I would feel the burning pain again. I was backed into the corner, dancing up and down on the bed, every bit of profanity I knew hovering on the tip of my tongue.

That morning I learned I could squeal like a girl. My squealing came both from the pain and from the fact that my daddy was deliberately causing the pain. And he would have continued had Mother not charged through the door.

"JB, you stop that right now."

"I'm just waking him up," Daddy said, poking at me, still laughing. This was as funny as hell to him. Across the room George had his head out from under the cover watching me leap and cavort. If he had not been half-asleep, he would have been laughing, too.

I have to tell you, if I was a steer and I knew that big building at the end of the chute was a slaughterhouse, I would charge ahead when poked by a five-battery cattle prod. I was still dancing in place, my knees coming up almost to my chin. "Daddy, I'm awake. I'm awake. I'm wide-awake."

Mother seized Daddy's arm. "Stop it," she ordered. "Now."

Reluctantly Daddy took his thumb off the button, and the frying noise ended. He dropped the five-battery cattle prod to his side. "I said I'm just waking him up," he told Mother. "We going to the fish camp tonight, and your son has a lot of work to do before then."

"JB, there are other ways to wake him up. You know that. Now come in the kitchen and eat your breakfast before it gets cold."

Daddy looked at Mother. He looked at me. The idea that his food was cooling off was more compelling than poking me again with the five-battery cattle prod. He waved the prod and said, "Young man, you better start getting up earlier on Saturdays. You got work to do."

I was still backed into the corner, standing on my tiptoes.

And that is when the answers to some of my questions came. It is amazing how a cattle prod can focus your thinking. A cattle prod can give you a philosophy about life.

Where is my life going?

Nowhere and fast.

What can I do to get the Sarge off my ass?

Nothing. He is the Sarge, and I am a recruit. I do not have a life, only boot camp.

Is it possible to find something, to do anything, that will enable me to fit in a bit better with my classmates?

Yes. And maybe at the same time it will cause the Sarge to lighten up, to do the equivalent of granting me a weekend pass.

That my idea would work was dim and unlikely, but if it did work, the Sarge might occasionally take his gimlet stare off me.

I was not getting out of Edison anytime soon. I was in bondage, just like the children of Israel that Brother Dunagan preached about. Until I was led to the promised land, which was anywhere beyond Edison, I had to stay out of range of Pharaoh, or he would wave his royal staff, the five-battery cattle prod. My sweet and gentle mother would help when she could, but I needed more.

My epiphany, brought on by the five-battery cattle prod, might be the answer. Next year I would become an athlete.

If that sounds like a simple solution to a vexing problem, consider these two things. First, I was not only the smallest boy in my class; I was also the smallest boy in high school. And second, you might say I did not have the proper frame of mind to be an athlete. Southwest Georgia, as much as any other part of America, places a premium on young men participating in sports. It is expected. It is a mystical priesthood, a gathering of gladiators. The problem was that I just didn't give a rat's ass about any sport you could name. But next year I would become an athlete.

A few minutes after Mother pulled Daddy into the kitchen, I was dressed and walking toward the table, far more awake than usual at this time of the morning. Daddy was seated at one end of the table, a scowl on his face as he read the *Atlanta Constitution*. When I think of my daddy, I always see that dour, scowling face. I don't think he was unhappy. I think that was his Army face.

Mother sat at the other end of the table, and as usual I sat next to her.

"George started his job yesterday," Daddy said without lifting his eyes from the paper. "Idn't it about time you started earning your allowance?"

"Yes, sir."

Daddy had decided that George and I should each have a job to justify our $2 per week allowance, something to teach us a sense of responsibility. Cleaning out Daddy's telephone truck and organizing the tools and equipment was George's job. For me, Daddy came up with a special job: washing dishes. Or, as he called it, "permanent KP."

"Can't I do something else?" I asked.

Every boy I knew had a job on the farm or around the house, so working for my allowance was reasonable. But my friends drove tractors and hay balers; they put screwworm medicine on cows, loaded pickup trucks with fertilizer, cut the grass, or painted the garage. They did a hundred things around their houses, things they could gripe about but were secretly proud of because their jobs showed the increased responsibilities their parents were giving them.

Boys did not wash dishes. But the Sarge had assigned me to KP duty, so I would wash dishes, dry them, and return them to their proper place. I also would not talk about my job, and I would hope to hell no one ever asked. The next time a friend said, "I almost got a hernia loading those hundred-pound bags of fertilizer," what was I going to say? . . . "Look at these dishpan hands."?

Mother put her hand on my shoulder and said, "You excited about going to the fish camp tonight? Rudy and Dorie and their family will be there."

"Yes, ma'am."

This had been a hell of a morning. Hit by lightning before daylight. A newfound philosophy. Then reminded of my he-man dishwashing job. A night at the fish camp would be good.

Rudy and Dorie were the only couple Mother and Daddy ever socialized with. Rudy owned a business that made concrete vaults. His crews went out and dug graves. They lowered the vault into the grave and then, after the casket had been lowered into the vault, sealed and covered the vault and placed the headstone on the grave. He had several other businesses that kept him on the road a lot, and I remember that he always dressed very well. Like most men in Edison, he was overweight, but he had the sleek and well-groomed look of a man who made a good living. He made enough money that he and Dorie had a house down in Panama City, Florida, the vacation spot of choice for people in Edison. Maybe that is why he smiled all the time. I don't think I ever saw Rudy without a big smile on his face.

Dorie always had a big smile, too, and was solicitous toward everyone, even children. She was active in every women's group around Edison. But most people agreed that she was a motormouth. Say good morning to her, and a half hour later you staggered away exhausted.

I don't know how the friendship between the two families got started or why it continued over the years. Daddy and Rudy seemed to have very little in common. Maybe it was because Mother did not mind listening to Dorie. That and the fact that Dorie sometimes came out to the house to help Mother get rid of her dandruff. Mother would lie on her back across her bed, her head hanging over the side, and Dorie would pull up a chair and use a big comb to part Mother's hair, then use the end of the comb to gently dislodge large flakes of dandruff and comb them onto the floor. This process went on for an hour or more. It was like a couple of howler monkeys, one grooming the other. Dorie chattered away the entire time, and Mother occasionally shrugged and said, "Uh-huh."

Our families met occasionally at the fish camp near Blakely, about twenty miles away. The fish camp was a ramshackle, unpainted building with big screen porches that perched on the banks of a creek that fed into the Chattahoochee River. No one fished at the fish camp. It was a restaurant that specialized in fried catfish, fried shrimp, fried hush puppies, fried apple fritters, fried everything. Like every other restaurant in southwest Georgia, it operated on a near-ecclesiastical mandate: If you fry it, they will come.

The fish camp was the only place I ever saw Daddy take a drink. When he was young, he drank often and a lot. But when I was born, he told Mother he did not want his children to see him the way he had been as a young man, and he pretty much stopped drinking. The one exception was at the fish camp, when Rudy brought out his paper bag with the bottle of bourbon inside and Daddy made what he called a "highball" for each of the grownups. After they had a couple of drinks, they would switch to the syrupy sweet tea that was about the only thing people in southwest Georgia drank with their meals.

What I remember about that particular night is that after dinner, while we were all full and contented, Rudy leaned across the table, flashed that big smile, and asked, "Robert, you want to dig some graves?"

I didn't know what the hell he was talking about. So while I'm staring at him, amazed to be included in the grown-up conversation, he said, "Another couple of years, I'll give you a job. Gotta tell you it's hard work. Digging graves in red clay ain't nobody's idea of fun. But I'll pay you good money."

Daddy didn't know what to make of this. He thought I was dumb as a stump-trained mule. But here is one of Edison's most successful businessmen saying that when I got a little older he wanted to hire me.

"Most funerals are on the weekend," Rudy continued. "That means on Saturday you'll be on a pick and shovel and on Sunday you'll be covering up the hole you dug Saturday." He turned to Daddy. "JB, we talking a year or so down the road, but I want you to think about whether or not he can miss church sometime."

"You will have to keep a close eye on him," Daddy said. I could always count on him to give me a full vote of confidence. "But maybe having a job will straighten him out and make something out of him. The discipline will do him good. I don't think it would matter if he missed church sometime."

The smile on Rudy's face grew even bigger. "Then we got a deal." He turned back to me. "Robert, if you want to learn the business, I'll start sending you out with a crew maybe next year. Can't pay you yet, gotta understand that. But you'd be learning how we do things."

Now Daddy nodded in approval. He liked the idea of my digging holes in concrete-hard red clay and not getting paid. Mother smiled across the table at Rudy and said, "Thank you."

It was settled. Soon I would begin my new career as a grave digger.

WHENEVER I went home with classmates after school there was always something fascinating to do on their farms, usually involving tractors or peanut pickers or big trucks. When I went home with Joe, we drove his big tractor up and down US Route 27, a primary north-south route for Yankees going to Florida in the fall and coming back in the spring. We drove slowly up a big hill as the cars lined up behind us, waiting for a stretch of road where they could press hard on the accelerator and leap around us, then get on down the road and out of southwest Georgia as fast as they could. Whether going north or south, Yankees did not like the heat of southwest Georgia. I was amazed at how little clothes some women wore in the car. As the long line of cars passed us, Joe and I would lean over and look into the open windows at the women with their dresses up around their waists or with no blouses on, sometimes even no brassieres. This happened often, and every time it did, Joe and I thought we had found the promised land.

"You see the titties on that woman in the Buick?"

"Yeah I did. That car was from New York."

"New York women got pretty titties."

"Sure do."

But back at my house, on our piddling little two acres, there was not a lot to do except get something to eat and maybe walk in the field of broom sedge.

One day Ollie came to the house after school, and that day I realized that if parents knew the innermost thoughts of their teenage boys, they would pray without ceasing. If parents knew the deeds of their teenage boys, they would lock them up. And if people from other parts of America knew about boys in southwest Georgia, it would fulfill every stereotype they had.

"You boys go outside and play," Mother said. "And don't you wander off."

Ollie and I each grabbed a biscuit left over from breakfast. Using a finger to poke a hole in it, we then filled the hole with thick cane syrup.

Pal came running up when he heard the back door slam behind us. His tail was up, and he was begging for food. I pinched off a piece of syrup-soaked biscuit and pitched it to him. He swallowed it without chewing and begged for more, following us, tail wagging.

Ollie glanced over his shoulder. When he did not see Mother at the screen door, he said, "You ever beat off your dog?"

This was not a question I heard every day. While I was trying to come up with, "Hell, no," Ollie said, "I do it for my dog all the time. He loves it."

"You beat off your dog?"

"You beat off your own self, don't you?"

I looked over my shoulder. "Every time I get half a chance."

"Then you oughta do it for your dog."

"Ollie, that don't make no sense." I looked over my shoulder again. "Let's go over behind the garage. I don't want Mother hearing this."

"Makes a lot of sense," Ollie said. "I'll show you." He threw Pal a piece of biscuit and said, "Pal, you about to go to heaven."

Behind the garage was a small wooded patch. We wandered among the scraggly oaks, found a shady spot, sat down, and munched on our biscuits.

"Ollie, you shitting me about beating off your dog?"

"Nah, I'd quit you 'fore I'd shit you." He finished his biscuit, licked his fingers, and said, "Lemme show you." He snapped his fingers. "Come here, Pal."

Pal did not need a second invitation. He was all over Ollie, licking his face and looking for another piece of biscuit. Ollie grabbed Pal's collar with his left hand and maneuvered Pal around a bit. "You can't get your hand all the way around his dick, so you got to hold your fingers like this," he said, showing me that his hand was cupped and his thumb and fingers vertical and tightly together. Holding Pal's collar with one hand, he reached out with the other and grabbed Pal's dick. The dog's eyes widened for a moment, then he rolled his eyes and looked over his shoulder to see what the hell was going on. He tried to maneuver away but Ollie held tight with one hand and moved his other faster and faster, and soon Pal was in a state of grace. As he ejaculated, he yelped and danced and began thrusting with his hips.

"He's air fucking," Ollie said. He giggled and released the dog. Pal wandered away a few feet, still thrusting his hips, and then after a few moments came over and licked Ollie's face. I mean he seriously licked Ollie's face. If ever a dog said "thank you," it was

Pal. Now I believed Ollie. Dogs like to get beat off. It makes sense when you think about it.

In my short life I had seen some strange things. But this one took the cake. "How often you do that to your dog?" I asked.

"Couple times a week. He wants me to do it more." Ollie reached into his pocket and pulled out a small piece of wire that formed a circle. "I made this in my daddy's shop," Ollie said. "Nothing to it." The tips of the wire were bent back in a "U" shape and hooked together. Opposite the connection the wire was bent into an inverted U shape.

"The hell is that?"

Pal was still trying to lick Ollie's face. "Get away, dog," Ollie said. He held up the wire again. "I took this piece of wire and bent it double. Then I bent it back double the other way to make this little bump in the middle. The hooks on the end hold it together."

"Yeah, but what is it?"

"I put it on my dog's dick when I beat him off. This little bulge in the wire mashes down the tube in the bottom of his dick. He shoots off, but it can't come out." Ollie giggled. "You oughta see him dance."

Pal was back again, still licking Ollie's face. "Want me to put it on Pal and show you how it works?" He looked up under Pal. "I think it will work. Their dicks are about the same size."

"Wait a minute. You mean he shoots off, but this thing keeps it from coming out? Where does it go?"

"Nowhere. Backs up, I guess, for a few seconds and then I take this gadget off. My dog sleeps for hours after I do this."

"Ollie, why the hell would you want to do that to a dog?"

"One time I squeezed my dick really hard when I was about to shoot off. God A-mighty. I was jumping around like I got hit by a truck. I couldn't hold it long." He waved the wire. "That's when I got the idea for this."

"Well, you ain't doing that to my dog."

Pal was nuzzling Ollie. "He wants me to."

"I don't care what he wants. You ain't doing it." I stood up. "Let's go back in the house and get another syrup biscuit."

Ollie was disappointed. "Okay."

Years later I met a man who boasted that he had seen a dancing bear and a woman preacher and had heard a Salvation Army band. He said that he had been to many places around the world and there was little that was new to him.

"You ever seen anybody beat off a dog?" I asked.

He stared at me, decided I was being serious, and said, "Can't say that I have."

"Then you ain't seen it all."

Ollie later went off to medical school and became a prominent psychiatrist. Still later he got into trouble selling prescription drugs. When I heard about his legal problems, I figured there was not that much between jerking off dogs and selling drugs. Ollie just wanted to bring happiness to the world.

One Monday after school I was sitting at the counter in the drugstore sipping on a cherry Coke when Ollie and Joe walked in, looked around, and then whispered urgently that one of the men whose name we had found in one of the decorated robes at the KKK house was next door in the barbershop. "That man is the imperial snapdragon," Joe said.

"The what?"

"Don't you remember all those titles Mr. Baxter told us about? That man is the imperial snapdragon."

"It is imperial wizard or grand . . . ."

Joe waved a hand in dismissal. "Who cares? Robert, you got to do this. The men in the barbershop saw us when we walked by. We can't turn around and go in there now. They will know that wudn't where we were going. You got to go. You need a haircut anyway."

"I never need a haircut. I always go before I need one."

"Well, you can get one."

It had been more than a month since we broke into the KKK house and we had heard nothing. The robes must have washed on down the creek where no one would ever find them. Mr. Baxter had never mentioned that episode on his porch again—not to us and apparently not to anyone else. But we knew the Klan would not let this thing go. We had stolen their property. We had insulted their role in the county. They had to be out beating the bushes for the guilty party. They had ears everywhere. With the Klan leader in the barbershop, this was our chance to learn how their search was going. The plan was for me to go next door, get a haircut, and see if the "imperial snapdragon" gave me the evil eye or said anything about the break-in.

I didn't want to do it. My mouth was as dry as a popcorn fart. "They won't be talking 'bout the Klan house, not in public," I said. "All everybody in Edison is talking about is that woman who killed her husband the other day."

"Prob'ly. But we need to find out if they talking about us. You got to do this."

I shrugged. "Okay."

"Listen," Joe said. "That dragon man smarts off at you, kick his bony ass and run."

"I ain't kicking no Klan man."

"Get on over there," Ollie said. "See what they talking about."

I walked out of the drugstore, turned left, and had taken no more than two steps when I heard a voice saying, "Coram." I turned, and Mr. Bill Israel was walking toward me. Mr. Bill was the most elegant man in Edison, a tall, slender, impeccably dressed man with a soft voice and a ready smile.

"You and your family liking it out there in the country?" he asked.

Daddy had bought two acres of pasture from Mr. Bill to build our house on. Mr. Bill and his wife and two boys lived in an enormous house on a hill about a halfmile across the pasture. Down at the bottom of the hill was a big fishpond. Not only had Mr. Bill sold part of his pasture land to Daddy, but he also had fenced the property in after we bought it.

"Yes, sir. We like it a lot."

"You ever need anything, you know where I live." He stuck out his hand. Not many grown-ups offered to shake hands with boys as young as me, but Mr. Bill did. I shook his hand, then turned and walked into the barbershop.

Judge looked up, nodded, and said, "Coram. Come in and have a seat."

A dozen of Edison's Big Possums were there, all lined up on the pew. Each one nodded as I walked past them toward the end of the pew, including the Klan leader, who murmured, "Coram."

Damn. He knew my name. He was lean and lanky like the sheriff and had the same hooded eyes and air of latent meanness oozing from his pores. He scared hell out of me.

"I see you talking to Mr. Bill," one of the farmers said.

"Yes, sir. He was asking me if I liked it out there in the country being his neighbor."

Judge stopped his scissors, looked up and down the pew, and said, "Mr. Bill is a fine man."

Nods of approval, and a few muttered, "Yep. Fine man." The dragon man nodded in agreement, too.

I sat down and picked up a newspaper. I had learned that if I stuck my head in a paper, the Big Possums would talk as if I wasn't there. It is that way with reading. If people see you reading a newspaper or a magazine or a book, they assume you are in another world and talk all around you. So it was on this day. Once I picked up the paper, the conversation that had been going on when I walked in the door picked up. As I thought, they were talking about the woman who for years had been beaten up by her husband every time he came home drunk, which was about every weekend. But this past Saturday night she was waiting for him at the door with a baseball bat. When he walked into the house, she stepped up behind him, and that was all she wrote. We were going to have a funeral come Tuesday.

"Lemme tell you what I heard happened," said one of the farmers. "That woman used to hide in the closet on Saturday nights to keep from getting beat up. Her husband never thought to look in there. After he stumbled around a little bit, he would pass out, and the next morning he had forgotten all about it."

"Yeah, but she was black-and- blue about every time I saw her," said another farmer. "He found her some of the time."

The first farmer smiled. "Well, now, he wudn't exactly predictable. He took to drinking weeknights. And when he came in, he beat her up something awful."

Another farmer spoke up. "She was a big woman. If she had her weight behind that baseball bat, she musta really worked him over."

The first farmer was determined to finish his story. "That's the reason she killed him," he said triumphantly.

The clicking of the scissors stopped. "She killed him because she was a big woman?" Judge asked.

"No. She got so big, she couldn't get in that closet to hide any- more. She didn't want a beating, so she pulled out the baseball bat and waited for him."

The Big Possums nodded and thought and digested this, and then one summed it up by saying, "That woman hadn't gotten so fat, her husband would still be alive."

"I spec you right," said the farmer next to me.

After a long silence the dragon man said. "I don't know about that."

When he spoke, it was as if someone had opened a refrigerator door and let a cold wave of air into the room. I could feel the man next to me go tense. He began studying the wall across the room. There was a long silence, and then the old man who operated the antiques store asked, "Well, who's going to preach his funeral?"

Blank stares.

"How 'bout that Methodist preacher y'all got?" Judge asked.

"Well, he called hisself a preacher. But I don't think he was much of nothing. We ran him off after that sermon he preached yesterday," said the antiques dealer.

"He preach against the Lord?" asked the dragon man. The temperature in the barbershop dropped another ten degrees.

Behind the newspaper I was lapping this up. If the dragon man was pissed at the Methodist preacher, he might burn a cross on the church lawn. That would be something to see. Or he and some lesser dragons might drag the preacher out on the church lawn and beat his ass. I'd heard of them doing that with people who crossed them. God knows what they would do to people who broke into the Klan house and stole their robes. I pulled the paper closer to my face so that now it was almost around my shoulders, leaving only my legs in sight.

"Well, not exactly. He was talking about Noah. Said that during the flood the whole earth was covered with water. Everything on earth, every living creature that wudn't on the ark, was dead. And in the middle of all that a bunch of Indians began shooting at the ark. That preacher said the Indians shot up the ark something awful. Filled it full of arrows."

"Where'd them Indians come from?" asked the dragon man. I could tell by his tone of voice he didn't appreciate a bunch of heathen Indians shooting at Noah. If he knew where they came from, he would gather his hooded, sheet-wearing buddies and get on over there and lay a Klan ass whipping on all their descendants.

The farmer raised his forefinger and said, "That is exactly what we asked him. Someone stood up in the middle of the sermon and said, 'Preacher, how 'bout them Indians?' The preacher hemmed and hawed and said they just showed up, that was all. Well, he was misquoting the Bible, and we ain't gonna stand for that foolishness. So we told him to pack his bag and get on the road. We can find us another preacher."

"So y'all ain't got a preacher?" Judge asked as his customer stepped down from the chair and stood there for a moment flicking hair from his shoulders. Judge whisked his little brush across the man's collar.

"Nope."

"Sounds like you didn't have much of one anyway," said the dragon man. He stood up and moved to the chair, then slid in like he was a snake coiling up. The Judge threw his barber's sheet across the dragon man and snugged it around his neck. "They's some sorry people in this county. I'm looking to identify some of them that been up to mischief here lately."

I froze. He was talking about Joe and Ollie and me. I wanted to get out of there while he was in the chair. I stood up and walked toward the door.

"You leaving?" the Judge asked. "Don't you want a haircut?"

"I'll be back."

Then a long bony finger snaked out from under the barber's sheet and the dragon man said, "Coram."

Oh, shit. Here it comes. I stopped and looked into the eyes of the man who led the Ku Klux Klan in Calhoun County.

"Yes, sir."

"Yo daddy is a good man."

How did the dragon man know my daddy that well?

"Yes, sir. Thank you." I was edging toward the door.

"Served his country in peace and war."

"Yes, sir. He did."

"A boy can do worse than following in his daddy's footsteps."

Now I was almost certain that Daddy was part of this man's klavern.

The Judge chuckled as he picked up his scissors. "Coram, how old are you?"

"Thirteen."

The Judge began clipping away. "Give him a few years. It's a little early for him to be thinking about joining the army."

"Ain't never too early to teach a boy right," said the dragon man. He pointed at me again. "Remember what I told you."

"Yes, sir." And I was out the door. The Klan had no idea who had broken into their house and stolen their robes. Joe and Ollie and I were safe.

In the drugstore, Joe and Ollie looked up, both big-eyed, when I sat down at the counter and let out a big sigh. "What'd you hear?" Joe asked. "Does Mr. Chief Snapdragon know about us?"

"He ain't no snapdragon. Don't you remember what Mr. Baxter said?"

"I ain't here to talk about Mr. Baxter. Tell me about the Klan man."

"If we keep our mouths shut and never tell anybody what we did, we won't have to worry about him."

Ollie looked at me in surprise. "We won't?"

"Nah. We got to worry about the Indians."

Ollie and Joe looked at me for a moment. Both took a sip of their Cokes. Joe nodded and said, "Somebody is always on our ass, ain't they?"

8

I don't remember what it was about. All I remember is that one morning Daddy rode me hard all through breakfast. His ridicule rolled over me and clung to me, and as he walked out the front door, his Army boots thumping, I ducked my head in frustration. I walked into the living room because I didn't want George to see how close to tears I was and sat on the sofa, my lips trembling, my arms crossed as I rocked back and forth.

I heard Mother tell Susie and Butch to eat their breakfast and then she got up from the table and followed me into the living room. She looked at me, and said, "Robert, I told your Aunt Clara I would come up today and help her rearrange the living room. Would you like to help move the furniture around?"

"Yes, ma'am. If you want me to."

She shut the door, her face serious. She stood in front of me, smiling, looking down with a look of utter compassion.

"What is it, son?"

"Mother, why does he do it?" I asked in barely controlled anguish. "Daddy picks on me about things I haven't even done. He just lays in wait for me to do something wrong. It never ends. It never ends."

There was more I wanted to say, more I wanted to know, but these were things I could not articulate. Why did Daddy demean me? Was I truly as incompetent and useless as he said? Hell, even a blind hog can find an acorn once in a while. I couldn't be all bad. I was his son, his firstborn son.

Frustration at my inability to express what I was feeling caused tears to roll down my cheeks, which made me all the more upset. Boys did not cry, not in southwest Georgia. And here I was crying like a girl. If Daddy saw me he would whip my ass out of general principle. He did not allow crying. I squeezed my hands into fists in frustration, staring up at Mother, hoping she could tell me something, anything, that would help me understand.

Mother moved around in front of me, kneeled down, and held my hands. She leaned close, her brow wrinkled as she gathered her thoughts. She squeezed my hands, then raised her eyes and stared long and hard into my eyes.

"Robert, before you were born, your daddy went out and bought every book about raising babies that he could find. He wanted to be a good daddy. He read those books. He did."

I snorted.

She pulled on my hands to emphasize her words. "Robert, listen to me. He did. He wanted to be a good daddy, and he read those books."

I stared at her, speechless, which was not my normal state. I usually had an opinion about everything. But I was struck dumb by the idea that the Sarge read books about how to raise children.

"I don't think it took," I said.

Mother smiled. "Robert, your daddy and I talked about those books, about what was in them. But..."

I waited a moment. "But what?"

She shook her head. "The Army." She paused for a long moment as if that explained everything. "That's all he knows. He was forty-three when you were born. That's too old to change." Another pause. "It was the Army."

"Why did you marry him?"

"Because I loved him. He is a good man, a good husband, a good daddy, a good provider for our family."

I had no response.

"Robert, it was the Army."

"Well, I ain't never joining the Army."

"Son, you need to think about what I just told you."

She paused a moment and continued. "You are his first child, his first son. He is learning. Every part of your life is new to him as a daddy." She paused again. "And Robert, you don't make it easy for him. Sometimes I think you go out of your way to aggravate him. It might help if you showed more interest in things he is interested in."

Because I loved my mother, my protector, my friend, my ally against the Sarge, I thought about those things. If Daddy had tried to be a good daddy, then I had to try harder to be a good son, to be the boy my daddy wanted me to be. I was not like other boys my age. They could repair a tractor transmission, and I was taxed just putting gas in a car. They could explain what the numbers on a bag of fertilizer meant and what variations in those numbers meant for various crops. I didn't know and didn't care. They loved to trek the wind-seared fields in the fall in search of quail and doves, but the one time Daddy took me hunting, I almost wept when I picked up the limp, shot-riddled body of a dove. When they talked about what they called "The War of Northern Aggression," as if we were in a lull between battles, I did not get it. They could name their maternal and paternal great-great-grandparents and talk at great length about each one. I was not big into ancestor worship. In fact, there were times when I thought I had been exchanged at birth, that aliens aboard a spaceship had abducted me from California or New York then thrown my ass out into the most desolate and remote part of America they could find.

I told Mother about my plan to become an athlete the next year, and she stared at me gently, then squeezed my hands again and said, "Son, that is a good idea. But is there anything you can do this year?"

For a long moment I could say nothing. Then Mother said, "You know how your daddy is about fitting in, about being like everybody else. Can't you find something that will make you fit in?"

My mind was racing. All my classmates except Dallas, whose daddy ran a grocery store, were sons of farmers. Southwest Georgia was farming country. Maybe I could find something to do that a farmer would do.

"Maybe I should join the FFA," I said. The FFA is the Future Farmers of America. I was the only boy in my class who was not a member. I knew that whatever I was going to be in life, it was not going to be a farmer, so I'd never joined.

"Son, that is a good idea."

"Then I'll get me a farm project like the other boys do."

Mother nodded and stood up. She tousled my hair. "Your daddy is going to be so proud of you."

So I joined the FFA and bought the royal blue corduroy jacket with the bright yellow emblem. Daddy liked the blue jacket. He said that he had seen them on boys around town and that the yellow emblem reminded him of the patch worn by some elite Army unit.

One day I announced to my agriculture teacher that, by God, I was going to raise me a hog. Mr. Wayne Dozier was a big-chested guy with reddish hair and a sandy mustache. He looked like a fice dog eating a corn shuck. He was always thumping his chest and philosophizing. One of his favorite bits of wisdom, which he delivered about once a month, was, "Well, boys, you got to remember one thing: A woman's love is like the morning dew. It would just as soon fall on a pile of cow manure as a rosebush."

When I announced that I was going to buy me a pig and raise him and show him and sell him, Mr. Dozier smiled and thumped his chest and said, "Well, Robert, what does the Sarge say about that?"

"He said I could do it."

"Your family has only got a couple of acres out there. You sure that's enough land for a hog? Your mama ain't goan like it if he is too close to the house. 'Specially in hot weather."

"I'll keep him in a pen away from the house."

Nobody in class was snickering, but I could tell that a few of the farm boys thought this was the silliest idea they had ever heard. Agriculture was not exactly my best class. Putting screwworm medicine on a cow, which we had to do in one class period, disgusted me. And when we had to castrate hogs with a single-edge razor blade, I could not do it. My classmates knew all this and were smiling their most indulgent smiles.

Mr. Dozier nodded. "You said 'him.' You sure you want to raise a boar? They get mighty frisky. Get yourself a female hog, and then later if she does well in the show, you can breed her and make a little money. You'll get class credit and make a profit."

I never thought of that. All I knew was that I wanted to raise me a hog. If I raised a hog, I could talk hog talk with the boys in my class. And if the hog made money—an idea I liked—I would show Daddy that I was not the shit bird he thought I was.

"Where do I get a hog?"

"I'll give you one," Joe said.

Mr. Dozier nodded in approval. "Joe's got him a sow that just dropped a litter. He will give you one of 'em. All you got to do is raise that female, breed her, and let Joe have the pick of the litter."

He was looking at Joe as he spoke, and Joe was nodding in agreement. I figured such an arrangement was standard in the hog world.

"How big a pen do I need?"

Joe smiled.

Mr. Dozier said, "Tell you what, Robert. Seeing as how you picked yourself a pretty big project for such a little piece of land, I'm gonna have my shop class come out and build you a pen—a pen that hog ain't gonna get out of. You pay for the lumber, and we'll build you a pen for that hog."

Joe raised his hand. "Mr. Dozier, we got a big pile of scrap lumber out by the barn just sitting there. I think there is enough good wood in it to build a hog pen. Won't be pretty, but it will keep a hog inside."

I was beginning to sense I had turned into a class project. My classmates were welcoming me into their world, helping me as they had seen their daddies help other farmers in times of need. I was on my way to being a farmer.

Daddy supported me with his usual strong belief in my ability to do a job. I think he agreed to let me raise a hog just so he would have one more thing to ride my ass about. "You don't feed that hog every day, you miss feeding it just one time, and you are giving it back. You understand me?"

"Yes, sir."

"That hog won't feed his own self. You got to take care of him. You have the responsibility of taking care of him."

I wanted to say it was a girl hog but it didn't matter so all I said was the standard, "Yes, sir."

I named my hog Bertha. I don't know why, just thought it was a good name. I put a couple of sheets of tin over one corner of the pen so that she would have a place out of the sun. I fed her hog food and table scraps, and I turned the hose onto the far corner of the pen and watered it until I had made a big mud hole, a place where Bertha could wallow. Hogs got to wallow.

Maybe it was because Bertha missed her siblings, or maybe it was just because she was a hog and it was her nature, but she was never a happy hog. She wanted out of the pen, and she rooted constantly. Time after time I had to patch the sides of the pen with barbed wire or a board or a stake to hold down the boards. And she oinked and squealed constantly. She was a very vocal pig.

Joe came out to help me repair the pen, and I said, "Joe, I think that hog is going to wear out her nose."

He shook his head and grinned. "Two things in this world you can't wear out—a pig's nose and a woman's pussy."

Then Mr. Dozier came out to the house to check on my pig project. When he got out of the truck, Pal came running and was all over him.

"Robert, that dog of yours sure is friendly."

I wanted to say, "You think he's friendly now, jerk him off one time." Instead I called Pal and said, "Get over here."

Mr. Dozier looked at Bertha, rubbed his chest, and said, "Robert, she's got good blood, and her color is good, but I can tell you her conformation is lacking. The show will be in a few months, and you need to think about showmanship. Get yourself a walking stick and train that hog. You don't teach a hog like you do a dog. You teach a hog with a walking stick. Teach her to stop when you put the stick in front of her nose, to move right or left when you tap her on the side. Show the judges you can control her. Do a good job, and you might place in showmanship."

So I got a big oak walking stick. It was as thick as my arm and heavy. I got in the pen with Bertha and began her training regimen. Trying to avoid piles of pig poop while running after her and attempting to stop her or turn her was an exercise in futility. If I put the stick in front of her, she wheeled hard and bolted. If I tapped her on the side, she ran straight ahead to get away. And she continued to squeal constantly, something Mr. Dozier said the judges at the show would not take kindly to.

"You got to make her stop that squealing," Mr. Dozier said.

"She squeals all the time. If she's out there in the pen all by herself, she squeals. I think she's just talking to herself."

"You got to stop the squealing."

"How do I do that?"

"I don't know. Some hogs just squeal. But you got to stop it if you want to get a ribbon for showmanship."

Daddy had observed a couple of my training sessions and left shaking his head and laughing. "Your son is trying to teach manners to a hog," he told Mother.

The day of the agricultural show was approaching, and I was desperate. Bertha remained as unruly as she had been the first day I'd climbed into the pen. Hours and hours and days and days of wading in pig crap and talking in a soft voice had had no effect. My pig was out of control. When she saw me coming, she planted her feet and oinked and stared with her little pig eyes. When I tapped her with the walking stick, she bolted, and when I put the stick in front of her, she ran in circles, squealing all the while. When she got tired of this nonsense, she ran over to the deepest pile of pig poop and stood there, daring me to come in after her.

On the morning of the show I went out to give Bertha a bath before moving her down to the warehouse where the show would be: horses and cows in the morning, pigs in the afternoon. My time in the ring would come about 2 p.m.

Bertha was not in her pen. She had snouted open the boards in one corner and finally found her freedom. Bertha had gone rabbit on me.

I looked across Mr. Bill's pasture and saw her perhaps a quarter mile away, clearly visible against the green grass, walking easily among Mr. Bill's horses. I grabbed a length of stout rope and my pig-training walking stick and ran across the field. The horses neighed warily as I approached and began ambling away, keeping an eye on me. But Bertha held her ground.

It was already hot in southwest Georgia and sweat dripped down my face. I made a loop at one end of the rope and crept closer. In my soft and low pig voice I said, "It's okay, Bertha. Good pig. Good pig. Let's go home. Good pig."

Bertha squealed, wheeled on her back feet, and ran about fifty feet. There she stopped and turned to keep her eyes on me. Again she let me approach to within five feet before she bolted. This happened several more times until I tired of the subtle approach and shifted tactics. I would run that damn hog down, put the rope around her neck, and walk her back to the pen.

For about six hours Bertha demonstrated that agility is better than speed. I could easily outrun her, with her little pig legs, but she could turn on a dime and avoid the rope. As the withering noonday sun beat down on us, Bertha began breathing harder and running shorter distances. Finally, wheezing and gasping, she stopped, hung her head, and let me put the rope around her neck and lead her back to the pen.

She stood still as I hosed her down, scrubbed her with soap, and wiped her off. She never squealed once, even when I buffed her hooves. Her black coat was shiny when I unloaded her from the truck and drove her into a small pen in the warehouse. I made the pig part of the show with about ten minutes to spare.

"Where you been?" Mr. Dozier asked in some agitation. "We been worried about you."

"Bertha got out. I had to catch her and clean her up."

"Bertha? Who's Bertha?"

"My pig."

His eyes widened. "You named your pig?"

"Yes sir." I paused. "Doesn't everybody?"

He walked away shaking his head and mumbling, "He named his pig."

As Mr. Dozier had predicted, Bertha didn't win anything in the conformation category. Whatever a prize pig needed, she didn't have. Then came the showmanship category, and Bertha was in the center of the ring with all eyes on her. About ten pigs and their handlers were in the ring, and there was a lot of oinking and confusion. When I put the walking stick in front of Bertha, she stopped dead in her tracks. She would not move even after I took the stick out of her sight. I tapped her on the side, and she turned in the proper direction. Stop. Start. Turn. And never an oink or a squeal.

"Boy, I ain't never seen a hog that well trained," the judge told me as he handed me the blue ribbon.

"Damnedest thing I ever saw," Mr. Dozier said as he helped me load Bertha into Joe's truck. She was going out to his farm to be bred and then would come back to her own pen at the house.

"Robert, how did you do that?" he asked.

"She's tired," I said. "She got out this morning, and I been chasing her all day. She's just too tired to do anything but what I tell her."

Daddy had nothing to say when I showed him my blue ribbon and told him I had the best-mannered pig in the whole show. I pinned the ribbon on the wall over my bed. It was the first award I had ever received, and after I turned out the lights that night, I stared at the dark shadow of the ribbon over my bed.

I was still feeling pretty good about this at breakfast the next morning when the phone rang. It was Joe. He said, "Robert, I got some bad news. Your hog is dead."

Even though Daddy had gone to work, I lowered my voice. "Dead? What happened?"

"She just lay down in a wallow and died. Daddy said she was overheated and just collapsed." He paused. "Coram, don't feel bad about this. Yesterday it was hotter than a blistered pussy in a pepper patch. It was just hot."

I could say nothing to that.

"You want her back, or you want me to bury her?"

"Is that any trouble?"

"Naw, happens from time to time out here. We just scrape out a hole with the tractor, push her in, and cover her up." He paused. "Sometimes we just leave 'em out and let the buzzards clean 'em up. Don't take long. Day or so."

"No, don't leave her out like that. Bury her."

"Okay. I'm sorry, but she musta got really hot yesterday."

"You tell Mr. Dozier?"

"Yeah, he knows about it. Said it wasn't my fault and not to worry. Said you chased the hog all over Calhoun County yesterday."

"Yeah, I did."

"Don't let it get you down."

"Yeah."

But it did. It grieved me that I had spent six months with that contrary, obstinate, squealing pig only to have her win me the first blue ribbon I had ever won in anything and then she up and died.

But Bertha's death got me down even more because I knew Daddy would rejoice. And he did. Being the telephone man who spent his days riding around three counties or hanging out at the barbershop, he was as up-to-date on gossip as anyone. He probably knew Bertha was dead two minutes after she collapsed. He came home that afternoon, walked into the bathroom to clean up, sat down at the table, and even before he said the blessing, looked down the table at me and said, "Well, Mr. Big Time Pig-Farmer, I hear you had a good day."

9

In the ninth grade I fell in love with Nellie. She had a smile that made my knees weak and eyes that danced like moonlight on the water. She sashayed when she walked, and she was smart and sassy. I thought she was the prettiest girl on God's green earth. I was, for the first time in my life, deeply in love — and to such a degree that when Daddy crawled my ass, I simply thought of Nellie, and nothing he said mattered.

When I went out with Nellie on Friday or Saturday night, it was always in someone else's car. I was only fifteen and too young to drive. That was a nonsense law to farmers, and most of the boys in my class had been driving for several years. But not me. Daddy wouldn't even let me sit behind the wheel of the car. So I had to plan ahead for doubledates.

One Friday evening about 6 p.m., Ollie came by the house to pick me up. He was driving his family's big white four-door Pontiac. I had on clean jeans and a white shirt with the short sleeves rolled up twice and the collar turned up. My hair was as long as I could get away with, which wasn't very long, and combed back in a weak imitation of a ducktail. Ollie was dressed the same, except his shirt was blue and he had a real ducktail. We were two cool cats.

"Let's go get 'em," he said.

"I'm ready."

"Got your rubber?"

I pulled out my billfold and showed him the round circle imprinted on the exterior caused by the condom inside. All the boys carried condoms, and we liked to pull out our billfolds as often as possible so everyone could see the round imprint. Most of us carried the same condom for four years of high school. In fact, I think we all did. Nobody ever got to use it, but we carried it nevertheless.

"Man, you ready. Let's ride."

Ollie drove slowly out of the driveway, knowing the Sarge was standing in the door watching. As soon as we passed the cemetery and were out of sight, he stuck it. We were climbing past eighty when we passed the city limits.

"Better slow down. Will Lawrence will catch you."

Will Lawrence was the city policeman. He was a lanky old hound dog of a man who stood at the main intersection in Edison and stared at everyone who drove down the street. He worked from about 10 a.m. until 3 or 4 p.m. and then went home. His official police car was a rattletrap that had seen its best days twenty years earlier.

Oliver laughed. "Will Lawrence couldn't catch a cold."

"You ever kissed Sandra?"

He looked sideways at me. "No, but I'm planning on doing it tonight. Think they will park?"

"Nah. They not gonna let us drive out in the woods and park."

Nice girls did not park, but there were ways around this. One was to back the car down a road that went through the middle of a cotton patch, the ostensible purpose being to watch cars going by on the main road, or to check to see when your daddy might be coming back from Blakely, or whatever. The main thing was to park without making it look as if you were parking.

I thought for a moment. "I like Nellie."

"You ever get any of that on you?"

The horror. The sacrilege. I stared at Ollie, unable to speak. Finally, I said, "Hell, no. She's a nice girl. All we've done is hold hands." I paused. "I did dance close to her one night."

"She got hard titties?"

"Yeah."

"Get a boner when you danced with her?"

"A bear shit in the woods?"

"Yeah, yeah. What'd she do?"

"Nothing."

"Nothing! You mean she let you push that old thing up against her?"

"You got to talk about something else. I like Nellie."

"Okay, gimme a dollar for gas."

"A dollar. That's three gallons. Damn, how far we riding tonight?"

"Daddy filled up the tank this afternoon. He said I could drive as far as I wanted but I'd better bring the car home with the tank full. I'll fill it up on the way home."

We picked up Sandra and Nellie, then drove up to Cuthbert and rode around the square. We drove down US Route 27 to Blakely and rode around the square. We returned to Edison and rode up and down, round and round, every street in Edison, just riding. Riding and talking.

Nellie and I were in the backseat sitting close together. My arm was around her, and her head was erect, neck straight, like a wild animal on alert. When we talked, she turned her head toward me but leaned away.

I was so nervous that you couldn't have driven a tack up my ass with a sledge hammer. All I could think of was kissing Nellie. I wanted to kiss her, but I didn't know how. Nellie sensed something.

"What time you gotta be home?" Ollie asked. He was talking to me. Usually this was a question asked of girls, but Ollie knew the Sarge.

"Nine o'clock," I said with resignation.

"That's so early," Nellie said, turning toward me. This time she did not lean away. I turned toward her, and her lips were an inch away. I kissed her, a chaste kiss, sweet and lingering and gentle. I heard angels singing and heavenly trumpets blowing. It was the first time I had ever kissed a girl and the first time Nellie had ever kissed a boy. I have never been happier.

I know the exact spot where this happened and today could take you there and show you the place. The road has since been paved, the nearby field is overgrown with briars, and the ditches are filled with trash. But I can take you to the exact spot where I first kissed a girl in the backseat of a white Pontiac. In fact, I have considered placing a historical marker on the spot.

Ollie saw us in the rearview mirror, and from the way he was jerking the car around, I thought we were about to have a wreck. I didn't care. Ollie couldn't keep his eyes off us. After we kissed, we both sat back, eyes wide, staring straight ahead, catatonic. In an effort to determine whether it was really possible to experience such heaven on earth, I reached out and turned Nellie's head toward me. Her eyes were half-closed as we kissed again, another butterfly-light kiss. To have touched her anywhere would have broken the magic. We continued to kiss — soft kisses that left us covered with pixie dust and filled with wonder. I lost all sense of time and space. I was transported to another place where there was nothing but happiness.

"We here," Ollie said.

I looked up, and we were at Nellie's house. She slid away from me. "Move over," she said. "Don't let Mama see you so close."

So I slid over and opened the door, then walked around to her side and opened her door. We did not even hold hands as we walked to the front door. There we paused for a split second. I wanted to kiss her good night, but her parents were in the living room and probably looking through the windows. So I said, "I had a very nice time," and she said, "I did, too." I opened the door for her, closed the door, walked on back to the car, and climbed into the backseat.

Ollie was giggling, about what I did not know.

Sandra lived only a few doors down the street. While Ollie walked Sandra to her door, I got into the front seat. I looked at my watch. It was five minutes until nine. Ollie and Sandra were standing on the front porch looking at each other. "Ollie, I need to go," I shouted.

He looked at me, made a grimace, then told Sandra good night and walked back to the car. As he got in, he said, "You need to go somewhere and beat off. When you came down the steps at Nellie's, you were toting the biggest boner I've ever seen. Sandra tried not to laugh, but I know she saw it."

Then he turned serious. "I was about to kiss Sandra there on the porch, and you messed it up when you hollered at me."

"I know—you would have screwed her there in the porch swing if I hadn't been here."

Ollie laughed and looked at his watch. "Yo daddy up waiting?"

"Better believe it."

The speedometer was on ninety when we left town. Ollie began braking a quarter mile from my house, causing the headlights to dive. When I opened the front door, Daddy was waiting. He looked at his watch. "Cutting it mighty close."

"JB, he got home before his curfew," Mother said. "Let him alone." She turned to me and said, "You have a good time?"

Still glassy-eyed, I edged toward the door to the hall. "Yes, ma'am. Yes, ma'am, I did."

"Good night, son." Her eyes stayed on me as if she knew something had happened.

"Night, Mother. Night, Daddy."

"Just because tomorrow is Saturday doesn't mean you can sleep late."

"Yes, sir."

I lay awake staring at the ceiling for hours.

SEVERAL months later, as I had done almost every day since that night we'd first kissed, I walked Nellie home from school. We had gotten our report cards that day and were taking them home to our parents. Nellie and I compared grades. She had all A's, and I had all B's.

Nellie's mother was a schoolteacher, and her daddy worked for the county. Neither would be home until around five. We put our books on a table by the door, and she turned to me and said, "You want a glass of sweet tea?"

"Not today." I reached for her hand, pulled her closer, and we kissed, the same sweet kiss we shared for several hours every afternoon. It was still magic.

"Let's sit down," I said and pulled her toward the sofa, where we usually sat and kissed. The innocent bliss we experienced on that sofa sanctified it for all time. I'm thinking of having it placed in the Smithsonian.

"I have to tell you something," Nellie said as we sat down. She was very serious.

"What?"

"You remember that first night?"

"Yes."

"I hated you when I came home that night."

"Why?" I was astonished.

"I don't know. I just did. That was my first kiss, and I just felt ... I don't know."

"You don't still feel that way, do you?"

She looked at me from a few inches away, and as we stared into each other's eyes, she said, "No." I leaned forward, and we kissed again. I think it was the conversation that caused us to kiss with a bit more passion than usual. I felt her lips part slightly, just a tiny fraction of an inch, and in that moment I remembered what I had heard about a "French kiss." Tentatively, very tentatively, I slid the tip of my tongue between her lips. My tongue touched her tongue and, oh, hallelulah, I was walking the streets of the promised land! I was quivering, never more alive, every nerve end singing. I trembled as we pulled apart and looked at each other in amazement, and then we were kissing again. We were on the sofa for half an hour, sprawled out and then lying down with our arms around each other, as we kissed and explored with our tongues. Those were some of the most glorious minutes of my life.

Years later I read a line of poetry that said, "The cheek of the beloved is more to be desired than the naked body of another," and I almost shouted "Yes!" because I knew exactly what the poet meant. Nellie and I never did anything but kiss, and that was all I wanted. Today I look back and wonder if she would have allowed more.

We levitated when we heard a car door slam. She straightened her hair and smoothed her blouse. "Mother is home early," she said in a panic.

A moment later her mother walked in the front door and looked at us in surprise. "Hey, Mother. Robert came by after school and we been talking. He was about to leave."

"No sense in leaving just because I'm here. Robert, would you like a glass of sweet tea?"

"Thank you, but I need to be going home."

"How you getting home?"

"I'm walking." I didn't tell her I had walked home almost every afternoon for the past several months.

"Walking?"

"It's only two miles."

"If you're walking home, you certainly need a glass of sweet tea."

"Yes, ma'am, if it is not a bother."

"Don't be silly." She reached to put her purse on a small table, when suddenly the three of us froze. The city's civil defense siren was sounding, wailing and moaning, rising and falling. The siren was in case we were attacked by Russian bombers and was our signal to duck and cover — to hunker down roll up under then nearest piece of furniture. The siren went off once a year to make sure it was operating properly. But those practice sessions were announced weeks in advance.

Were we being attacked by the Soviets? Was an atomic bomb about to fall on Edison?

Nellie's mother picked up the telephone to see what was going on. Everyone else in Edison must have been calling the switchboard at the same time, because for several minutes she stood there, eyebrows raised in exasperation, as Nellie and I waited.

"Yes," she said. "I'm calling to ... "

It was clear she had been interrupted by the operator. She waited and listened, and then her eyes came to rest on me. She nodded several times, still staring at me, then said, "We on our way."

She hung up the phone, turned to me, and said, "Robert, that was your daddy on the telephone. He is the one who set off the siren. He just told I don't know how many people who were on hold that your brother George has run away. He's somewhere down around Bay Branch, and your daddy is asking everyone in Edison to help find him."

I stared at Nellie's mother. "Run away? Why?"

Her eyes were unflinching. "Your daddy said he got all Cs on his report card."

I nodded in embarrassment. "Daddy doesn't allow Cs on a report card."

In the background the siren continued to wail. I knew that people all over Edison were calling the switchboard office to find out if the Russians were about to bomb Edison.

Nellie's mother sighed. "I guess we better go down to Bay Branch." She turned to me and said, "Why in the world would George want to go down there if he was running away?"

"He was scared to go home."

Nellie's mother looked at me without speaking. I answered her unasked question. "Yes, ma'am, he's that scared of Daddy."

"Well, I gave him one of those Cs," she said defiantly.

"Yes, ma'am."

I didn't care if she had given him a D or an F. I just wanted to know what Daddy was going to do now that his favorite son had run away from home.

As we walked out on the front porch, we heard from somewhere across town faint snatches of a voice, an imploring voice, rising and falling, words indistinguishable but clearly pleading, almost begging.

"What in the world is that?" Nellie asked. It was not until the next day I discovered that Brother Dunagan had put a couple of extension cords on his pulpit microphone, unhooked the speakers that carried piano music throughout the church, and taken them outside to the top of the steps. There, half crying into his improvised sound system, he was waving his claw hand and wailing, "Geooooorrge. Come home, Geooooorrge. Yo mama and daddy are worried. Geooooorrge. Come home, Geooooorrge."

I rode with Nellie and her mother about a mile south to Bay Branch. Nellie's mother had a lot of school supplies and books in the front seat, so Nellie and I sat in the back. We sat on opposite sides of the seat but with our arms stretched out, holding hands out of sight of her mother.

"My, my," Nellie's mother said as we approached Bay Branch. Cars lined both sides of the road for several hundred yards on either side of the small bridge over the creek, and more were arriving by the minute. Will Lawrence, all bowed up with self-importance, had parked his car on the edge of the road, red light flashing, and now was directing traffic. We pulled off the road and sat there, watching the spectacle unfolding before us. People, mostly men and boys, were getting out of their cars. The women either stayed in their cars, or got out and started to look for Mother, so they could console her and at the same time do a little prying into our family business as they clucked in mock sympathy. Men and boys were fanning out on both sides of the creek, looking under trees and bushes as they moved down the creek calling, "Hey, George. Where you at? Come on out." This was turning into a real goat roping.

We heard a blaring of horns and looked up as Mother's car, followed by Daddy's telephone truck, came drove down the road to the bridge, where both stopped. Now the road was blocked, but no one seemed to care. Telling new arrivals to pull off the road and park, Will Lawrence held out his arms, then spread them apart, as if he was parting the waters.

Mother and Daddy, both distraught, met in the middle of the bridge. Daddy put his arms around Mother, and I knew he was telling her everything would be allright.

After they separated, a dozen or so women materialized around Mother and began hovering, convincing her to sit in her car and wait while the menfolk did the searching. Daddy pulled a bull-horn out of his truck — where the hell had he gotten a bullhorn? It must have been part of his Shriner equipment. He fiddled with the button, then held it up to his mouth and began talking. His voice was loud enough that he didn't need a bullhorn.

"Thank y'all for coming out to help me find my boy," he said. "We know he is down here at Bay Branch. Fan out on both sides of the creek and look everywhere you can. We got to find him before dark."

We had a full-blown three-ring circus going on. The road was blocked, darkness was approaching, and now a couple of sheriff's deputies arrived with flashing lights. Daddy went over to talk with them. After an intense conversation one of the deputies nodded and began talking on his police radio. I wondered what Daddy had said to him.

Suddenly Will Lawrence was waving his arms again, clearing the way, as Mother and a carful of women raced back toward town.

"I wonder where she's going," I said.

Several hundred people were milling around, stomping through the woods, shouting, "Hey, George. Come on out, George. Yo mama is worried about you and wants you home for dinner. Where you at? Come on out."

Nellie and her mother and I were quiet. Then, out of nowhere, Nellie's mother shook her head, sighed, and said, "Robert, what would your Daddy do that made George so scared?"

"He said if we made a C, we would get a whipping and have to stay at home for six weeks until the next report card came out."

She shook her head in disbelief.

I was beginning to get a bit worried about Daddy. He was on the bullhorn imploring George to come out from wherever he was, and the anguish in his voice was clear. "George, son, this is your daddy. Come on out, son. Your mother is worried about you. George, come on out, now."

Mother returned, stopped in the middle of the road, and handed something to Daddy.

"I wonder what that was," Nellie said.

"I don't know. Looks like a wad of cloth."

Several minutes later a pickup truck arrived with flashing lights. In the back was a cage filled with yipping and barking dogs. Bloodhounds. Holy shit. Daddy had asked the sheriff to turn the bloodhounds loose to track George. We were going big time here.

This was the biggest thing to happen in Edison since the circus came to town the year before. We had heard that when elephants screwed, they did it for twenty-four hours at a time. So several of us had lain out in the grass all one day and half the night watching to see if the elephants were going to get any that weekend.

A deputy wearing big boots and dark clothes snapped leashes on the dog, and now they were on the ground, yipping, jumping, and sniffing. Daddy ran up and handed something to the deputy, who unfolded it. It was one of George's shirts. I knew that George wore a shirt one day, put it in the closet, and then several days later wore it again, repeating that process until Mother made him put it in the washing machine. The dogs would have no trouble finding a scent on that shirt.

Now people were yelping as loudly as the bloodhounds. "Dawgs is here. Dawgs is here. Sheriff done brought his bloodhounds. They goan track George down. No doubt about it. They will find him. Them dawgs is good. They track jail breakers. They will find old George."

The deputy and his dogs, along with about fifty people, took off down the creek bank. It was the biggest cacophony I'd ever heard: dogs barking and people shouting, as the beams from dozens of flashlights darted through the trees..

"They ain't got the scent yet," I heard one man say as he walked by the car. "You'll hear it in their voice when they get his scent."

"Yeah, it won't take long to find him now," said his companion.

"Robert, maybe you ought to go sit with your mother," Nellie's mother said. "I know she is upset by all this."

I squeezed Nellie's hand. "Yes, ma'am, I will. Thank you for letting me ride down here with you."

"Don't you worry," she said. "They will find George."

When I arrived at the car, Mother said, "Robert, where have you been? Your brother is out there lost somewhere."

"I've been here. I was sitting with Nellie and her mother."

"Well, I think..." She stopped speaking and her eyes widened. She was looking over my shoulder. I turned and there was George, crawling up the creek bank, muddy and dirty, and looking scared.

"George!" Mother shouted, opening the door. "Your daddy and I have been worried sick. Where have you been?"

"In that big drain pipe under the road," he said, looking around. "Dogs scared me, and I came out."

Mother was out of the car, her arms around George. Daddy ran up, dropped his bullhorn, and put his arms around George, too. He held George tightly, his face contorted in anguish.

"Daddy, you goan whip me?" George said in a muffled voice.

I almost laughed.

"No, son. Don't you worry about that. Let's get you home and get you some supper and a hot bath." He ushered George into the backseat of the car and said to Mother, "You drive. I'll get in the back with George."

"What about your truck?" Mother asked.

"Oh, yeah." Daddy looked around, found his bullhorn, and said, "My boy is here. We found him. Thank you all for coming out and helping. George is okay, and now we're gonna take him home and get him warm and put some hot food into him. Thank you all again."

He turned to a deputy and handed him the keys to his telephone truck. The deputy nodded and said, "I'll park it in your front yard."

I saw another deputy emerge from the creek, a dingy gray bundle under his arm, walk up to the sheriff and begin talking in urgent manner, occasionally pointing at the bundle. The sheriff tensed, stroked his chin and looked around, and I realized that the bundle was the three KKK robes. The sheriff leaned toward the deputy, said something, and the deputy put the bundle in the trunk of the sheriff's car.

A second of raw fear swept over me. Then I realized that while Klan members might continue asking questions, they would settle down a bit now that they had found their missing robes. Joe and Ollie and I were safe. I hoped.

Daddy crawled into the backseat. He put his arms around George, hugging him and saying over and over as we drove home, "Don't you worry about anything. Everything is okay."

"Daddy, my stomach hurts."

"Bad?"

"No, sir. Not too bad. Just a little bit."

I sat in the front seat staring straight ahead, saying nothing.

The next day at recess I looked across the school yard to where the kids in George's class were gathered. I walked closer and saw that George was the center of attention. He had a stick and was drawing in the sand. "I started out here," he said. "Then I went here for a half hour. After that I walked down the railroad tracks to Bay Branch." He dug his stick into the sand. "I sat there for a while, and then when I heard the siren, I moved over here." He pointed to a place on a line he had drawn. "That's the drain pipe under the road. When I heard the siren and saw all the cars coming, I got in there." He looked around the circle of rapt listeners. He was a star. "When I heard the dogs, I got out."

About a week before school ended, Daddy said, "Robert, you going back to your aunt Grace's this summer." It was a flat statement, an order. I was about to remind him of his promise that I could ride with him and be his helper when Mother said, "JB, don't you remember?"

"Remember what?"

"Your mama has been sick, and Grace and Felix are having to look after her. They don't have time to have Robert underfoot all summer."

Daddy grimaced.

I grinned. "That means I can ride with you and be your helper for the rest of the summer."

"Yes, it does," Mother said. She turned to Daddy for his approval.

Daddy was squirming. I could almost hear the wheels turning in his head. We all, Daddy included, knew that he had no way out. After a long moment he said, "I already told George he could go, so both of you will be my helpers. He will show you what to do." He turned and walked off, clearly displeased. But I didn't care. I would do such a good job that he would have to tell me he was proud of me. This was my big chance, and I was going to make the most of it. I might be a pig killer, but I knew I could be a better helper than George.

Monday morning, as we walked out to Daddy's truck, I asked, "Do you want us in the cab or in the back?"

"Usually we have to ride for a while before we get to where we going," George said. "So we ride in the cab in the mornings."

Nothing is worse than a self-righteous tour guide.

Daddy nodded in approval. "Let's go down to the office to see what we got."

George sat next to Daddy, and I sat by the window as we drove the two miles into Edison. The telephone company office was located in a small wooden building, just a short block from the main intersection. Inside two women wearing headsets sat at the switchboard. When someone picked up the phone at home, a light flashed on the switchboard. In front of each operator was a flat panel out of which protruded plugs attached to cords. The operator picked up a plug and stuck it into a hole under the blinking light, then said, "Number please?" When the person on the other end gave the operator a number, she pushed another plug into the hole representing that number, then pressed a button to make the phone ring, and everyone was in business.

The fire alarm system and the civil defense siren also were operated through Daddy's office. An administrator sat at a desk to the side of the single large, open room and picked up several papers and offered them to Daddy as he walked in. "Morning, Sarge. I see you got your helpers with you today," she said.

"We'll see how much help they are," Daddy said as he sorted through his "trouble sheets," the papers indicating whose phone was out of order, where a line was down, or where a pole had been broken or insulators shot off the poles. Daddy covered Calhoun, Clay, and Randolph Counties, a pretty good piece of southwest Georgia. He stayed busy.

As Daddy sorted through the sheets, I wandered over to watch the switchboard operators, in awe of how — after they asked "Number please?" — they quickly found the number on the vertical board before them and connected the two parties.

Daddy stuffed the sheets in his pocket and said, "Let's go, boys. We got lots of work to do today."

Our first call was in Fort Gaines, a half-hour drive away. As we drove out past the city limits, George pointed to an oncoming truck and said, "Forty-eight Ford." He pointed again, "Packard. Nineteen forty-two, no forty-three."

"What are you doing?" I asked.

"George can identify the make and model of just about every car or truck we meet," Daddy said. "He never misses."

What the hell good is that? I wondered. *Who cares what kind of car we see?*

"You want to play?" George asked.

"Go ahead," Daddy encouraged. "When you boys see a car, sing out. See who can identify it first." He lifted a finger from the steering wheel. "There's one coming now."

George and I looked up just as the car disappeared behind the crest of a hill. We knew that in a moment it would reappear much closer. George leaned forward, tense as a bird dog sniffing quail. The car popped up over the hill. I was studying the grill, the shape of the hood, anything to identify it, when George said, "Studebaker. Nineteen fifty."

We waited a minute as the car swept past. It was a 1950 Studebaker. Daddy laughed in appreciation.

George pointed. "One's coming." Far ahead was a pickup truck. Most local farmers were Chevrolet people, so I took a guess and shouted, "Chevrolet."

"What year?" Daddy said.

I looked again. George was thrumming with tension. "Nope. That's a Ford pickup," he said. "Nineteen forty seven."

And that's what it was.

I stuck my arm out the window, held it parallel to the ground, and then by tilting it slightly up or slightly down caused it to porpoise rapidly. "Look at that," I said. "Like an airplane."

Daddy shook his head and said, "Robert, you need to get more serious."

ABOUT midafternoon as we were about to leave Fort Gaines, George and I got into the back of the truck. We sat behind the cab, looking over Daddy's shoulder. He stared straight ahead, ignoring us. Every few minutes George would sing out the make and model of a car or truck. "Don't you want to play?" he asked.

But I was looking at something else. Daddy's left hand was on the steering wheel, and his right hand was on his penis. He was squeezing and fondling his penis, but nothing was happening. And he was talking to himself. I looked into the rear view mirror and saw that he was having a very intense conversation with himself. All he had to do was glance into the mirror, and our eyes would meet. But he was staring straight ahead, mumbling and fondling. I couldn't figure out what was going on. I could look at a frog and get an erection. Why wasn't Daddy's thing getting hard?

"George, you got good eyes. Tell me something."

"What?"

"Why doesn't Daddy's dick get hard? He is playing with it constantly, but look, there where he is grabbing, it is limp as a dishrag."

"Wow. A Packard. You don't see many of those."

10

I<small>N</small> addition to slow, peculiar, and not right, we had people in Edison who were "different." In southwest Georgia, the word could be both pejorative and kind, depending on how it was used.

If someone said "Negroes" rather than "niggers," he was different in the worst possible way. That word was used in New York or Washington, or in Atlanta by Ralph McGill. We sensed at some deep level that we might be wrong in saying "niggers" and that people in New York or Washington or Atlanta just might be right. We sensed, but could not admit, that this was another area in which the world had passed us by. But we did not want to be wrong, as that would have meant that our worst fears were well-founded: we were uninformed and out-of-date, and the rest of the world looked down on us. We had to cling to our ways. Those who did not were different.

A more common use of the word "different," one usually preceded by the word "well," applied if someone, say, added salt to the cream of mushroom soup that was the base for every casserole Edison cooks made. Those who ate the soup would nod in an indulgent fashion and say, "Well, that's different." If a housewife tried to make lilacs grow in southwest Georgia, we would notice the flowers and say, "Well, she's different." If a man wore a striped shirt rather than a white shirt to church, we'd say, "Well, he's different." This use of "different" was nonthreatening and often had a slightly patronizing tone.

A more edgy use of the word was when we said, "He just wants to be different." There was little patience with someone who wanted to be different, because that meant the person did not like things as they were.

It is this last translation that Daddy had in mind one morning when he looked down the table at me and said, "Robert, you trying to be different?"

I was sitting there having what Daddy called a "staring spell," and he didn't like it.

George went on full alert, wide eyes jumping between Daddy and me. Susie and Butch, as usual, were oblivious to everything going on around them. Susie was off in that distant kingdom inhabited by young girls, and Butch in that permanent happy place where the last and unexpected child lives. Butch was an indulged child. He still drank milk from his baby bottle.

"Sir?"

"You doing it again, just sitting there staring off into space. What's the matter with you?"

"Nothing."

"Well, nothing or not, I'm thinking seriously of sending you up to Riverside Academy in Gainesville, Georgia. I hear that is a fine military school. They will straighten you out. And when you graduate, its's only a few miles up the road to Dahlonega, Georgia, and North Georgia College. You got to learn how to be a man, and a military school will do it. Then when you get out of college, or flunk out, you can join the Army."

I took a sip of milk and didn't say anything. For a change.

"Something the matter, son?" Mother asked.

"No, ma'am. I'm just thinking."

"Thinking about what?"

Daddy jumped in. "Just like he said, nothing." He shook his head, pruned up, and returned to the newspaper.

I had decided to put off my athletic career for a year. I was too small to play anything but tiddlywinks, and we didn't have a tiddlywinks team. Trying to figure out how to be more like my classmates and do something of which Daddy would approve came to be an obsession during my sophomore year. Not only had pig farming been a disaster, but an attempt to grow a crop of tomatoes had been worse. I had convinced Daddy to let me plant tomatoes on an acre and a half of the two acres of land we owned. He grumbled, but he let me do it. I picked the crop too early, and as a result the warehouse paid so little that I wound up losing money. Or Daddy wound up losing money, and he would gripe about that forever. "Is there anything you can do right?" he asked.

Mr. Wayne Dozier was the only one impressed. He stood in front of the ag class and said, "Old Robert here, his family owns just two acres of land, and Robert farmed an acre and a half of it. That's a pretty good percentage. 'Course he lost money, but he tried."

The farmer boys in class nodded and smiled. "Can't have many years like that if you gonna be a farmer," one of them said.

Well, I wasn't going to grow hogs, and I wasn't going to farm. So what the hell else was there?

Night after night I went to bed at nine o'clock, pulled the blanket up over me, turned on my flashlight, and read until after midnight. Mother, who always stuck her head in the door to take a look around before she went to bed, finally decided I just liked to sleep under a blanket, no matter how hot it was. I lay there, in pools of sweat, reading, anxious that I would read too late, oversleep, and not hear Daddy when he called for George and me to get up and get ready for school. If I lingered for more than a few seconds, I would hear the buzzing of the five-battery cattle prod and feel its burning prongs on my legs. Daddy still loved to wave that thing around.

I think that cattle prod is the reason I have never been able to sleep past 6 a.m. No matter what time I go to bed, I awaken around six, eyes wide and my feet on the floor. I look around in near panic, still half expecting to be popped with the cattle prod.

At breakfast and at dinner I had my staring fits. Daddy grew weary of my staring and chewing, staring and chewing, and one night he said, "I talked to Rudy today. He says you can start digging graves this weekend. You want to stare at something, you can stare at a hole in the ground."

Mother's eyes lit up. "He is letting Robert work out at his place? That is so nice. We should buy him and Dorie supper one night at the fish camp."

"Yeah, he's letting Robert work. Even going to pay him a little bit. And he says if one of us will drive him out there, he will drive him home. I got things to do on Saturday, so you're going to have to take your son to his job." He paused and looked at me. "Maybe digging graves will teach you something."

Yeah, long-term prospects for grave diggers are really good, I thought.

SATURDAY around 7 a.m. Mother drove me out to Rudy's place of business a few miles west of Edison.

"Morning, Gussie," he said with his usual big smile. "You up early this morning. How you doing? And how's that boy of yours doing?" He reached, out and we shook hands.

"Morning, Mr. Rudy," I said.

"He's ready to go to work," Mother said.

"Well, we goan take good care of him today, so don't you worry." Rudy looked at me. "Go on down there and meet Jesse. You'll be working with him. I'll be right there."

He turned to walk Mother to her car, and I went across the parking lot and opened the door of the tin-covered building. Jesse was black, about age fifty, with a wiry build and a proud bearing. His face was lined and showed years of poverty and hard work. He wore heavy brogans, jeans, and a shirt that was soft from many washings. His close-cropped hair was black, touched with gray. Atop his head sat an old hat that gave him an air of dignity. I think he wore it because he was always attending funerals, and most men at funerals wore hats.

"Morning, Mr. Robert," he said when I walked in the door. He was collecting tools, getting the truck ready for the day, moving with the slow economy of one who is saving his energy for a long, hard day. He barely glanced my way. We did not shake hands. "Mr. Rudy told me you would be here today."

"Yeah, he wants me to be a good grave digger."

I looked around. Rudy's office sat in one corner and all the rest of the building was open and filled with piles of sand, bags of cement, tools, and vaults — the large concrete containers into which caskets were placed.

"Well, sir, Mr. Rudy said he wanted me to learn you the business. We just got one grave to dig today, so it won't be a long day."

"Where we going?"

"We going to Wesley Chapel. That's a white folks' church up on the road to Fort Gaines. You gonna drive the truck up there, and then we gonna dig a grave and put in the vault. Then we gonna pitch the tent, spread the grass, set up the chairs, and get everything ready for the funeral tomorrow morning. After the funeral, when everybody done gone home, we put the lid on the vault, seal it, and cover it up." He looked around. "Then we got to load everything we take up there today and bring it back down here."

All I heard was, "You gonna drive the truck."

I looked behind him to where one of Rudy's big blue trucks sat, a gray concrete vault perched on the flat bed behind the cab. Rudy had two trucks, each with a square frame of heavy angle iron around the bed. The frame extended maybe six feet high above the bed. It had a pulley and a block-and-tackle arrangement attached to a heavy chain to lower the concrete vaults into the grave. Inside the cab the floor-mounted gearshift probably had four forward gears, and I didn't know where the first of them was. I couldn't drive anything, much less one of Rudy's big trucks.

I looked around. Where the hell was Rudy?

"How much one of them vaults weigh?" I asked Jesse.

"Don't know. They heavy."

"How deep we got to dig the grave?"

"Mr. Rudy, he say we dig 'em peter deep." He grinned. "You so short we might dig it waist deep on you." Amused by his own joke, he said, "Yes, sir. I know that's right."

"What's this grass you talking about that we got to spread?"

"Like a rug. Except it's green. We put it out to cover all the raw dirt and have a nice level place to put the chairs for the family. It ain't grass. More like a bunch of little rugs. But we call it grass."

Just then Rudy walked in, beaming. "Robert, you ready to go to work? Jesse tell you what you doing?"

"I can't drive," I said.

His eyes widened. "You can't ... ? Don't you worry. Jesse can drive. He usually does anyway." He looked toward Jesse, who had two picks in one hand and two shovels in the other. "Jesse, you about ready?"

"Yes, sir. Just about. Still got a few things to load."

"Ah-ite. You go ahead and load up. You drive today. Show Mr. Robert here a little bit about operating that truck and what he's supposed to do. Don't work him too hard on his first day, or his mama will be upset with me."

"Yes, sir," Jesse said, not looking at either one of us. He put the tools in the truck and began loading the grass and chairs.

Jesse was working to put food on the table, and here he was having to indulge his boss and take along a jackleg boy who couldn't find his ass with both hands. I was fifteen and knew absolutely nothing about this job, and if I went to the cemetery and didn't dig one shovelful of dirt, that would be okay. If I said it was too hot and went out and sat in the shade, that would be okay. If I stretched out on the seat and slept, that would be okay. Just about anything I wanted to do would be okay, because I was white, I was a friend of his boss, and Jesse was black.

"You bring any water today?" Rudy asked.

"No, sir. I didn't think about that."

"Well, don't want you drinking behind Jesse. So let's see if we got a gallon jug back here that I can put some ice water in." He rummaged around behind his desk, picked up a clear gallon jug, and handed it to me. "One of my white helpers used this the other day. It's okay. Go out there to the faucet and rinse it out. Get you some ice out of the 'frigerator and fill it up with water. You bring something to eat?"

"No, sir. I didn't think of that either." I shrugged. "This is my first job."

Jessie gave no indication that he heard the conversation. He continued loading the truck, impassive, just doing his job, accepting life as it was in southwest Georgia.

"You got any money?" Rudy asked.

"A dollar or so."

Rudy reached into his pocket. "Well, that should be enough. But here's another dollar just in case. You tell Jesse to stop at Sutton's Cross Roads on the way up. Buy your own self a pack of crackers and a Co-Cola for dinner. I'll take the dollar out of your pay."

"Thanks."

Jesse, you ready yet?"

"I'm ready to go, Mr. Rudy. Yes, sir."

Rudy looked at the back of the truck, paying close attention to the rolls of grass wedged against the back of the cab. "That grass weighed down okay? Don't want it blowing off."

"Yes, sir. I put all my tools on it to hold it down, just like I always do."

Rudy turned to me and said, "You got to watch these niggers every minute." Then he smiled. "Robert, your mama and daddy doing okay? We haven't been out to the fish camp in a while. About time to go again."

We stood there side by side watching Jesse checking out the truck.

"Yes, sir. They doing okay."

"You making any plans about what you wanna do when you get out of school? You goan stay here, or you going off to school?"

I scuffed the toe of my shoe on the floor. "I haven't decided yet."

"Well, I can tell you, your mama has high hopes for you." He nodded and added, "She does. She sure does." He took a halfstep toward the truck. "Jesse, you know where that church is? You know which plot the grave site is in?" He turned to me and with little attempt to lower his voice said, "Niggers. He might dig a grave in the wrong plot."

Jesse rubbed his hands together and looked at Rudy, giving no indication he had heard anything except the question. "Yes, sir. I know where the church is. I know where to dig the grave. I ain't never dug one in the wrong place, have I, Mr. Rudolph?"

Rudy nodded. "No, you ain't." He turned to me and said, "Jesse is a good nigger. You gonna be okay with him today. All you got to do is dig a hole in the ground and get everything ready for the funeral. You should be through by the middle of the afternoon. I'll be up to check on things. Give you a ride home." He pushed on my shoulder, and I walked to the passenger side of the truck.

"Okay, Jesse," I said. "I'm ready."

"Yes, sir, Mr. Robert."

In December Ralph McGill wrote a column saying that segregation was finished, that Negroes had been graduating from medical schools and law schools all around the South. He said that southern churches sent missionaries to convert Negroes and then pointed out that those same Negroes could not enter white churches, that whites and blacks could not worship together. Christianity could not afford to be on the wrong side of a moral force, McGill said. The very idea of segregation implied inferiority. Segregation was on the way out.

Daddy read the column and said, "Negroes." He pronounced it "knee-grows" with a derisive snort. He shook his head and again said, "Negroes. The dumb son of a bitch can't even spell. It is n-i-g-g-e-r-s." He shook his head, this time slowly, and said, "The man just doesn't know what he is talking about. Is he talking about Atlanta? Is he talking about New York? He sure as hell ain't talking about Edison. The things he says will never happen in Edison. Never."

"Remember your blood pressure, JB," Mother said.

Daddy took a sip of his coffee. "Sweetheart, my blood pressure is okay, but my coffee cup is empty." As Mother brought the coffeepot to the table and refilled his cup, Daddy said, "What world does he live in? Is he a Communist? Nobody cares what Ralph McGill says." He folded the paper and looked at McGill's picture. "He oughta be in the funny pages. Or back there with the hemorrhoid ads."

"JB, you're at the table," Mother said.

I sensed in Daddy's anger a distant fear that McGill might be right. Plus, reading McGill's column was almost like reading the Bible. There was both an Old Testament certitude to his words and a summons to rise higher and do better. Just like in the Bible. And people didn't read McGill, nod, and move on to something else. They lingered over his column and — at least in Edison — grew so angry that they sputtered when they talked about him. What was there about him that affected people that way?

Daddy moved the paper and looked down the table. "Where is Butch?"

Instantly Mother ran to the front window, Daddy a halfstep behind. George and I were grinning, and Susie was watching Mother and Daddy.

"There he is," Mother said.

"Damn," Daddy said. "How did he get out of the house with nobody hearing him?" They both ran for the front door.

"The beaver at it again?" I laughed.

Daddy looked over his shoulder, glared, and shook his finger toward me.

As Mother and Daddy ran down the front steps, George and I broke out laughing. Susie stared at us with all the disapproval a nine-year-old girl can show toward for her older brothers.

We looked through the window and saw Mother and Daddy hovering over Butch, Mother wiping at his mouth, Daddy shaking his head. When they returned, each holding one of Butch's hands, Daddy said, "Sweetheart, we just have to keep a closer eye on him. And we have to keep the doors locked. Look at his mouth."

Mother took Butch into the kitchen, where she kept some concoction that was supposed to remove turpentine without hurting Butch's skin. Daddy sat back down at the table and looked at me. "You think it's funny that your baby brother eats pine trees?"

"Yes, sir. I think that's funny."

"Well, it's not. It's not funny at all. You're his big brother, and part of your job is to keep him from eating pine trees."

There is a mandate not many sons get: keep your baby brother from eating pine trees. I was still grinning. "Yes, sir. I'll watch him."

"What are you doing at school, Mr. Big Shot? You got any more projects going? Like pig farming or growing tomatoes?"

"No, sir. But I've been thinking about going out for some sports next year. I think I'm going out for basketball."

Daddy looked at me in disbelief. "You can't play basketball."

"You always tell me a person doesn't know what he can do until he tries. So I'm going to try."

Big grimace. Daddy didn't like it when I threw his words back at him to prove a point. Mother smiled and did not say a word.

"You're not big enough," Daddy said.

"No, but I'm real fast."

"What about practice? You got to practice. When will you do that?"

"They have practice every day after school."

"You still have things to do around the house. You got to study. And how will you get home from practice? We have supper here at five o'clock, young man."

"I thought maybe Mother could pick me up."

Mother nodded in agreement. "That's no problem …"

Daddy interrupted. "Your mother has other things to do. She's got to fix supper for the rest of us, not go gallivanting around picking you up like she is your own chauffeur."

"Maybe somebody on the team. They all drive."

"I don't want you bumming rides from other people."

"Maybe somebody will be coming this way."

"Well, young man, if they are not, you walk. You understand that?"

"Yes, sir." With that sort of strong encouragement from my daddy, how could I be anything but a basketball star?

"Daddy?"

Daddy picked up the paper, opened it, and grumbled, "What?"

"Coach said I was really fast. I mean really *fast*."

"Uhhhh."

"After basketball season I'm probably going out for track."

Daddy folded the paper and looked at me for a moment without speaking. Then he said, "I guess next thing I know you goan be in the Olympics." He retreated behind the paper.

"I hadn't thought of that."

Mother held up her hand and shook her head. I finished my breakfast and pushed back my chair. The noise of the chair caused Daddy to pull the paper away from his face and look at me.

"You gonna be a big-time athlete, you need to get in shape. Working on weekends for Rudy won't cut it. I'm sending you up to your aunt Grace's this summer, and I expect you to work eight hours a day for them." He paused. "I bet you hadn't thought of that either."

As a matter of fact, I had not.

"I thought I was going to ride with you and be your helper. George does it all the time. Why can't I ride with you? I thought this was my summer."

"Well, you thought wrong, young man. You thought wrong."

11

I expected to have several weeks at home before I was sent up to Aunt Grace's. I thought the whole family would go up there after church one Sunday. We would eat a big dinner and sit around on the front porch for a few hours, then Mother and Daddy and the other kids would go back to Edison. But it didn't work that way. Daddy wanted to get rid of my sorry ass as quickly as he could.

The last day of school, when I got off the bus and walked up the steps and into the house, Mother was waiting for me, an anxious expression on her face. "Your daddy is on the way home to take you up to Aunt Grace's," she said. "Go ahead and pack your suitcase. And don't forget your church clothes."

"I thought..."

"Robert, your daddy is on the way home right now. He wants you ready to go when he gets here. I put your suitcase on the bed. You know how your daddy is, so get in there and pack."

For a moment I stood still, acting as if I had just been knocked up side the head with a ball-peen hammer. Daddy seemed unable to shake his belief that I was a worthless piece of shit. But I would prove him wrong, no matter what I had to do or however long it took. Just because Daddy spent thirty years in the Army did not mean he knew everything that was worth knowing.

George was Daddy's favorite. Susie was a girl, a very smart girl, and studious. She was a princess who could do no wrong and was above any need for discipline. Butch was indulged and pampered even more than Susie. That left me, Mr. Shit Bird. Daddy got to practice everything he learned in all those baby books on me. Standing in the living room on the last day of school at the end of my sophomore year, I realized that my plan to impress Daddy was not working. But come the fall, by God, when I went out for basketball, I would show him.

I was mad as a hornet as I threw a couple of pairs of short pants, a change of underwear, a white shirt, one pair of dark pants, and my good shoes into the suitcase and snapped it shut. Most of the time at Aunt Grace's I would wear only short pants and be barefoot. I didn't need a lot.

I heard the front door slam, and then Daddy was standing there tapping his watch. "Robert, get a move on. I want to get up there and get back before suppertime."

People in southwest Georgia were funny about time. Here was a corner of America lost in time, a place where people thought slavery was not a bad thing, thought integration would never happen, and even if they went off to college and came back with more degrees than a thermometer, were usually successful in hiding the fact. But for reasons I never figured out, people in southwest Georgia were dominated by their clocks, especially at mealtime and at the end of Sunday church. You could pick a ten-year period; mark the times that a family in southwest Georgia ate breakfast, dinner, and supper; and find no more than a five-minute variation for each meal over that ten years. People got grouchy and ill-tempered if a meal was a couple of minutes late.

As for church, people started looking at their watches around 11:50 a.m. And if the preacher had not wrapped up everything by noon, one of two things would happen: a deacon would stand up and remind the preacher that his time was up, or people would begin drifting out of church, going home to finish cooking that Sunday dinner that had to be served on time.

Daddy grew up in that world and then had it reinforced during thirty years in the Army. If his supper was not ready within one minute of 5 p.m., he would really put on a show. So when he said he wanted to get back home for supper, I knew things had to move according to his plan, or there would be hell to pay.

Mother gave me a big hug, kissed me on the cheek, and said that she would miss me this summer and that I should work hard and help Aunt Grace and Daddy's Mama every way I could. Her eyes were moist, and her hand lingered on my shoulder as I turned and followed Daddy out the door. When I crawled into the front seat of Daddy's truck, I looked toward the house and saw her on the front porch, her shoulders pulled together almost as if in pain, and her hand fluttered one more goodbye.

I was so pissed off about being shuffled off to the farm again that I slammed the door of the truck and turned to Daddy, determined to ask if he was a member of the Klan. But the expression on his face stopped me. He had things on his mind.

Daddy didn't talk during the twenty-minute ride up to Aunt Grace's. He sat there staring straight ahead, eyes on the road but with a thousand-yard stare. Out of the corner of my eye I could see that he was moving his lips in a half mumble and fondling his dick. But no words were coming out of his mouth, and his dick was not getting hard.

That reaming out operation down at the VA hospital must have been a doozy.

At Aunt Grace's I wouldn't exactly say that Daddy ordered me out of his moving truck, but I will say that as we drove into the sandy yard — which needed raking — Daddy moved the gearshift to neutral and began racing the engine. I wanted to hug my daddy. Rather, I wanted him to hug me. But Daddy was not a hugger. He had never hugged me. Never. And he was not about to start.

As the truck stopped, I looked at Daddy without speaking for maybe half a second, which is how long it took him to say, "Behave yourself this summer. No foolishness." He leaned out the window. Daddy's Mama was sitting on the front porch rocking, just watching us with all the placidity in the world.

"Where's Grace and Felix?" Daddy asked.

"Grace is fixing dinner, and Felix is tending to that dawg," Daddy's Mama said. I could tell from the timbre of her voice that she was into her cough medicine.

"What's the matter with Dog?" Daddy asked.

She waved a hand in dismissal. "Rattlesnake bit him. Right on the nose. He's laid up back there under the house. Way Felix is carrying on, you'd think it was a child that got bit."

"Mama, I've got to get home to supper," Daddy shouted. "He's all yours. Tell Grace and Felix I said to give him a spanking if he needs it."

Daddy's Mama smiled indulgently. "JB, he's too big to spank. Everybody knows that but you. Besides, he ain't no trouble." She paused, but Daddy didn't say anything. Then she added, "Sure you won't get out and set a spell?"

"Got to get home."

"Well, tell Gussie we all said hello."

I stepped down from the truck, closed the door, backed up a couple of steps, and nodded toward Daddy. He put the truck in gear, and as he moved away he said, "No foolishness. Do everything they tell you."

"Yes, sir." I stood watching as his truck disappeared quickly down the dirt road, pulling a big cloud of red dust. After a few seconds I couldn't see the truck, but I watched the dust, knowing Daddy's truck was somewhere at the head of that cloud, in the sunshine, leaving all the dust and debris behind.

The yard was quiet in the late afternoon, wrapped in the lassitude that comes near the end of the day. I watched the dust cloud until Daddy's Mama said, "Robert, I swan. How long you goan stand out there daydreaming? Get on out back and wash your hands. We 'bout to have supper."

"Yes, ma'am."

"And tomorrow morning I want you to sweep that yard." She drained the last of her cough medicine, looked around, and to no one in particular said, "Where's supper?"

I dropped my suitcase inside the house, got a big hug from Aunt Grace, and asked if I had time to see what Uncle Felix was doing with Dog.

"Yes, just for a minute. And you tell him I said to be in here in five minutes, or his dinner will be cold." She turned from the stove and waved a spoon at me. "You wash your hands good after being with that dawg."

I threw open the screen door, scampered down the steps, and looked around. "Uncle Felix," I called. "Where you?"

"Right here, boy." He was behind me, up under the edge of the house only a few feet away, sitting on a croker sack. Dog's head was in his lap. Uncle Felix was gently stroking Dog's neck and back. Dog's eyes were closed, and his breathing was slow and shallow. Dog heard my voice and half opened his eyes, and his long tail flopped one time. Then he closed his eyes, and his tail lay limp.

I squatted and patted Dog's shoulder. "Dog got snakebit?" I asked.

"Sure did," Uncle Felix said in an unusually soft voice, his big, work-gnarled hands easy and gentle as he continued stroking Dog. "Rattler popped him good. Right up side the head." The side of Dog's face was puffy and discolored.

"When?"

"Couple days ago." Uncle Felix pointed. "Down there by the barn. I killed that snake. Killed him dead."

"How'd you kill him?"

"Hoe. Chopped him into giblets."

I petted Dog's back. "He goan make it?"

"I don't know, boy. He's just about got past going. That was a big rattler, almost six feet, and fat. Snake that big packs a lot of poison. I've done everything I know how to do for Dawg, but I just don't know. If he makes it through one more night, he might be okay."

"What'd you do for him?"

Uncle Felix pointed to a small Coca-Cola bottle under the back steps. "Gave him six ounces of kerosene."

I sat back on my heels and stared at Uncle Felix. I had never heard of a dose of kerosene as a treatment for snakebite.

"He drink that kerosene?"

"Didn't want to."

"Where'd you hear about kerosene for a snakebite?"

"Don't know. Just heard."

"What does it do for a snakebite?"

"I hope it makes him well." He raised his head and looked at me. "Boy, I'm glad you're here. Dawg has missed you."

For some reason a wave of emotion swept over me. I waited a moment, then said, "Aunt Grace said supper is ready."

"Well, I guess we better go inside then." Very tenderly he lifted Dog's head out of his lap and placed it on the croker sack. "I'll be back down after supper to see about you, Dawg," he said.

Uncle Felix ate his supper quickly, then pushed his chair back and said, "I got to go look after Dawg." Intending to follow him, I pushed my chair back and stood up. Aunt Grace said, "Sit right there, young man, and finish your supper." So I sat back down.

"After you get through, I got a job for you," she said.

"I just wanted to — ...."

"I know what you want to do. You want to get up under the porch with Felix and nurse that dawg of his. You do that later. Right now I got something else for you to do."

Daddy's Mama looked across the table and said, "And don't you forget that yard. Tomorrow morning I want you to sweep the yard and do it good. All the sweeping in the same direction."

Damn. Everybody's nerves were shot today. I was angry even before Daddy dumped me like an unwanted hitchhiker. Aunt Grace snapped at me during supper. Daddy's Mama wanted clean dirt in the front yard. And Uncle Felix was preoccupied with Dog.

After dinner Aunt Grace went out on the back porch, poured the churn full of cream that had been skimmed off the cow's milk, and said, "Robert, get a chair from the table and come out here and churn us up some butter."

As I went outside, I heard a cat meowing. I mean, the cat was wound up. Constant, imperious meowing.

The cat scampered up the steps and stood there, a big gray cat with feral eyes and a skittish manner. "That your cat?" I asked.

Aunt Grace shook her head. "Most aggravating noise I ever heard. That cat just showed up. It wudn't nothing but skin and bones, so I started giving it a saucer of milk every night, and now we can't get rid of it."

"That a boy cat or a girl cat?"

"It's a mean cat. Couple days ago that cat stood up on its back feet, bit Dawg on the nose, and then clawed him on both ears. All at the same time. Scared Dawg half to death. Sent him scampering off down there toward the barn." She paused. "That's when the rattler got him."

As Aunt Grace opened the screen door, she looked over her shoulder and said, "Call me when you got butter. We'll give the leftover milk to the cat. Maybe it will stop that noise."

"Yes, Ma'am," I said.

When cream turns to butter, a small amount of milk is left. That was what Aunt Grace wanted me to save for the cat. So I sat there, churn between my legs, dasher in my hands, pushing and pulling, up and down, up and down, beginning the interminable process of turning cream into butter. And all the while the cat was meowing.

Uncle Felix was so close by, sitting up under the porch, that I didn't have to raise my voice to speak to him. "Uncle Felix, is Dog doing better?"

"Don't know yet. But I don't think he likes the noise that cat is making." Pause. "Don't think I do either." Another pause. "I know I don't like that cat."

I took a long look at the cat. Scuzzy. A bag of bones. Demanding and standoffish. Stalking around, circling, glaring at me with those glittering eyes as if it wanted to chase me away from the churn. I think that cat believed it owned the churn and all its contents. But it was the noise that got me. I've never liked repetitive noise, and that cat was a meow machine. "Meow. Meow. Meow. Meow."

"Shut up, cat," I said, churning faster, making the dasher plunge up and down, hoping the noise would make the cat move away. Instead, my excess force caused cream to spurt up through the hole on top of the churn and spray out onto the porch. The cat came running, lapping it up in an instant, then looking at me and demanding more. "Meow. Meow. Meow."

"Get away, cat," I said, swinging my foot out to the side to push the cat away. It danced aside, then dashed closer to the churn, licking the edges for drops of milk.

I don't know what I was thinking at the time, but with one quick motion I grabbed the cat by the scruff of the neck, lifted the lid off the churn, and shoved the cat inside. Then I began working that dasher up and down, up and down. By God, if that cat wanted cream, I would give it cream.

The cat set up a racket you could hear a mile away. Somehow it snaked it way upward through the angled wooden blades of the dasher and was riding the dasher up and down as if it was being baptized over and over, caterwauling like a born-again fundamentalist and trying to get out of the churn with an energy I did not know an animal that small could possess. The cat blew the lid off the churn, crawled up on the edge, and launched itself with such force that it tipped the churn over. It ran like hell for the sanctuary of the fig tree, one royally pissed-off, cream-covered cat.

Aunt Grace threw open the screen door at the same time Uncle Felix came up on the steps. "Robert, what was that noise?" Aunt Grace said. "What on earth is going on out here?"

I looked at the overturned churn and the cream pooling on the porch, then I said, "I think the cat got caught in the churn."

"You think … you think the cat got caught in the churn?" Aunt Grace's lips were tight and her face stern. "Robert, I got to tell you right now. This is no way to start your summer here."

"No, ma'am."

"You clean up this mess. And lemme tell you something. Tomorrow morning you go down there to the barn and milk those cows, and when the cream has separated you get yourself back up here, refill that churn, and make us some butter. And you better do it right this time. You hear me?"

Before I could answer, she spun around and said, "Where is that cat?"

"Out there under the fig tree. Probably licking its own self."

"You have wasted two gallons of cream, and we just can't afford that. And why would you put a poor dumb animal in a churn?"

"I guess because it is a dumb animal."

Aunt Grace was all puffed up and her elbows stuck out from her side. She took a step toward me and said, "Don't you get smart with me, you young scalawag." She shook her finger, something she did not do unless she was really mad.

Uncle Felix was now on the porch, standing behind Aunt Grace, not saying a word..

"Clean this mess up right now. You hear me?"

"Yes, ma'am."

She went inside, and the door slammed behind her.

Sometimes I thought my only conversation with adults was "Yes, ma'am" and "No, ma'am," "Yes, sir" and "No, sir." But that was all they wanted to hear.

"Better clean it up, boy," Uncle Felix said. "Yo Aunt Grace is mighty upset."

"About the cream or the cat?"

"Both. Mostly about the cat." He stopped and looked hard at me. "Robert, I ain't never heard of nobody putting a cat in a churn. What made you do such a thing?"

"I don't know."

"Uh-huh." Uncle Felix paused a moment, playing this out in his mind, then decided there was no explanation and said, "I don't think you put a hurting on that cat. You just scared it." He paused. "Right now you better clean up like she said. Yo aunt Grace has had her hissy fit. She will get over it. But you better lay low tonight. Go to bed early and don't say nothing."

"What are you going to do about Dog?"

"Wait until morning. That's all I can do."

As I began cleaning up the porch, the screen door shut, and I heard Uncle Felix say, "Putting a cat in a churn. If that don't beat all."

Early the next morning I heard Uncle Felix getting dressed. I threw off the sheet covering me and slid on a pair of short pants. Uncle Felix nodded as we walked silently through the dining room, through the kitchen where Aunt Grace was cooking breakfast, and out the back door. "Don't y'all hang out down there all morning with that dawg," she said. "Breakfast is just about ready."

"I gotta look after Dawg," Uncle Felix said.

Dog heard us bouncing down the steps and was struggling to sit up when we stooped over and waddled up under the porch. "Hey, looks like you feeling better," Uncle Felix said. Dog couldn't get on his feet, but his eyes were open and his tail was moving. "I wonder if he will eat anything."

"I guess that kerosene worked," I said.

"Guess it did."

Overhead I heard the back door slam. Aunt Grace thumped her shoe on the back porch. "You two get up here and wash your hands and eat breakfast," she said. "And Robert, as soon as you get up from the table, you go down to the barn and milk those cows and make us some butter."

THAT night I looked at the mantel and saw that the collected works of Edgar Allan Poe and been replaced by a single book, an almost-new book. That it had no dust jacket was not unusual. People in southwest Georgia looked on books the same way they looked on apples and oranges: you had to peel them to get to the good stuff.

The title of the book was *The Foxes of Harrow*, and the author was Frank Yerby. I had never heard of the book or the author, but that didn't mean anything.

"Where'd this book come from?" I asked as I picked up the book. But as had been the case with Poe, Aunt Grace did not know.

"It just showed up," she said.

"How long has it been here?"

Aunt Grace smiled. Everyone in the house seemed to be in a better mood now that Dog was on the mend. "Robert, you ask a lot of questions. I don't know how long it has been there. I didn't even know it was there."

It didn't make sense that, given the scarcity of books in Aunt Grace's house, a new book would arrive and no one would know where it came from. I was beginning to think that a cosmic rolling store delivered books in the middle of the night to southwest Georgia and a capricious angel looked at each title and said, "If I throw it out at this house, the right person will find it." I wondered who else out there had books that they didn't know were there.

I sat down and opened the book with a half sigh. My friend Edgar Allan Poe was gone, and Aunt Grace didn't know what had happened to him. The Bible was there, but I figured Daddy's Mama read that enough for all of us. This was all I had to read.

Daddy's Mama was rocking peacefully, a beatific smile on her face, filled with cough medicine and happy memories. Aunt Grace appeared deep in thought, her worn face lined in the dim light. Uncle Felix had his shoes off and was pulling at his toes and smiling. I moved my chair beyond his reach. He chuckled, continued to pull at his toes as if he was exercising them, and said, "Boy, get your nose out of that book for a minute. I want to ask you about something."

"Yes, sir. What is it?"

"Did you hear about — I seem to recall it was some months ago — that fellow what drove a rocket ship out in California?"

"Yes, sir, I heard about that in the barbershop."

"Yeah, what'd you hear?"

"His name was Chuck something. He went pretty fast."

Uncle Felix leaned toward me. "You know how fast?"

"More than a thousand miles an hour. I don't remember exactly."

"Well, I do. One thousand and six hundred miles an hour." Uncle Felix sat back, nodding his head.

"That's fast." I opened the book on my lap.

"I been studying about that. You know what I think?"

"No, sir. What?"

"If he was really going that fast, I don't think he left a shadow." Uncle Felix sat back, chuckled to himself, and said, "I'm going to bed. If you goan read, get your own self out there in the dining room."

"And turn off the light when you come to bed," Aunt Grace said.

So they all toddled off to bed, and I sat down in a straight-backed, cane-bottomed chair at the dining room table and opened the book.

The novel was set in Louisiana in the mid-1800s, and on the first page was a description of the Mississippi River such as I had never read. On that first page I saw and felt and smelled and heard the river. I knew how it lingered on the curves and raced down the straightaways. I felt the power of that mighty river, and in the background loomed intimations of a wonderful story.

Stephen Fox was tossed off a riverboat and left on a sandbar in the Mississippi River. Fox was a gambler, a rogue with a golden snuffbox and, as it turned out later, an eye for golden-skinned quadroons. He was picked up by a "pig boat," a flat-bottomed scow loaded with pigs, which took him to New Orleans. He had only a few dollars and the clothes on his back. Within a few years he owned the biggest plantation and the most majestic house in all of Louisiana. He married the most beautiful daughter of the most aristocratic French family in the state.

I stuck my forefinger in the book to hold my place and closed the book to look at the cover. Frank Yerby. Frank Yerby.

Well, that night Mr. Frank Yerby grabbed me by the scruff of the neck and pulled me into another world. I had never known that in Louisiana there had been such haughty French aristocrats and plainspoken Americans. I had never known, except in the vaguest of ways, about plantation society, about gambling and grand balls, duels and of days in the fields. French phrases were sprinkled throughout the book. I was taken with the phrase "Ma foi," which was used often by the elegant young men in the book which I mentally pronounced as "Ma foy." I rolled the phrase around on my tongue, repeating it softly, savoring it. I was not quite sure what it meant, but judging by the context, I thought it was something like "Damn right" or "You bet your ass" or "No shit."

"Night, Robert," Aunt Grace said from the other room.

"Night, Aunt Grace." I paused. "I'll turn out the light when I go to bed."

"See you in the morning."

Behind her I heard Uncle Felix. "That boy gets his nose in a book, and he can't hear it thunder."

"Yes, ma'am," I finally replied. And immediately I was back in the book.

Never before had I encountered a writer who could spin such a compelling story. Never had I given myself up to such a master. Frank Yerby wrote of Stephen Fox's revulsion toward black women until he met a young black woman who was everything he had ever wanted and more. He wrote of social and cultural barriers between the French and the Americans, but underneath that was the story of the barriers between blacks and whites. Mr. Yerby wrote of highly accomplished, multilingual black people who had been educated in France but condemned to servitude for one reason and one reason alone: the color of their skin. At the core of the story, moving slowly and with all the power of the Mississippi River, was Mr. Yerby's heartfelt pain for the South as it was and his bittersweet longing for the South that might have been.

It was nearly dawn when I reverently closed the book and sat back, letting the story settle inside me. I was deeply disturbed. The book had forced me to consider whether what I thought I knew about black people could be wrong. If there were in reality black people such as those Frank Yerby described, they were clearly superior to many of the white people I knew. The scope of such a heretical idea was, at the time, simply too much for me to assimilate.

And there was something else. That night, leaning over the dining room table, reading by the light of a bare bulb and listening to the sporadic buzzing of dying flies stuck to the flypaper hanging over my head, I realized at some subliminal level that a book is more than pages covered with printed words. A book is a package of wonder, a container of bliss, a vale of emotion, an unexploded bomb. A book can not only draw the reader into a new world and toward new friends but also separate him from the old world and old friends. Almost always, the new world and new friends are better than the old. That is the magic of books. One book can change a person's life. A library can change the world.

THAT Sunday we went to a little country church about a mile away. Daddy's Mama carried her Bible cradled in her arm like it was a baby. Aunt Grace carried herself with the pride and dignity that come with grinding poverty. And Uncle Felix rolled along with the resignation of a man who is terribly uncomfortable in his one pair of dress slacks and his one white shirt.

When we arrived, we stood in front of the Vilulah church, milling around with several dozen other people although we knew it would be a few degrees cooler inside the church, where we would be out of the sun and where wooden-handled fans would allow us to generate a tiny zephyr across our faces. We stood outside, waiting for some silent signal impelling us to troop inside.

Daddy's Mama put her hand on my arm and pointed across the road to the cemetery. "All yo people buried there."

I was fifteen and thought I would never die. I didn't care one bit if all my people were buried there. "Ma foy," I said.

"Say what?"

"Yes, ma'am."

"Yo aunt Grace and your uncle Felix and me, we all goan be buried there." She pointed. "You see those plots on either side?"

177

"Yes, ma'am."

"Yo cousins, all yo relatives, and most of the men served in the Army. Yo daddy has a plot there, right behind the plot where yo granddaddy is buried. He and yo mama will be buried there. I hope you and yo brothers and yo sister will be buried there."

"Not anytime soon, I hope," I said.

"Not anytime soon for you. But one day. For me it will be sooner."

This was turning out to be a very uplifting morning. I was still thinking about Frank Yerby's book and how Stephen Fox had risen from the pig boat to marry a beautiful woman and become the most prominent man in Louisiana. And Daddy's Mama was parading dead relatives.

"No, ma'am. It will be a long time before you are there."

She looked off into the distance. "Well, the Lord is mindful of his own," she murmured. She turned back to me. "Robert, you just remember what I said about yo people."

As if on cue, we all walked up the stairs, into the shadowy confines of the church, and down the single center aisle toward the front, where Daddy's Mama liked to sit. As I sat down next to her, she leaned over and in a loud whisper said, "Before I forget it, after dinner today you go out and sweep that front yard."

"Ma, foy."

She looked hard at me, wondering if her hearing was getting worse, and then the preacher stood up, and the service began.

I did not know it then, but this would be my last summer at Aunt Grace's, and the next time I would entered the Vilulah church would be for my daddy's funeral. After the funeral we would slowly walk across the road to where Daddy would be buried, to the first grave in the Coram family plot.

12

LIKE almost everyone else in Edison, I had little concern for current events. But I do remember 1953 because that was the year Ralph McGill's column moved to the front page of the *Atlanta Constitution*. Daddy unfolded the paper one morning, shook it, stared at the front page for a full half minute, and said, "I'll just be a striped-ass ape."

"What is it, JB?" Mother asked.

In the same tone of horror and disbelief Daddy would have used if he were telling Mother he had walked into a customer's house and found the toilet had not been flushed, he said, "They put Ralph McGill on the front page of the paper."

"What do you mean they put him on the front page?"

"I mean they moved him from there in the back where he belonged, and they put him on the front page. His column and his picture are on the front page."

"Hmmm," Mother said as she busied herself at the stove.

"Now I got to look at his face when I open up the paper."

"Don't look at him if he bothers you all that much."

Daddy shook the paper as if it were covered with fleas. "Sweetheart, he's on the front page. I got to look at him."

I don't think Daddy ever got over seeing Ralph McGill's column on the front page. But there were a lot of things that year he never got over. That summer peace talks in Korea ended in a truce. Daddy couldn't figure out if we had won or lost. "I don't understand a truce," he said. "They never called it a war; they called it a police action. What does that mean? Now we got a truce. Somebody has got to win. America has got to win."

That was also the year it seemed that if you combed your hair wrong, Senator Joseph McCarthy called you a Communist and your life turned to crap. People thought Communists were coming out of the woodwork. Because we didn't really know what a Communist was, and because being one was considered such a horrible thing, if you wanted to get into a fight, all you had to do was call someone a Communist, which was worse than calling him a shit ass or a morphydite. Being a Communist was nothing to joke about. It got so bad that someone wrote that since Robin Hood stole from the rich and gave to the poor, he was a Communist. It made national news when a reporter contacted the mayor of Nottingham, England, and asked him if Robin Hood was a Communist. "If he was, it's news to me," the mayor said.

But there was one constant, and that was the ritual that attended a new school year. I began the eleventh grade the same way I did the eighth, ninth, and tenth: with a trip to Z. Israel & Son to buy new clothes. In the past, Daddy had considered the trip women's work and Mother had taken George and me down to the department store for the ritualistic purchase of two pairs of Levi's and four shirts—two with short sleeves and two heavier long-sleeved shirts for winter. But this year Daddy decided to tag along, and I knew it was not going to be an easy trip.

If seniors were the kings and queens of high school, juniors were the princes and princesses, full of the knowledge that next year we would be the kings and queens, and then we would be out of school and off to wherever we were going. Some in the class were already talking about college. Daddy was pushing North Georgia

College, a military school that he described as "almost up there with West Point." But I was thinking about North Carolina State, in part because Mother was from North Carolina. So here I am a prince of Edison High School, and both my mother and daddy are accompanying me to do something as simple as buying jeans and shirts.

Daddy barreled down the aisle toward the rear of the store with Mother behind him; George and I were the caboose. Mr. Z. Israel, the oldest man God ever made, moved from his spot by the window to greet us. He was small and frail, and by the time he shuffled across the store, I was the only one within speaking distance.

"Hey, Mr. Z," I said. "How you doing?"

"I'm here," he said. "Thank God, I'm here." This was his standard reply. He grimaced and shook his head. His voice was heavily accented, and people in Edison knew he came from somewhere else. We heard it was Poland, but that was too far away to imagine.

Mr. Z and his son Bill, daughter-in-law Dorothy, and two grandsons Phil and Jack went to church every Saturday in Fitzgerald, a small town about fifty miles from Edison. We knew vaguely that Mr. Z was a big wheel in the church — no one ever used the word "synagogue" — and we didn't really think much about the fact that the Israels went to church on Saturday.

The Israels were the most prominent family in town. Mr. Bill, who was somewhere around age forty, gave to every charity in town. Tall and slender, he was soft-spoken and had iron-gray hair. In a few more years he would be voted the Man of the Century in Edison.

After I left Edison, when I would hear about anti-Semitism in the rural South, I would tell people about Mr. Bill and how he was voted not the Man of the Year or the Man of the Decade, but the Man of the Century, and they would not believe me. But the truth is that in Edison, Georgia, in the 1950s, there was no anti-Semitism. We were bigots and racists who could muster a cold contempt for black people, and we looked upon Catholics with suspicion, but we were not anti-Semitic.

Up ahead Daddy was telling Mr. Bill that he was bringing us in to get outfitted for the coming year. Daddy looked over his shoulder, saw me talking with Mr. Z, and shouted, "Robert, get on up here so you can tell Mr. Bill what you need."

"Ma foy," I said without thinking.

Daddy's eyes narrowed. He walked up to me and, with his back to Mr. Bill, got right in my face, bowed up like a butterbean tick and said, "You smart-mouth me again, and I'll show you that you are not too big for me to dust your britches. You understand me?"

"Yes, sir," I said in my rarely used contrite voice.

Daddy and George wandered off, George checking the waist and length of the Levi's, then looking at the shirts. Mother and I trailed behind.

Miss Dorothy walked up close to Mother and said, "Gussie, thank you for coming over and helping me the other day."

"Dottie, it was nothing. You would have done the same for me."

Miss Dorothy squeezed Mother's arm and said, "Thank you."

Mother turned to me and said, "Robert, besides your jeans, do you know what you want?"

"Yes, ma'am. I need two short-sleeved nylon shirts. One of 'em pink."

"Pink?"

I picked up a pink shirt and a blue shirt. "Here they are."

Mother ran her hand inside the shirt. "Robert, you can see through these shirts."

"I'll be wearing an undershirt."

Down the aisle a few steps was a large open bin of boys' winter shirts. I checked the size and picked up two. Nothing really mattered except the pink nylon shirt. With the short sleeves folded twice and the collar pulled up in the back, I would be ready for the school year.

"Is that a pink shirt?" Daddy asked. His voice was somewhere between scorn and anger. "You got a pink shirt?" He pulled it out of my hand.

What could I say? It was a pink shirt.

"You can see through this thing," Daddy said. "A boy wearing a see-through pink shirt?"

"JB, if that's what he wants to wear, let him wear it," Mother said.

Daddy shook his head. He looked at Mr. Bill, who was standing a few feet away and saying nothing. "Mr. Bill, you see any boys from around here wearing pink shirts? I know you see girls wearing pink, but I'm talking about boys."

Mr. Bill laughed. "JB, I've sold pink shirts to half the boys at Edison High School. It's all the thing this year."

"You mean everybody will be wearing these things?"

"Afraid so."

"Hmmmm!" Daddy paused. If that many boys were wearing pink shirts, then they were almost like a uniform. And uniforms were good. "Well, I don't like them. But if that many boys are wearing them . . . "

Mr. Bill looked at me. "You tell your folks about the jacket the other boys will be wearing?"

I looked at him in gratitude. "No, sir. Not yet."

I turned toward Mother and Daddy. "I need a new winter jacket." I paused. "A suede jacket."

Daddy snorted and turned his back. "A pink shirt and a suede jacket. What the . . . "

"Try this on, Robert," Mr. Bill said, handing me a beautiful tan suede jacket. "Whatever you do, don't let it rain on you when you are wearing this. You don't want to get this jacket wet. It will spot."

I slipped my arms into the sleeves and felt the jacket nestle over my shoulders. It was a perfect fit. I moved around Daddy to look into the full-length mirror.

"Robert, it does look good on you," Mother said.

"Sure does," Mr. Bill said. "That jacket was made for you." He turned to Daddy. "JB, you want that jacket for your boy? It's only thirty dollars."

Daddy winced. "Thirty dollars?"

Mr. Bill reached into the pocket of the jacket and pulled out what appeared to be a sponge. It was the size of a pack of cigarettes. "This is what you clean it with," he said. "Just rub the jacket with this. Make sure you go with the nap. If you don't get rained on, this jacket will look like it was new a year from now." He backed off a step, smiled, and said, "Nice-looking piece of clothing."

Daddy had too much respect for Mr. Bill to turn him down.

"He does need a winter coat," Mother said.

Daddy's face was all pruned up. I fingered the tan suede and said, "Look at this, Daddy. The color is just like your Army uniforms."

That did it. I was over the top. I could put cow turds on each shoulder, tell Daddy they looked like Army insignia, and he would go for it.

"Thirty dollars," was all he could say.

Mr. Bill knew this sale was wrapped up. "Robert, let me put that jacket in a box for you. It's too nice to put in a bag." He looked at George. "George, you want one of these?"

Daddy's eyes widened, but George said, "No, thank you, sir. I can still wear the jacket I got last year."

George might not have been much, but he was practical.

"Anything else your family needs, JB?"

"No, Mr. Bill, I think that's about it."

I leaned over and whispered in Mother's ear, "I need a pair of tennis shoes. Black."

She drew back and looked at me. "For what?"

"I'm going out for basketball."

"You what?"

"What's he talking about?" Daddy asked.

"He says he is going out for basketball and needs a pair of ... "

"Basketball!" Daddy laughed. He would have exploded, but he wouldn't do that in front of Mr. Bill. But he could act the part of a tough daddy. "I thought you were over that foolishness. Like I told you before, you too short to play basketball. You'll never make the team."

"I can try."

"You can't play basketball."

"You know I cut the price on my tennis shoes for boys going out for basketball?" Mr. Bill asked. "I can sell you a pair of black tennis shoes — that's what everyone on the team wears — for six dollars. What size do you wear?" He walked a few steps toward the shoe section, looking over his shoulder at my feet. "Those shoes fit you okay? They look pretty small."

"I wear a five and a half. Same size shoe Daddy wears."

"They look small for you." He pulled down a box of shoes. "You want to try them on?"

"No, sir. They'll fit."

The idea that my feet might be bigger than Daddy's had never occurred to me.

Daddy was overwhelmed. The words "team" and "everyone" had temporarily blown his circuits. Both words reminded him of the Army and therefore were good. But he still didn't think I could play basketball. And there I was with a box of tennis shoes under my arm.

"How are you going ... ?" He stopped, and I knew I would hear more about this later.

"George, you got everything you need?" Mr. Bill asked. George had been standing back with that big-eyed owlish stare of his.

"Yes, sir. I'm okay."

"All right, then. JB, you want to charge these goods?"

"No, Mr. Bill, I appreciate that, but I'll pay cash," Daddy said, reaching into his back pocket for his billfold. "I don't like to owe money."

He looked over his shoulder at me. How the hell had I wound up with a pair of tennis shoes so quickly?

"Good way to be," Mr. Bill said, as he pushed the clothes across the counter to Miss Dorothy, who began putting them in bags. She put a piece of soft white paper around my suede jacket and then slid it into a box. "Robert, you want to put those shoes in a bag?"

"No, ma'am, Miss Dorothy. I'll carry them."

We marched out of the store like a line of ducks, Daddy Duck up front, leading the way, mumbling and grimacing, with Mama Duck right behind him. George and me brought up the rear.

Mr. Z was standing by the door. "Thank you," he said. "Thank you."

Daddy and Mother and George nodded. Mr. Z smiled, reached out and touched my arm, and said, "Boy, you ready for school?"

"Yes, sir, Mr. Z. I'm ready."

Daddy opened the trunk, and we put all the clothes in there. He looked at me and said, "You don't know anything about basketball. And here you have basketball shoes." He slammed the trunk shut.

"JB, stop it. He can't get on the court without those shoes."

"He's too short to play basketball."

"He's as big as you are."

"I ain't playing basketball."

Daddy opened the car door and turned to me. "Besides that, your dog needs some training. He's crawling all over people, begging."

"Daddy, I haven't noticed anything different about him." That was not really true. Getting a hand job had changed Pal's life. He expected everyone to do for him what Ollie had done.

"Well, I saw him slobbering all over George the other day."

George began nodding in agreement.

"Robert, you train that dog."

"Yes, sir," I said, thinking that what I really needed to do was untrain him. But I didn't know how to do that.

THE first week of school I went into the library. Three walls were lined with books and the fourth with a row of windows. Even with the light that came through the windows and the overhead lights, the library always seemed dim and shrouded in quietness.

The teacher who sat at the far end of the room looked up as I entered and said, "Robert, anything I can help you with?" We didn't have a full-time librarian. The job rotated among the teachers, depending on which one did not have a class during a particular period. I had drawn Mrs. Pierce, the English teacher.

"Yes, ma'am. Do you have any books by Frank Yerby?"

She raised an eyebrow. "This is not for a classroom assignment."

"No, ma'am. I just want to read it. I already read *The Foxes of Harrow,* and I wondered if Mr. Yerby wrote any other books."

"*Mr.* Yerby?"

"Yes, ma'am. He wrote it."

"I know that. I like to see students reading beyond their assignments. But... you've already read one of his books, you say?"

"Yes, ma'am."

"Ah-ite. Over there, off to your right. Third row from the top. There. Right in front of you."

I was in awe There were three books by Frank Yerby. That many books by one man. "How many books has he written?"

"I don't know. I think six or seven. He turns them out."

From the shelf I pulled *The Vixens.* "Mrs. Pierce, what's a vixen?"

"A female fox."

The book had no dust jacket, but I sensed this was not a nature book. I opened to the first page and read about a steamboat coming down the Chattahoochee River. The Chattahoochee? That was less than twenty miles away. A book that took place in southwest Georgia? I thumbed through the book and my eyes fell on a passage that said the reason the devil did not make Georgia his home was because hell had a better climate. Hey, I agreed with that 100 percent.

I spotted another passage where Mr. Yerby said that men in the South were "too enamored by the mystical brotherhood of whiteness to comprehend democracy" and that the rise of black men did not mean the fall of whiteness. Whoa! This guy could set the pages on fire. I had never read or heard, nor had I ever known of grown-ups discussing, such inflammatory ideas. I could not wait to get home and start reading. I snapped the book shut and walked over to Mrs. Pierce. "I'll take this one."

She pulled the library card from the back of the book and said, "Robert, I'm not sure you are old enough to read this book." She looked at the cover and in a low voice, almost as if speaking to herself, added, "I don't know why we even have it in here."

I didn't say anything.

"You always return books early, so don't pay any attention to the date." She wrote my name on the card, the date I checked it out, and the return date, then handed me the book.

I took *The Vixens* home hidden between my schoolbooks. When I walked into the house, I said hi to Mother, sat on the sofa in the living room, and opened up the big loose-leaf binder in which I kept notes and I wrote my homework assignments. I hid the novel behind the notebook and began reading. When Daddy walked in and saw me staring into what he thought was a homework assignment, he said, "Glad to see you are doing your homework."

One of Daddy's many rules was that his children be in bed by 9 p.m. So that night when I went to bed, I pulled out my old Boy Scout flashlight and crawled under the sheet. I knew the light would be visible through the sheet, so I took a blanket from the closet and pulled it over me, turned on the flashlight, and continued to read, carried away by Mr. Yerby's story.

"Why you under a blanket again?" George asked from across the room.

I stuck my head out long enough to say, "Go shit in your hat, your turd roller."

"You cussing. I'm gonna tell Daddy on you."

"Do and I'll whip your scrawny ass."

As she always did, Mother stuck her head in the door about 10 p.m. to see if we were asleep. "Robert, you awake?" she whispered. I was right in the middle of a story about white aristocrats who were unfulfilled by beautiful but disturbed wives and who found their dreams in the arms of black women. Of course I was awake. My eyes were as big as saucers. I turned off the flashlight, emerged from under the covers, pretended to be half-asleep, and looked at Mother in the dim light.

She came across the room and pressed the back of her hand against my forehead. "As hot as it is, why are you under a blanket? Don't you feel well?" She scratched her head, waited a moment, and said, "You don't have a fever."

"I'm okay. Just a little chilly."

"I don't see how you can be chilly. It must be more than eighty degrees."

"I'm going back to sleep."

"You call me if you don't feel well."

"Night, Mother."

"Good night, son."

Around 2 a.m. the flashlight grew dim, and I was forced to put the book away. That probably was a good thing. I was soaked with perspiration, and the mattress was damp. "Ma foy," I murmured and drifted off to sleep.

In the next few weeks I read *Floodtide*, *Golden Hawk*, *A Woman Called Fancy*, and *Benton's Row*. I almost missed the newly-published *Benton's Row* because it had a dust jacket. I saw Mr. Yerby's name on the dust jacket and pulled the book off the shelf. If this one had a dust jacket, it must be special. It was. On the back was a photograph of Frank Yerby and a biographical sketch.

I stared at the photo, eyes wide. I could not have moved if someone had shouted, "Fire!" I could not have moved if Daddy had come in the door and said, "Front and center!"

I continued to stare at the photo, trying desperately to find another truth. But there was only one truth. *Frank Yerby was a black man.*

The greatest writer I had ever known, the man who had turned my world upside down, was a black man. I trembled as I read about him with spiraling astonishment.

Frank Yerby was from Georgia, the great-grandson of slaves and the son of a hotel doorman. He had written eight novels. *The Foxes of Harrow* had sold more than a million copies and not only was made into a movie, the movie was nominated for an Oscar. Two other books of his had been made into movies.

I was rigid. I squeezed the book until my knuckles whitened. I was still trying to force another truth.

I was obsessed—there is no other word for it—with the discovery that Frank Yerby, the greatest writer that God ever put on earth, was from Georgia. And he was black. I realized why Mrs. Pierce had looked at me in an odd fashion when I said "Mr. Yerby." She knew he was black. But she was the English teacher. How many other people in Edison had heard about this man from Georgia who had written a book that sold more than a million copies? He was *famous*. People all over the world knew about him, but I felt as if he was all mine—my discovery, my writer, my hero.

And he was a black man!

If Daddy found out I was reading books written by a black man, it would be worse than admiring a column by Ralph McGill. Daddy would have my ass for breakfast.

But it did not matter, not at that moment. All that mattered was the raw and undiluted sense of wonder about the stories Frank Yerby told. I was captivated, enthralled, consumed by his ability to tell a story.

I was still squeezing the book, still trying to force some understanding from my discovery. I stared at Frank Yerby's face. Full. Sensitive. Soft eyes that recognized everything and saw through everything.

He had once been young like me. He had started somewhere. How had he begun his career? How does a black man begin a career as a writer? It had to have been difficult in the extreme. I shook my head in amazement.

Today when I look back at the hidden patterns of my life, at the recovered memory that comes from looking over one's shoulder, I know that Frank Yerby changed my life. He planted the giddy idea that I might one day become a writer. For a poorly educated, shirttail boy coming out of rural southwest Georgia in the 1950s, you cannot begin to imagine what an impossible dream that was. You simply cannot imagine.

But perhaps even more important, Frank Yerby opened a door and the light that came through that door awakened me. The racism that was in the marrow of my bones would, like a virulent poison, take years to eradicate. And the deep sense of insecurity about being from the rural South, and therefore inferior in all ways to city people, would take even longer. But this was the beginning. The books of Frank Yerby were a yeasty concoction that would ferment for years and make me question the things I had been taught about black people, about the South, about my family, about the very roots of my existence.

13

THE next Sunday after church I was tingling with excitement when my family drove up to have dinner at Aunt Grace's house. It took me a while to get Aunt Grace off by herself, but eventually I went up to her on the front porch, leaned over, and whispered, "Aunt Grace, I need to talk to you."

Aunt Grace always had a liking for me. She smiled indulgently and said to Mother and Daddy, "Robert wants to tell me something." We walked off the front porch and around the corner of the house, then stopped under the big pecan tree in which some birds were singing. I grinned in excitement and bounced from one leg to the other.

She laughed. "Robert, what is going on with you?"

"Aunt Grace, you know that book you got, the one by Frank Yerby, *The Foxes of Harrow*?"

"Well, I haven't read it."

"But you remember it? It is on your shelf. I read it last summer when I was here."

"Is that the one you stayed up all one night reading?"

"Yes, ma'am."

"I never did know where that book came from." She folded her arms and looked at me indulgently. "Well, what about it?"

"Aunt Grace … Aunt Grace … did you know that it was written by Frank Yerby?"

"If you say so." She smiled that sweet winsome smile of hers and said, "Robert, what do you want?"

"He's a … he's a … " And then I blurted, "black man." That was the first time I ever said "black man."

"Who is?"

"Frank Yerby. The man who wrote *The Foxes of Harrow.*"

She stared, brow wrinkled, not saying anything.

"Frank Yerby is a black man," I repeated. "And he's from Georgia."

"And you say he wrote that book in there?"

"Yes, ma'am. And about a half dozen others. He is a famous writer, and you got one of his books."

Aunt Grace laughed and shook her head. "Robert, where do you get such foolish ideas?" She turned and began walking toward the front of the house.

"His great-grandparents were slaves," I said. She threw up her hands in a dismissive wave and kept walking. I stood there, feet rooted in the sandy yard, not fully understanding how the stories told by Frank Yerby could be so glorious and liberating, how they could fill me with such exultation and wonder, and how Aunt Grace, my sweet and wonderful aunt who loved me deeply, did not understand any of this.

I took a deep breath. The warm, dry air, sweet with the scents of the fields, filled my lungs. I looked up through the leaves of the pecan tree toward the blue sky, and in that moment I realized that if I'd ever had the slightest doubt that I would leave southwest Georgia one day, that doubt was gone.

I didn't give two hoots in hell about basketball. But if I made the team, if somehow I could play just thirty seconds in one game—enough to win a letter—I would get a black wool sweater with a big red E sewn on the front, and I would belong. No longer would I be the short and faintly odd oldest son of the Sarge, who, by the way, was not a farmer but instead climbed telephone poles for a living. I would be a member of the only fraternity that existed at Edison High School in the fall of 1954: that of the athlete. Athletes owned the school. Good grades meant little. In fact, a boy who was an A student was looked down on with the patronizing, anti-intellectual air that was the hallmark of rural Georgia.

The dozen or so boys who wore black school sweaters festooned with a small basketball, baseball bat, or a winged foot had no equal at school, in town, or in all of Calhoun County. Grown-ups spoke to them on the street as if they were equals. And these godlike boys had all mastered the essence of cool, manifesting the knowledge that they were superior to all other life forms.

The conversations between townspeople and athletes were so understated that an outsider would have thought everyone in Edison cared as little for sports as I did. If one of these boys walked into the barbershop before a big game, the Judge would stop clipping, nod, and in a flat, impassive voice say, "I see y'all playing Attapulgus Friday night."

The boy, in the same tone, would reply "Yes, sir."

Then the Judge would say, "You goan take care of bidness?"

"We goan take care of bidness," the boy would say, and Judge would nod in approval.

A book could have been written about the underlying messages in these brief exchanges: the school rivalry between Edison and Attapulgus; personal animosities between Edison families and Attapulgus families, the origins of which went back generations; the fact that Attapulgus was on the edge of a big swamp; defensiveness toward everything and everyone beyond the Edison city limits; the ever-simmering anger toward the entire world. Translated, the preceding conversation would have sounded something like this:

"I see y'all are playing that swamp-rat bunch of morphydites from Attapulgus. I wouldn't be a bit surprised to find out every one of those snot-nosed shit asses was a twenty-five-year-old retard."

"Yeah, well, some strange people come out of that swamp down there. They worse than those people what put butter beans in their Brunswick stew. But that's who we scheduled to play."

"You goan stomp a mud hole in their ass and then wade it dry?"

"Goan beat 'em like they was rented mules."

"Damn right. Uh-huh."

I wanted to be a part of that fraternity. I wanted to belong. I was too short to play basketball. Daddy was right about that. And I didn't have the loose-limbed, catlike grace possessed by most of the baseball players. But I was fast. I was greased lightning. I could outrun any boy at Edison High School except Gerald and he didn't count. His daddy made moonshine, and he had grown up running from the law. Besides, he was too lazy to go out for any sport. He was too lazy to swat a fly.

Speed would be my weapon. I would specialize in the fast break. I would be Mr. Speed Demon.

At breakfast I said, "Daddy, this is the first day of basketball practice, and if I get to your office by about ten to five, can I ride home with you?"

Daddy snorted. "Why you wasting your time? You ain't never gonna play a minute, and you know it."

"JB, you let him alone," Mother said. "You ought to encourage him on playing sports."

"Well, I'm not coming by the office today. I'll be coming back from Bluffton, and I'm not stopping."

"What if I'm on the corner waiting?"

"I might be early. Don't count on it."

I looked down at my plate.

"I'll tell you something else, too. And I told you this before. This family schedule is not going to be interrupted for you. If you want to play basketball, fine. But your mother is not holding up supper. If you are not here at five o'clock, we eat without you."

"Robert, you call when you are ready to go, and I'll come down in the car and pick you up," Mother said.

Daddy's head snapped toward her. "How you gonna go down and pick him up when it is suppertime? What about the rest of the family?"

"JB, it's only five minutes into town. If I don't pick him up, how will he get home?"

"He can walk home. That's how." Daddy slapped the table. "He is not going to change our schedule."

"Okay, okay. JB, remember your blood pressure." Mother looked at me and shrugged.

"And one more thing, young man," Daddy said. "One C on your report card, and your basketball days are over."

"Yes, sir."

THIRTEEN of us showed up to try out for the basketball team. The tryouts were being held in the shell, which is, for reasons I never knew, what we called the basketball gymnasium. The shell was built of concrete blocks and had a tin roof. It contained bathrooms, dressing rooms, and a glistening basketball floor. The court had been painted with the requisite stripes delineating the playing area, then coated with high-gloss polyurethane. After that a half dozen coats of wax had been applied. To walk on that floor in street shoes was sacrilegious.

There was something prophetic about the fact that of the thirteen who showed up that day, ten arrived early and were dressing out when the last three arrived. We were the three misfits. The first weighed about 210 pounds and broke into a sweat putting on his tennis shoes, the second was so uncoordinated that every time he combed his hair, he stuck the comb in his eye. The third was me, shorter by a head than anyone else on the team. But fast, damn fast.

The Magnificent Ten, those boys who would make up the first and second teams and who would play 99 percent of the time, looked up when we walked deferentially into the dressing room.

"Everybody better look out," Joe said. "Ain't nobody safe no more." Everyone snickered. The coach knew who would be on the first team and who would be on the second. So did the players. So did we three misfits.

JOE was leaning against a locker, naked as a jaybird and idly scratching the jock itch that ran from his groin up to the edge of his lower abdomen. Even before the season started, Joe had a great case of jock itch going. So did several other boys who would be playing on the first and second team. Jock itch was a symbol of the nobility, a scarlet escutcheon, the suppurating badge of the athlete. When those boys scratched, the rest of us sighed with envy.

I could tell by the way Joe's mouth was pooched out that he was working on a chaw of tobacco, a suspicion that was confirmed when he let loose and spit what seemed to be a pint of juice through a crack in the floor without a drop flying off on either side.

I was carrying a bathing suit, a T-shirt, and my tennis shoes all rolled in a towel. I found an empty space on the bench, unrolled the towel, and undressed. When I slid my bathing suit over my underwear, Joe said, "Hey, Coram. You ain't wearing no jockstrap?"

Damn. I didn't know I was supposed to wear a jockstrap. I had heard of them but never worn one. From the grins on their faces, I knew that every one of the Magnificent Ten would be wearing a jockstrap. I looked at my two fellow misfits, and their faces told me they had no jockstraps either.

"It's in the washing machine."

Joe hustled his balls, looked around the dressing room at his grinning teammates, and said, "Maybe you don't need one. Maybe you ain't got nothing to put in it."

Across the dressing room a naked member of the Magnificent Ten was sitting on the bench. He slid his jockstrap up his legs, stood up, and carefully pushed his penis and testicles into the pouch. He adjusted everything, bent and stretched, adjusted again, and used his forefingers to gently scratch the red rash reaching from his groin to his abdomen and a few inches down his legs. "Damn jock itch," he mumbled. The ritual completed, he pulled on his bathing suit, sat down and began lacing up his black high-topped tennis shoes.

We all wore bathing suits and T-shirts that day because the coach had not issued uniforms. The same uniforms were used year after year at Edison. No one could remember when the uniforms had been new. The Magnificent Ten would get the same uniforms they had worn the previous year, so they would have little sewing or adjusting to do. If I got a uniform, Mother was going to have to do some serious tailoring. Those uniforms were meant for much taller boys.

The coach walked into the dressing room, slapped his hands together, and started to say something. He bowed his head in resignation for a moment, then said, "I've told y'all this before. Not getting the jock itch is a simple matter of cleanliness. Cleanliness, boys, that's all there is to it. You got to stay clean down there. Clean and dry. Wash yourselves good, especially after a game when you get sweaty. Then put on some Johnson's Baby Powder. I mean, really pour on that baby powder. Use a whole can if you want to. But you stay clean and you stay dry, and you won't get the jock itch."

He looked around the room. "Anybody got any questions about this?" No one said anything. "Ah-ite, guys. Let's hit the court."

Joe casually turned his head away from the coach and in what seemed a seamless motion, spat another pint of tobacco juice through the crack in the floor and then spat his chaw into a trash can.

The coach looked at the misfits. "That goes for you new fellows, too. Let's move it."

The coach would have been satisfied with the Magnificent Ten. All had played basketball the previous year. Ten boys had dressed out for each game, and those ten, now juniors and seniors, had won more games than they had lost. They'd had a good year. For several of them this would be their final year of high school basketball, and they were determined to make it a great year for the Edison Dynamos.

We practiced hard two or three days a week for the next two months. If the coach had had his way, we would have practiced every day. But his players were the sons of farmers, and they were needed at home during the harvest season to work in the fields. Some days there were only three or four of us at practice, and I was able to demonstrate my fast-break skills. I could be under the basket at the far end of the court before anyone else crossed the center line. I often missed the basket on that all-important first shot, but at least I got down there in a hurry.

"Coram, you fast," the coach always said. "You really fast." But in his eyes I saw the unspoken afterthought: "If only you were about six feet tall."

Every day after basketball practice I walked home. Walked and ran. I thought of it as extra training. It took maybe ten minutes to walk across town to the city limits and then another half hour to reach the house. I passed the fire tower on the right, then Frog's little honky-tonk beer joint on the outskirts of town. I continued down the hill and through the swamp and thick woods, on past the church and cemetery, and into the driveway.

Mother always looked up and smiled when I came through the front door, then she'd say, "Robert, your supper is in the oven. I'll fix you a plate."

But before she could move, Daddy would snap, "He's old enough to fix his own supper." Then he'd glare at me and say,. "I expect you to work on your homework until it is finished."

Daddy was always in a bad mood. "Somebody bust the Nelly Hoover curve again?" I would ask.

"No, but they will. Your friends don't know how to drive."

A week before the first game of the season, I walked into the dressing room after school, and the Magnificent Ten were sitting there on the benches, all clad in their red-and-black uniforms. There was a big cardboard box beside the coach. Everyone looked at me and the coach said, "Where's the other two?"

I looked over my shoulder as "Big Boy," breathing hard, and "Spaz," spun half around because his shoulder hit the door, walked in. I saw their anxiety in their eyes. Would we be dressing out this season?

The coach was a nice guy, and he knew that it wasn't going to do any harm to have us on the team. He turned to the Magnificent Ten, smiled, and said, "Men, I want you to welcome our three new members." He reached down to the bottom of the cardboard box and handed each of us a pair of black pants and a red jersey with a black number on the front and back.

"Coram, you like number thirty-three?" he asked.

"Yes, sir."

"Good thing," he said. "Get yo mama to adjust it for you."

To Big Boy he said, "I want you to lose some weight. Lots of weight. Otherwise, we goan have to devise some special plays around you."

Overcome with emotion, Big Boy, his hands caressing the uniform, nodded.

The three of us knew that it would take a miracle for us to get our letters. Basketball games in southwest Georgia were often closely matched, with only six or eight points separating the winner and loser. But we would dress out, and we would travel to the away games. We would be part of the team. I don't know about the other two misfits, but deep in my heart I was petrified some night I might be called on to play.

MOTHER must have been looking out the window, waiting for me, because as I walked up the front steps, she threw open the screen door, locked her arms around me, and said, "Oh, son, I am so glad for you." She touched the rolled-up towel, fingered the red satin material hanging out the end, then turned and said, "JB, your son made the team. Aren't you proud of him?"

Daddy did not answer. I was standing straight when I walked into the kitchen where Daddy lingered over his dessert. Mother linked her arm through mine and smiled. She laughed, touched my shoulder, and said, "Son, I'm proud of you."

Daddy half turned, looked me up and down with his wide-eyed confused-owl stare, and said, "How many times you think you goan play this year?"

"The coach says I'm the fastest person on the team."

"Fast ain't everything." Daddy shook his head. "You'll never get on the court. Not unless Edison is fifty points ahead with ten seconds to play."

He turned back to his dessert, carefully pushed a piece of cake around to make sure it was dripping with chicken gravy, leaned over his plate, and lifted the cake to his mouth. "Good dessert, Sweetheart."

Mother squeezed my shoulder as I stood there mute. As always I was immensely pleased at Daddy's enthusiastic support of my athletic career. A boy could go for a long time with that kind of support.

"I'm going to play, and I'm going to be good."

"Go do your homework."

"Yes, sir."

THE Dynamos won their first three games, which were played at home, and then it was time to go on the road. We were playing Jakin, a town about the size of Edison and located about an hour south.

"I need a big breakfast today," I said as I sat down at the table that morning.

"JB, why don't we drive down tonight and watch the game," Mother said. "Jakin is not very good. Robert might get to play, and I want to be there so I can see him."

Daddy's face twisted into an annoyed rictus. "I'm too tired when I get off work to drive down to Jakin." He looked up at Mother as she poured him another cup of coffee. "And you are not going down to the school in the middle of the night to pick him up. He knew when he started this foolishness that we weren't going to be his drivers."

"But JB, either the parents of the other players are there to pick them up or they drive themselves home."

"Well, we ain't everybody else."

"It's going to be almost midnight when the bus gets back to Edison."

"He can walk."

"Can't he ask somebody to give him a ride?"

"No. He needs to learn some discipline."

"At midnight? JB, he's just a boy."

"He should be in bed by nine o'clock." Daddy shrugged. "He's a basketball hero. Ain't nobody going to bother him."

"It's okay, Mother. I'm not afraid."

"Good thing," Daddy said. "You tell George when you goan be gone so he will feed Pal." He shook his head. "That dog has gotten strange. I'm thinking about getting rid of him."

"I'm training him, Daddy. I been putting him on a leash. He will be okay."

"Well, he better."

So that night and on several dozen other nights, I rode the team bus to Jakin, Iron City, Colquitt, Donalsonville, Climax, Morgan, Fort Gaines, and other little towns scattered across deep southwest Georgia. On the ride out of Edison I was always filled with good humor and boastful basketball talk. But then there was the game. I always dressed out but never played. That might have been a good thing, because the pants of my black satin uniform were so big that Mother had to take an enormous tuck in the back. The extra material was gathered in a big knot making me look as if I had some sort of abnormal growth on my ass. After the game we'd climb back aboard the bus, the other players sitting with their girlfriends or a cheerleader, while I sat up front with the teachers who were chaperones and tried not to think about what lay ahead.

The bus stopped in the parking lot by the shell, and we'd all slowly climb down- boisterous and boastful if we had won, which was most of the time, and subdued if we had lost. As older boys looked for their cars and the others looked for their parents, the parking lot was filled with red dust and brake lights, school cheers and shouted farewells. I hunched my shoulders inside my suede jacket and lingered in the shadows. If anyone saw me, they assumed that Mother or Daddy was on the way to pick me up. When all the cars were gone and the dust had settled, I began the long midnight walk toward home.

Once beyond the streetlights I was enveloped in unrelieved blackness. I walked down the middle of the road because all I could see was the faint blur of intermittent whiteness that was the centerline. Because farmers in southwest Georgia were long abed, most nights I never saw a car or truck. I walked with teeth gritted in fear as I crossed the fearful swamp outside of town. The cacophony of a thousand night creatures ushered me through the darkness, my eyes on the blur of a white line.

After I climbed the hill that took me out of the swamp, ahead of me was the creek. The thick woods in that vicinity made the night seem even darker, and the mysterious noises emanating from them hastened my feet. Then there was the cemetery which fell to the very edge of the road. On clear nights the white tombstones shone in the moonlight, and the ghosts of those long gone hovered over the land. On dark, rainy nights when the wind was blowing, the cemetery was an unseen but even more palpable presence.

Often the sound of a limb breaking or an owl screeching covered me with fear, and I ran all-out, breathing hard, the rhythmic slapping of my shoes on the asphalt taking my mind away from the swamp and the creek and the cemetery. As the damp night air filled my nostrils and unfamiliar sounds assaulted me, I knew that everything I had ever been afraid of, real and imagined, was in those woods and in that swamp.

I went to every away game that fall and winter, in fair weather and foul, in the mild and languid autumn and the bitter-cold of winter. And afterward I followed the white line. No matter how great my fear of the night, I was not going to let Daddy dominate me. And at the end of every one of those solitary runs, I opened the front door and heard two recognizable sounds: Daddy's snoring and Mother's whispered, "Are you okay, son?"

14

As the bus pulled out of the school parking lot, the coach seized the chrome pole at the door, pulled himself up, and turned to face us. He was a kind man, too kind to be a great coach, and when he put on his war face and began exhorting us to victory, we found it difficult to hide our smiles.

"Ah-ite, you boys, listen up. This is our last game of the season, and we going up against a strong and hungry team in Attapulgus. They beat us twice this year, but it was close both times, real close, four points and six points. Other than that, you won just about every game, and I'm proud of you. Edison is proud of you."

He smiled. "You boys are winners. This has been a great season. Folks are gonna talk about you for years to come. But I want more. I want a win tonight, and I want a big win. I want you to show these folks in Attapulgus what champions look like."

He went on for about five minutes and we stared up at him with straight faces. When he sat down, members of the Magnificent Ten looked at one another and smiled. They were relaxed and confident, so much so that several of them put a wad of Red Man chewing tobacco into their mouths—not big enough to pooch out of their cheeks, but big enough—and began chewing with all the contentment of cows chewing their cuds. Then the cheerleaders, some of whom were standing in the aisle, began singing the school fight song and practicing their cheers.

"Hey, Coram," Joe said. "What's the coach doing?"

"Talking to the driver."

Joe raised a window, leaned out, spit out a dark plume of tobacco juice, closed the window, and sat down, all in the space of a few seconds.

"What's he doing now?"

"Still talking to the driver."

So many windows were going up and down that gusts of wind were blasting through the bus. The coach stood up and tried to put on a stern face as he looked toward the back of the bus. "Ah-ite," he growled. "Who's opening the windows? Y'all know you not supposed to open any windows."

The players and cheerleaders looked at one another in mock bewilderment and then looked at the coach. Joe said, "Coach, ain't no windows open back here."

"Y'all better not open any windows," the coach said again and then he sat down.

That Joe, with a chaw in his mouth, had the nerve to speak up to the coach, and that he pulled it off, made him even more of a hero in my eyes.

We pulled up close to the gym in Attapulgus and parked in the spot reserved for the out-of-town players' bus. The coach stood up and said, "I'll talk to you in the dressing room." We filed off the bus, walking slowly — swaggering, really — with studied coolness, acting as if we owned the town of Attapulgus. We were warriors as we filed into the gym, each holding in one hand a white towel wrapped around a red-and-black uniform, with enough of the uniform showing to let everyone know who we were.

The gym was packed to overflowing, the fans from Attapulgus on one side and those from Edison on the other. It was loud and raucous. The Edison fans were shouting, "The swamp rats gonna get stepped on tonight" and "Do swamp rats eat cheese?" From the Attapulgus side came, "Dynamos goan get turned off tonight."

"Everybody in Edison must be here," Big Boy mumbled.

"Not everybody," I said.

The fans from Edison stood up and cheered as we walked along the edge of the court toward the dressing room. Inside there was little conversation as we shucked our jeans and shirts and began dressing out. Joe prompted some laughter when he stood naked in the center of the room, lifted his testicles, bent over and looked at his groin, and said, "If this jock itch gets any worse, I'm goan have an ass red as an Indian's."

"Knock it off, Joe," the coach said. And from his tone we knew he was nervous. As coach, he had more riding on this game than we did.

The Attapulgus fans looked on with wary respect when the Magnificent Ten ran onto the floor, but they laughed openly as we three misfits came out. Big Boy was breathing hard after running maybe twenty or thirty paces, and Spaz was shuffling and jerking like a marionette. I was the last player out of the dressing room, but I cut off to the side and arrived near the front of the Magnificent Ten as they began the pregame drills. Damn, I was fast. I ran in place until the end of the line came around, then did my high-speed dribble down our half of the court and took my shot. I could run like a bat out of hell.

A couple of Attapulgus boys who had probably graduated three or four years earlier and were now working on their daddies' farms, leaned against the wall behind the basket, grinning.

"Hey, you little short shit," one of them said. "You ain't big as a minute. You in the third grade?"

"Naw, he's in the fourth," another said. "Bet he's still on a sugar teat."

"Shit-eating swamp rats," I said over my shoulder as I ran back up the court.

By then Joe was taking his shot behind me, and he heard the exchange. He stopped, bounced the basketball hard behind him, causing it to continue bouncing up the court, walked right up to those two boys. I mean he was in their faces. He stared from one to the other and said, "If y'all looking for trouble, you damn sure came to the right place."

The boys bowed up, but by then our coach and the Attapulgus coach were running down the court. "You boys sit down and behave," the Attapulgus coach ordered, and the boys slunk off to the bleachers. Coaches were minor deities in southwest Georgia, and no one argued with them on the court.

THAT night the Edison Dynamos fulfilled the coach's dream. The Magnificent Ten never played better. By the beginning of the fourth quarter Edison was ahead by more than thirty points. The second-string players continued dominating Attapulgus. They got so cocky that one went charging down the floor on a fast break, then stopped in front of our bench, right in the heart of the Edison fans, and put on the most dazzling display of dribbling I have ever seen. No doubt he had been influenced by a movie about the Harlem Globetrotters that had come out a couple of years earlier. He was trying to show that he could dribble as well as any of them.

Joe was sitting in the second row, chewing a celebratory plug of tobacco and spitting the juice through a crack in the floor. "What do you think of that, Coram?" he asked. "You do that?"

"No way."

Three of the Attapulgus players clustered around the dribbler, determined to take the ball away. But he bent over the ball, bouncing it only inches high, moving it from hand to hand, moving it behind his back, and between his legs, at arm's length and tucked in close, faking one way and moving another, leaving the Attapulgus players red-faced with embarrassment. Then he dribbled out of the crowd, danced around the ball a few times and stopped in front of the coach. With the ball still bouncing and him still dancing, he said grinning impishly, "Coach, I can flat ass dribble a basketball." Then he twirled and was off down the court, making another two points for Edison.

The coach laughed and slapped his hands together, then stood up and called a time-out. He looked at Big Boy and said, "We need a change of pace. Get in there and replace that dribbling wizard. He's tired."

"You, too," he said, pointing toward Spaz.

The Attapulgus team knew the end was in sight when Big Boy rolled onto the court and Spaz jerked along behind him, both firm-faced and staring straight ahead. Those two boys were panic-stricken but you wouldn't have known it if you weren't up close. Both were so pale, they looked as if all their blood had been drained.

The Edison side of the gym was in bedlam. The greatest basketball season anyone in Edison could remember was about to come to an end.

Joe shook his head and said, "Don't that beat all?" He tapped one of the cheerleaders on the shoulder and, when she looked at him, he made a chewing motion. She darted a glance at the coach, then reached into her purse and handed Joe his package of Red Man. Joe handed it to me and said, "Take a chew. And get ready. You 'bout to earn your letter."

I froze. For me practicing, dressing out, and traveling with the team was enough. I never thought I would get in a game. But Joe was right. If Big Boy and Spaz were on the court, I would be next. In a panic, I grabbed the tobacco and said, "How much?"

"However much you want."

I pulled off a plug of the dark, sticky stuff, stuck it in my mouth, and began chewing. I passed the plug back to Joe, who looked at it, then looked at me in surprise and said, "Damn, Coram."

I was chewing fast, watching the court, hoping the coach would play Big Boy and Spaz until the end of the game. I did not want to play. After one more year of school I would graduate and go somewhere, anywhere. Not being part of Edison, not fitting in, was something I could live with for one more year. To hell with getting a letter. I leaned forward, elbows on my knees, head swiveling as I watched the two teams.

Big Boy had a simple strategy. He stayed in the middle of the court, not straying more than three or four steps from the center-line. As the two teams raced up and down the floor, he was like a big rock in the middle of a creek: everything flowed around him. Everyone on the Edison side of the gym was howling. Even the Magnificent Ten had abandoned their studied indifference and were rocking back and forth in laughter.

But there was no joy across the court. A sea of grim faces stared from the Attapulgus side. Of course there were a few exhortations about coming back and a few voices shouting, "You can still beat 'em. Come on!" But they knew the clock was running out. With three members of the Magnificent Ten plus Big Boy and Spaz, Edison had allowed Attapulgus only six points. In a little less than four minutes, the game would be over.

The coach called a time-out. He stalked out from the bench, almost to the middle of the court, and twirled around, hands on his hips, a big grin on his face.

"Get ready, Coram," Joe said.

By then I had built up enough tobacco juice to float a boat. "Joe, I got to spit." My mouth was so full of tobacco juice, I could feel it dribbling down my chin as I tried to talk. I wiped it off quickly.

The Edison crowd had erupted in a cheer that could be heard for a mile. They knew what was coming. The coach's grin was so wide he couldn't talk. He held up a hand for silence, but the crowd continued to roar. Across the court the Attapulgus fans wore quizzical expressions. What the hell was going on?

"You what?"

"I got to spit."

"All this time you ain't been spitting?"

I moved my head from side to side. "I forgot."

The coach stared up at me, shouted "Coram," and jerked his thumb over his shoulder. "Get in here."

"Swallow it," Joe said laughing.

I didn't have a better plan, so I swallowed what seemed to be a half gallon of tobacco juice and a plug of tobacco that had doubled in size.

Most of the people on the Edison side were standing and applauding, whistling and cheering. The Sarge's oldest boy was about to play, about to get his letter. They were looking around the gym for Mother and Daddy but could not find them. Edison was stomping a mud hole in the collective ass of Attapulgus, and now I was being sent in to wade it dry. The steady, rumbling roar that signified the end of the game was beginning to build. I would be on the court when the last game of the greatest basketball season in memory ended.

I stood up and everything began spinning. I was looking out at the world through a green haze. I stepped down from the bench I had been sitting on to the one below and the impact sent the wad of tobacco and tobacco juice jolting to the bottom of my stomach. I paused. Now the gym was spinning rapidly in one direction and the green haze in another.

Far in the distance I could hear a thunderous "Coram! Coram! Coram!" from the Edison fans, and I knew the Attapulgus crowd must be wondering what new secret weapon, what scoring machine, what hell was about to be visited upon them.

My eyes teared up, my nose got congested, and my stomach rebelled. I leaned over and was violently ill, vomiting tobacco juice and bile and God knows what else all over the Magnificent Ten. I sank to my knees, then collapsed across the bench and onto the edge of the court, sprawled in ignominy and vomit. Then rolling to my side and lifting my head, spewed another spectacular stream across the shoes of Edison's most important fans, the Big Possums allowed to sit on the bench next to the players.

As I convulsed with dry heaves, I shut my eyes and prayed for death.

THAT night, when I left the parking lot behind Edison High School, I did not run down the white line toward home. I walked. No...I lollygagged, just poking along, too sick to worry about swamp noises, forest creatures, or haints from the cemetery. I wondered only whether it was possible for anyone, anywhere, at any time in the history of the world, to sink deeper into the pit of embarrassment and humiliation in which I now wallowed. The weeks ahead were going to be long and painful, with frequent references to tobacco chewing and vomiting and how the Dynamos defeated Attapulgus without my help.

I opened the front door quietly, then closed it, turned the lock, and tiptoed across the living room toward the hall. I had not made a sound. But as I turned toward my bedroom, Mother appeared in the doorway of her bedroom and whispered, "Son, you okay?"

"Yes, ma'am."

"Did you all win tonight?"

"Yes, ma'am, we did. We beat Attapulgus."

"Did you get to play?"

I paused. "No, ma'am."

"I'm sorry, son. I know that meant a lot to you. Maybe next year you can play."

"Yes, ma'am."

"Good night, son."

"Night, Mother."

DADDY did not look up when I sat down at the far end of the table the next morning. As was the case every weekday morning, he was dressed for work, wearing a khaki shirt and pants and his Army boots. His fatigue jacket was draped over the back of the chair. The newspaper in front of his face never moved. "Your mother tells me Edison beat Attapulgus last night."

"Thank you," I said to Mother as she slid a plate of grits and sausage and sunny-side-up eggs in front of me. Two pieces of sugar toast were perched atop the grits. I recoiled, stomach roiling. Mother smiled and touched my shoulder. "Yes, sir," I said.

I looked up at Mother and said, "I'm not hungry this morning. I think I'll just have a bowl of cornflakes."

"Son, you okay?"

"Yes, ma'am. I'm just not hungry."

She slid the plate down the table and said, "George can eat this." She turned as George came out of the bedroom. "Son, your breakfast is on the table."

George did not acknowledge Mother. He said, "Hey, Daddy," then sat down and began eating.

"Morning, son."

From behind the paper he said, "Sweetheart, idn't it about time you got Susie and Butch in here?"

She looked down at her breakfast then stood up and walked down the hall.

Daddy moved the paper aside and said to me, raising his voice, "How much?"

I looked down the table, eyebrows raised in confusion. "How much what, sir?"

"How much Edison beat Attapulgus?"

"Twenty-eight points."

"And you didn't play."

"No, sir."

He smirked. "I told you last fall you would never play. But no, Mr. Hardhead, you had to do it your way." He shook his head in disgust.

Mother put a bowl of cornflakes in front of me. I poured on sugar and milk, then stirred and stirred and stirred. Then I shoved a spoonful into my mouth.

Daddy glared at me through his steel-rimmed glasses. He believed that if something was worth saying once, it was worth saying two or three more times. "Well, didn't I tell you that last fall?"

I nodded.

"Robert, you just a know-it-all. You get my goat because you don't listen to anybody. Sometimes I wonder if you will ever amount to anything. You got to listen, son. You got to listen."

I chewed and nodded, thinking that today he would hear about my vomiting over half the population of Edison. Then I would have to listen to him tell me how I had embarrassed him.

"I want you to think about going to North Georgia College up in Dahlonega. That's a good school. I am not sure you would make a good officer, but you can go to North Georgia and enter the Army as a second lieutenant. You keep your nose clean, and you might retire as a lieutenant colonel."

Daddy knew I wanted to go to college in North Carolina, in mother's home state. For a moment I sat there staring at my bowl, knowing that anything I said would be the wrong thing. Mother returned with Susie and Butch and seated them, then put her hand on my shoulder and said, "JB, he's just a junior in high school. He doesn't have to decide about college until next year."

"North Georgia College would straighten him out. He would learn to listen to people and do what he is told." He looked at me, waiting for an answer.

Mother squeezed my shoulder, silently telling me to say nothing. But I had to say something, weak though it might be.

"I think I'll wait before I decide."

I took another bite of cornflakes and stared at my bowl.

"Well, one thing is for sure, Mr. Big-Time Athlete. You'll need the financial help that ROTC provides, because you sure ain't going to get an athletic scholarship."

George snickered.

Daddy, pleased with himself, opened the paper and began reading. "Basketball season is over. What are you going to do now?"

"Practice starts next week for the track team. I'm going out for track."

Daddy froze. He didn't even move the paper to stare at me. Mother retreated to the kitchen. George looked at Daddy, waiting for his reaction.

"I mentioned that some time back," I said.

After about ten seconds, Daddy crumpled the paper and pushed it into the empty chair to his right. He stood up and put on his field jacket. "Sweetheart, I'm going to work."

Mother came across the kitchen and kissed Daddy. "Be careful. And don't be climbing poles. Remember what the doctor said about your blood pressure."

Daddy looked at me, shook his head and said, "Track." He spit out the word. "Only thing you ought to run for is the state line." And he was gone.

I pushed my bowl of cornflakes aside and watched as Daddy's truck left the driveway and turned toward Edison. "I see he is in his usual good mood," I said.

"I think something in the paper set him off," Mother said.

"George, pass me that paper," I said.

He looked up, eyes wide like a surprised owl. "You want it, come get it. I ain't no waiter."

I pushed back my chair, walked to the end of the table, and sat down in Daddy's chair. George, eyes even wider, looked at me, then at Mother, then back at me. All he could say was, "Mother."

I pulled the paper toward me and bean reading Ralph McGill's column. It was about how talented young black people were being held back by the evils of segregation.

I wondered if Ralph McGill had ever met Frank Yerby. I thought they would have liked each other.

15

THE spring of 1954 was the second half of my junior year and the most glorious time of my high school years. Everything I did was successful. I was writing for the *High Voltage*, the school newspaper, and one of my teachers, Myrlene Tye, liked my writing. She was the only teacher who encouraged me in anything. For all the others I had long since disappeared.

America exploded the first H-bomb on March 1, and we in Edison were so proud that you would have thought the thing had been concocted in the chemistry lab at Edison High School. Dien Bien Phu, a place in Vietnam no one in Edison had ever heard of, fell to the Communists in 1954, and newspapers announced that for the first time in more than twenty years, there was no shooting war going on anywhere on earth. The world was at peace. In May the U.S. Supreme Court said that no child could be barred from public school because of his color, but that decision did not affect Edison. On the radio Kitty Kallen was singing "Little Things Mean a Lot," the Crew Cuts were singing "Sh-Boom," and Doris Day was singing "Secret Love."

Daddy bought a black-and-white television set that spring. We could pick up a station in Albany and another in Columbus. When Daddy wanted to change channels, he pressed a device on top of the set and ordered me outside to observe the herky-jerky motion of the antenna, which was about forty feet tall, as it ratcheted around to reorient itself from one town to the other. Every few seconds I shouted my report: "It's started moving... It's about half-way there... Almost there." And as the antenna jerked to a stop, "It's there. It's all the way there."

Nellie had dropped me for one of the Magnificent Ten. It was that way in high school, a series of girlfriends. But I was in love again. I was seeing Dina, Edison's most privileged daughter, the only child of E. E. Earl—commonly referred to as "Triple E"—one of the most prominent businessmen in Calhoun County. Dina was a dark-haired beauty with a smile as bright as the dawn, and when she sashayed down the street dressed in her expensive clothes, everyone looked upon her as Edison's very own fairy princess. And in a sweet and entirely inoffensive way, she looked upon herself in the same fashion.

Two or three days a week I walked to her house after school, and we sat on the sofa in her living room and held hands and kissed, always aware that her mother was fluttering around in the kitchen or humming away in a nearby room. Dina said "yes" when I invited her to the Junior-Senior Banquet, the biggest social event of the year for juniors and seniors at Edison High School.

Dina's parents had a house on the beach in Panama City, Florida, and I had been their guest for several weekends. They were always hovering around, but they did allow Dina and me to walk the beach holding hands. Girls stared at her in envy and boys in admiration.

One night Dina's parents dropped us off at the Hang Out, a big, open-air dance floor on the beach, and Dina and I slow-danced for hours. I held her close, and her freshly shampooed hair filled my nostrils with an ambrosial sweetness that several times caused me to miscount on the box step and stumble. But she didn't care. When she saw other boys coming up to tap me on the shoulder to cut in, she just smiled and shook her head.

Once when her parents went out for a few hours, Dina and I snuggled on a daybed on the back porch. I unbuttoned her blouse and, for the first time in my life, held a girl's breast. This visit to heaven was brief. Too soon she murmured, "No," and buttoned her blouse. I stood up and looked across the sandspurs growing in an adjacent lot and tears ran down my cheeks. When Dina stood beside me and asked, "Why are you crying?" I had no answer.

Daddy's reaction to my dating Dina was predictable: "What in hell does the daughter of a man like E. E. Earl see in you? Why should she give a continental damn about you?"

"Because I'm a smart and good-looking boy. I think it comes from Mother's side of the family."

Mother laughed. Daddy snorted.

He still clawed my ass every chance he got, which was often, but I was in love with Dina that spring, and his scorn didn't matter. When he went on a tirade, I simply thought of how Dina pulled gently at my hair when we kissed, pictured her lightning flash of a smile, or dreamed of the day when I might again hold her breast, and nothing Daddy said bothered me.

In a few months everything would collapse, and my life would be changed forever. But in the spring of 1954, and for the last time in many years, I was truly happy.

Being the star of the track team was a big part of my happiness.

Edison High School was small. There were twelve boys and thirteen girls in my class, and we were the largest class in years. Because the school was so small, we had neither the money nor the bodies to have a football team. Some years we had a baseball team. But basketball was our big sport, followed closely by track.

Those of us who tried out for track did not think it unusual that when we dressed out, our uniform was a bathing suit and a T-shirt, both of which we provided, and a pair of tired baseball cleats, which the school provided.

"What size shoes you wear, Coram?" the coach asked the first day of tryouts.

"Five and a half."

He shuffled through a bag of scuffed and run-over baseball shoes and threw a pair in my direction. "Nine is the smallest size I got. Stuff you some newspaper in the toe. Old rags will do. I'll give you some duct tape to put around the instep so that shoe will stay on you."

I packed newspaper in the toes but those cleats still curled up like clown shoes. I looked around at the other members of the track team. In our bathing suits and old T-shirts, we may not have been the prime example of how a track team should look, but we were convinced we were the best.

Most of us tried out for every event but pole-vaulting and throwing the discus. The boy who was the vaulter was a loner and he had that sport all to himself. Ollie threw the discus and was so erratic that the coach sent him off way down the field to practice. The rest of us sometime stood around watching Ollie swing his arm back and forth a few times, then do a hop, skip, and a jump before twirling in a circle and flinging the discus down the field or across the road into a cotton patch or God knows where.

The sprinters and distance runners were all jumbled together. Everyone had to run more than one event. So when the coach bellowed, "On your mark," maybe ten or fifteen boys stood on the line, hunkered down, and curled our fingers back so that our knuckles supported our weight.

"Get set."

We raised our hips, lifted our heads, and looked down the track.

"Go."

And away we went.

I knew I had found my place in the athletic pantheon of Edison High School when after several weeks of practice and only a few days before our first meet, the coach came to me and said, in front of the other members of the team, "Coram, we got a problem with you."

Ears perked up. I looked around warily and asked, "What's that, Coach?"

"The rules say no member of any track team can participate in more than four events. I'm putting you in the hundred-yard dash, the two-twenty, the four-forty, and the anchor leg of the relay."

Even with my curly-toed baseball shoes, I could run the hundred in under eleven seconds. For the two-twenty and the four-forty, I could outrun anyone else on the team. And because I was so fast, I had the anchor position—the runner whose job it was to take the baton across the finish line—on the relay team. Not only was I on the track team, but I was, for the first time in my life, the most important member of anything. This may have been the greatest moment of my high school athletic career.

The other members of the team stared at me. I was the only person on the team running four events, and my sprints were punishing events calling for both speed and endurance. They had to be run flat out at full speed. The four-forty was the most brutal. Every time I ran the four-forty, the large muscles in my legs cramped up and throbbed as I gasped for breath.

Joe looked up at the coach and said, "Coach, sounds pretty good to us. What's the problem?"

"The problem is..." he paused dramatically and looked around the room. "I need him to run the low hurdles."

Everyone laughed.

The coach had a little trick to help us train for the low hurdles. He put a nickel atop each hurdle and challenged us to dislodge the nickel without knocking over the hurdle. Most of the boys would hit the hurdle with their trailing knee, but I found that little zone where I could "tickle the nickel" and nudge it off without knocking over the hurdle, and I could do it consistently. Two other could run the hurdles faster, but they knocked over as many hurdles as they cleared.

During that glorious spring of 1954, the Edison Dynamos outran, out-broad-jumped, out-high-jumped, and out-pole-vaulted almost everyone we went up against. Ollie was a big strong boy and could throw the discus as far as anyone. But he never learned control, and several times he threw the discus toward the spectator stands causing people to scatter like a covey of quail. We were good in the sprints, and we were good in the distance events. We won enough events that spring that we were considered the best track team in southwest Georgia.

I won or tied every hundred-yard and two-twenty I ran. The four-forty was my weak spot. After running the shorter sprints, I just didn't have the horsepower to do well in such a punishing race, especially when I was up against some long-legged farm boy whose only event was the four-forty. In the relay I sat in my lane dancing in anticipation as the first three legs were run, and then I cranked it up and was at full speed when the baton was passed, carrying the mail on home. I liked the relay. It was usually the last of the sprinting events, and being anchorman was a big deal. Several times it was my hauling the baton across the finish line that signified we had won the meet, and the cheering was loud and prolonged. Those cheers were more for the team's victory than they were for me. But I had never been cheered for anything, and I liked it.

One day toward the end of the season the coach walked out to where we were warming up. He put his hands on his hips, looked around, and in a voice that showed he was pleased with himself, he said, "Well, boys, y'all so good that I got us a track meet with Albany."

Our eyes widened, and there was a collective gasp. Albany High School had twice as many students in any one grade as we had in our entire school. Albany spent more money on track than we spent on our entire athletic program. Albany was, for crying out loud, the biggest town in southwest Georgia, and knowing we were going up against them sent us into full defensive mode. We were country boys going up against city people, and all the insecurities we felt toward the outside world surfaced.

"There will be three or four other schools there, too," the coach said. "But you fellows have beat all of them. You don't have to worry."

"Coach, we ain't worried," Joe said.

The coach nodded. "That's good. Just remember, they put on their britches the same way you do — one leg at the time. So they go to Albany High School. So what? Just do what you been doing all year, and you'll be okay."

THAT spring George had another of his terrible stomachaches and this time Daddy took him to the hospital in Cuthbert. Thinking George had appendicitis, the doctor operated. A half hour or so after the surgery began, the doctor, brow wrinkled, came down the hall to the waiting room. He told Daddy that nothing about George's intestines was where it was supposed to be, that he could not even locate George's appendix. He had never seen anything like it. He had sewn George back up and given him a massive dose of antibiotics, and now he told Daddy that George needed exploratory surgery at a major hospital. He suggested the hospital at Duke University in Durham, North Carolina.

George was in pain for a day or so, but he milked that operation for all it was worth. Daddy could have gotten a nursing degree for all the attention he paid to George over the next few weeks. George's surgery at Duke was scheduled for June.

THE Edison track team got off the school bus looking around like a bunch of steers released into a corral at the slaughterhouse. Everything we saw at Albany High School was new, and new was bad. Albany had an enormous oval cinder track. Sprints were run along one side and the white lines marking off the lanes for the races were so precise, the track looked like a table set with sterling silver. We had never seen a cinder track, and we had never seen a track so beautifully organized.

Several hundred people sat in the stands, something else we had never seen. Usually we saw a few farmers in overalls standing around mumbling, "Y'all go get 'em, you hear?" Or, "Get out there and put a hurting on them people." Where had all these spectators come from?

In the corners of the big field were separate areas for the pole vault, discus throw, and broad jump. These were permanent areas, not a pile of sand or a circle scuffed in the dirt or a section of red clay turned over with a shovel. The Albany track team was warming up, and they were wearing long pants and jackets in their school colors. They looked sophisticated and glorious. They looked like athletes. Olympic athletes. Several of them paused to watch us get off the bus. They smiled in a lordly fashion, made comments to one another, and laughed. They were so easy in their warm up motions that they looked almost indolent.

"What's that they wearing?" I asked.

"Warm-up suits," Joe said.

"They need suits just to warm up? Where's their uniforms?"

"Underneath the warm-up suits."

"No shit?"

"No shit."

"They laughing at us."

"So what. They a bunch of shit asses."

A moment later I heard a soft "Hey, Robert." I looked around and saw Dina walking toward me, her mother a few steps behind. That sunburst of a smile brightened Dina's face. Albany may have been ahead of us in almost everything, but Edison had at least one girl who was prettier than anyone at Albany High School.

I grinned in surprise. "What are you doing here?"

She reached out and clasped my hands. "Mother and I came over to do some shopping, and I made her bring me by here so I could see you and wish you good luck." She leaned forward, kissed me on the cheek, and whispered, "I hope you win."

"Dina," her mother said.

"I have to go," Dina said, and she wheeled and was gone, her perfume lingering in the air. There was a certain stillness in her absence as some of the boys stared in open envy.

"Coram, you one lucky guy," said David, a big boy who threw the shot put. David was not the brightest boy in class, but he was handsome. David stared after Dina, and I sensed more than appreciation in his comment.

"Stop all this lollygagging," the coach said. He pointed toward a low building. "Visitors' dressing rooms. Y'all get dressed out, then come on out here and warm up. We got bidness to do."

When we came out of the dressing room in our bathing suits, grungy T-shirts, and baseball shoes, one of the boys from Albany called to his teammates, and suddenly the entire Albany team was looking at us and making no secret of their disdain. One of them, a tall, lanky, movie-star-handsome boy with blond hair and a warm-up jacket sporting a winged track shoe, a basketball, a football, and a baseball, pointed and laughed when he saw the tape around my curly-toed baseball shoes.

"Who's that shit ass?" I asked.

"Team captain," David said. "Runs the hundred. Damn fast."

I looked again. I had never seen shoes such as he was wearing. They fit like gloves and looked as light as smoke. When one boy bent his leg to check the bottom of his shoe, I saw what appeared to be the tips of little ice picks.

"Coach, what kinda shoes is that they wearing?"

"Track shoes."

"Shoes ain't got no heels."

"Track shoes don't have heels."

We were rolling our shoulders and jogging in place and looking around furtively. A cinder track with white lines painted on it. Warm-up suits. Track shoes. What was next?

Mr. Movie Star walked over, a big smile on his face. He was followed by a half dozen of his teammates. He had a baton in his hand, so I guessed he ran the relay, too. Slumping in his indolent fashion, he leaned over and swung his head back and forth as he made a big deal of staring at our feet.

"You guys always run in baseball cleats?" he asked. Before anyone could answer, he added, "I thought you Alabama boys ran barefooted."

"Alabama?" I snapped. "We ain't from Alabama."

Suddenly the coach was there waving his arms. "You boys from Albany get on back over on your side of the field. Go on. Get out of here."

Mr. Movie Star and his buddies walked off, jostling one another and looking over their shoulders and laughing, cocky beyond description. They were big city boys, and we were from a little town most of them had never heard of.

Joe tugged at my arm. "Robert, he's messing with you. Can't you see that?"

"I thought he was stupid."

"No, you stupid."

"I ain't stupid."

"Well, you running against him in the hundred. You better save your wind."

I started to say something, but then I noticed little angled pieces of wood at the starting line in each lane. "Hey, Coach," I said, "what are those things at the starting line?"

"Starting blocks."

"I saw those in a picture show one time. You brace your toes up against them for a better start."

"That's right. And you can adjust them for whatever spacing you want."

I shook my head, jogging in place to relieve the tension. As I jogged, I looked to the right and saw that a man in a striped shirt was standing near the starting line and examining a pistol.

I jogged over to the coach, touched his arm, and said, "Coach, that man over there has got a gun."

"Coram, that's a starting pistol." He raised his voice. "I told you fellows that they use a starting pistol here at Albany. They will do the regular commands, but instead of saying 'Go,' they fire that pistol."

Joe smiled. "I thought he was goan shoot the losers."

The coach laughed. "It shoots blanks."

Joe looked at the Albany team and said, "I hope we ain't shooting blanks today."

We weren't. Well, most of us weren't. I came in second to Mr. Movie Star in the hundred. And I came in second in both the two-twenty and the four-forty. I could tell you that I was not used to the starting blocks and couldn't adjust them properly. I could tell you that the starting pistol scared hell out of me. But the truth is, Mr. Movie Star was faster than I was, and he beat me fair and square.

Despite my lack of any blue ribbons, the Edison Dynamos won or came in second in enough events that when the relay race was called, we were ahead of all the other schools and tied with Albany. If we won the relay, we would win the meet.

As the coach called together the relay team — Nick, Joe, John, and me — Joe laughed his infectious laugh and said, "Coach, we hotter than a damn two-dollar pistol."

The coach glared. "Joe, you know I don't tolerate profanity on my teams."

"Sorry, coach," he said. But he wasn't.

The air around the five of us crackled with excitement. The coach was grinning and dancing from one foot to the other. He was about to become one of Edison's Big Possums. When he walked into the barbershop, everyone in there would call out, "Hey, Coach," and jump up to shake his hand.

The coach wasn't big on inspirational speeches. He simply told us what he expected, and that he expected us to win. "You boys have done good today," he said. "Real good. All you got to do now is just keep on doing what you been doing, and we will win this thing." He looked carefully at each of us and grew intense. "The main thing you got to remember is make sure you are in the box when you pass the baton. Don't get anxious and start too soon." He turned to me. "Robert, I expect we will be ahead when Joe passes the baton to you for the last leg. You just bring it on home. That's all you got to do." He paused. "Anybody got any questions?"

"You goan let us out of school tomorrow if we win?" Joe asked.

Even the coach laughed.

"You boys get out there and show them what your backsides look like."

Nick was the first box. Down the track and around the first turn, John stood in the second. Joe was in the third, I was all the way around the track in the last box. I looked around. Mr. Movie Star was the anchorman for Albany. He was in the inside lane, while I was in the fourth lane. He grinned and waved. "Hey, short man," he said. "Beat you once. This will make twice."

I gave him the finger.

"Oooooh," he said in mock alarm. "Isn't that unsportsman-like conduct?"

The track was still neat and the lines crisp, and it was all still a bit foreign to me. But this was my lane. All I had to do was take the handoff from Joe and sprint to the finish line.

All the anchormen turned and faced the starting line. We heard the starting commands and the sharp crack of the pistol and saw six boys leap out of the blocks. The lanes were staggered, so it was hard to tell who was ahead, but it seemed that on the second leg John received the handoff a split second ahead of the next team. The spectators in the seats were beginning to stand up, and most of them were cheering on the Albany team. On the third leg there was no doubt that Edison was winning. Joe had the baton maybe two seconds before anyone else. I started jogging in place, standing at the very back of the box, looking over my shoulder, waiting to judge it just right so I would be at full speed but still in the box when Joe passed the baton to me. I began running, hand behind me, and felt Joe slap the baton into my hand. I knew the handoff was good.

By now everyone in the stands were on their feet, and the noise was deafening. I had my head up, arms pumping, legs driving, giving it everything I had. This was the event that would seal Albany's fate, and I was the man who was going to seal the victory.

I rounded the turn, driving hard. Out of the corner of my eye I sensed Mr. Movie Star moving closer. I stayed in my lane and moved into a gear I did not know I had. Then over the crowd I heard the coach's voice shouting, but I couldn't understand what he was saying. Up ahead I saw him throwing his arm to the side, over and over, flailing and pointing and shouting. Then Mr. Movie Star was ahead, and he crossed the line a full second ahead of me.

Head back, breathing hard, legs trembling, I coasted to a stop and stood there, hands on my knees, head bent over, gasping. Suddenly the coach was beside me, and he was sputtering in frustration. "Robert, I kept telling you to move over. You were ahead. You didn't have to stay in your lane. You ran twenty yards farther than anybody else." He threw his arms wide. "I thought you knew that."

I raised my head enough to look at him and shake my head.

"It's my fault," he said.

But somehow I sensed that it was not his fault.

Nobody talked much on the one-hour bus ride back to Edison. Joe did stand up and say, "Where's Coram?" I don't know why he asked that. I was sitting across the aisle from him. "Oh, there you are," he said. He paused, grinned, and said, "Coram, you think you could push a wheelbarrow without breaking it?"

Everyone laughed.

Joe sat down, leaned across the aisle, and said, "I bet you got a case of the down yonders."

When I didn't say anything, he clapped me on the shoulder and laughed. "Ain't as bad as the can't hep its." He leaned closer. "And it sho ain't as bad as the epizootics."

I laughed. But I knew everything was not okay.

My track career earned me a respect I had never known. I was awarded a black school sweater. Mother sewed a big red E on it, and on the E she sewed the winged foot that told the world I was a member of the track team. I had realized my greatest high school dream. But I was too ashamed to wear the sweater.

16

Several mornings later, as I stumbled into the kitchen, Daddy folded his paper and stared. Not good. I sat down and looked at my plate.

Daddy remained silent as Mother opened the oven and gingerly removed two pieces of hot sugar toast. I raised my head and sniffed the aroma of melted butter and slightly burned sugar. Now Daddy was smiling. What was this all about? I look at him warily.

"Sir?" I said.

The first shot of his morning salvo was more devastating than usual. "Robert, you never goan amount to anything. You sorry as gully dirt."

Mother slammed the oven shut and snapped, "JB, that is no way to talk to your son." She slid the sugar toast and a sausage patty onto my plate. "Robert, don't pay any attention to your daddy."

She glared at Daddy, defiant, as if daring him to continue.

Of course Daddy ignored her. He leaned toward me, still smiling. "You didn't tell me the real reason Edison lost the track meet, did you? No, sir, you didn't. You didn't tell me that you, Mr. Hog Killer, Mr. Puking Basketball Star, Mr. Greased Lightning, didn't know enough to move over on the track. You just stayed over there by yourself, doing it your own way as usual, and losing the track meet for Edison. You ought to be proud of yourself."

"We never ran on a real track before."

"Don't make excuses. You know how I feel about people who make excuses."

"JB, your blood pressure," Mother said. "Remember what the doctor told you."

"My blood pressure is fine." Daddy turned as George came into the room followed by Susie and Butch. "Morning, son. You feeling okay today?"

"Yes, sir." As George sat down to Daddy's right, Daddy reached out and patted his hand. He turned back toward me and said, "Don't forget to feed that dog of yours before you leave." He paused. "By the way, your dog-training program needs an update. I'm tired of telling you to make that dog behave."

"Yes, sir," I mumbled as I picked up my sugar toast. I wanted to say, "That dog is living in hope. Play with his pecker, and he'll be okay."

Mother placed a plate of sugar toast and sausage in front of George. He took a bite of toast and, staring out the window, said, "Daddy, I like your new truck."

Daddy looked over his shoulder out the kitchen window. His new truck was a glaring shade of orangish brown. I had never seen a truck or a car or anything else that color. I wondered if someone at the phone company had sent it to Daddy because nobody else would ride in it. Behind the shiny new orangish cab sat the old once-green body, scratched and mottled and leaning to one side because two telephone poles were tied up top to the frame atop the truck and extending maybe fifteen feet in front of the truck and fifteen feet behind. The truck looked like something out of a comic book: brand-new on the front end, old and gnarly on the back end, and everything topped by two telephone poles.

"Thank you, son."

"Robert says it is the color of dog crap."

"George, don't talk that way at the table," Mother said.

"He did, did he?" Daddy said, looking at me.

"Yes, sir. He did."

"You say that?" Daddy asked, no longer smiling.

"Yes, sir."

"Well, that's too bad because that's what you are driving tonight."

I looked up, eyes wide. "You told me I could have the car." This was to have been the first night I was allowed to drive the new car.

A few weeks earlier we had heard a horn blowing in the driveway and looked out to see a brand-new red-and-white Chrysler. The door opened, and Daddy, beaming from ear to ear, jumped out. The car was a sleek two-door model, a young man's car. Mother was as surprised by it as we were. Now we had the only Chrysler in a town of Chevrolets and Fords. That shiny red-and-white car was the envy of every boy in Edison, and I had missed sleep thinking of how Dina would like riding in it.

"Your mother and I are using the car."

"We are?" Mother asked. "Where we going?"

"I got a date with Dina," I said.

"She won't mind riding in the truck. Her daddy sells trucks."

"I'm double-dating with Ollie and Sandra."

"Four people can fit in the cab."

"Daddy," I wailed. "I can't go on a date in the phone company truck. It's got two telephone poles on top."

Daddy picked up his paper and stared at the front page. "Then stay at home and do your homework."

"There's no radio."

"Music you listen to ain't worth listening to."

I bit my lip and leaned over my plate, very close to tears. Mother put her hand on my shoulder.

"JB, you said he could use the car tonight. You gave him your word."

"I changed my mind, and that is all there is to it."

That evening Mother followed me out of the house. When I stopped a few feet from the truck, looking at it in dismay, she reached out and put her hand on my shoulder. "Mother," I whispered in anguish, "All I did was make a comment about the color of his truck. And it is true."

She reached out and touched my arm. "Son, he tries."

"No he doesn't. He is just mean."

She dug her fingers into my shoulder. "Don't you talk that way about your daddy." She relaxed her grip and said, "You remember what I told you before. He wants to be a good daddy. He just doesn't know how."

On some deep level I sensed that she was right. My daddy had been formed by the Army and had spent thirty years hardening his shell. Once an Army sergeant, always an Army sergeant. But my understanding was not deep enough for me to like driving a pickup truck the color of dog crap with two smelly creosote-leaking telephone poles tied to the top, on a date with the Princess of Edison.

Earlier, Ollie and I had talked about taking our dates to a movie. But I had no intention of having everyone on the main street in Edison see the four of us pour out of both sides like a pack of dogs running from a skunk. So I changed our plans for the evening. We would go up to Cuthbert and ride around the square. Then we'd drive down US 27 to Blakely and back through Bluffton, staying on backcountry roads until it was time to go home. Somewhere in there I thought we should stop for a Coke, but I didn't know of any place where we could hide the truck when we went inside. And while parking on a back road or behind a church or out in the middle of a cotton field and smooching with our dates was the ideal, no way that was going to happen, not with four of us jammed into the cab of the truck.

I drove out to Ollie's house in the country. The two telephone poles were very much in my vision, as was the long rope tied around the poles and stretching down to the front bumper. As I drove, the rubbing of the poles against each other made guttural sounds and the rubbing of the poles against the steel frame made erratic squeaking noises, high-pitched and grating. The grunts and squeaks were accompanied by a multitude of sounds coming from the back of the truck: glass insulators clanking, rolls of steel wire grinding, tools and parts bumping, and an occasional flapping sound, the source of which I did not know.

I beeped the horn as I drove into Ollie's yard, and almost immediately he was pushing open the screen door. He stopped, eyes wide in surprise, then folded over in laughter.

"We double-dating in the phone truck?" he asked. "I thought we were going in that new red-and-white Chrysler."

"Get in."

He stuck his head through the open window and looked around. "Ain't no backseat. How am I goan get any titty tonight?"

"You ain't. Get in."

Ollie looked over his shoulder. "If I had known, I could have used the Pontiac. But Daddy won't let me have it on such short notice." He shook his head. "We ain't goan get none on us tonight."

He opened the door and climbed in. "What the hell happened? Why you driving this thing?"

I put the truck into gear and drove down the driveway. "You know my daddy."

Ollie shook his head. "Yeah." He shook his head. "I gotta tell you, my daddy treated me the way your daddy treats you, I'd put on a wooden beak and peck shit with the chickens."

He laughed. "The cab still smells new."

As I turned onto the main road and moved up through the gears, Ollie laughed again.

"What are you laughing at?"

"I was wondering what Miss Sugar Britches is goan say about riding in a truck."

"Don't call her that. You call her that again, and I'm goan tell people you been jerking off my dog."

He shrugged. Ollie didn't care. He smiled and said, "If we go to Blakely, we got to go the long way, out through Sutton's Cross Roads."

"Why?"

He thrust his thumb over his shoulder. "With those poles on top, you'd have go around the Nelly Hoover curve at two miles an hour. Otherwise you'd have telephone poles in Miss Nelly's front yard."

"Well, then, we'll go the long way."

He settled back in the seat. "No radio?"

"Phone company doesn't put in a radio."

"Damn."

He tilted his head, smiled, and said, "We don't need a radio. We can listen to the noises the truck makes. This thing sounds like a junk pile in motion."

"You think I like this?"

"If we meet somebody we don't like, just point the truck at them and jam on the brakes. Those two telephone poles will gig 'em like they was a bullfrog."

Sandra giggled from the moment she got into the truck. And when we drove up the long driveway to Dina's house, I saw out of the corner of my eye that she was looking at Ollie and he was shaking his head. I knew both were wondering how the Princess of Edison was going to react when she came out and saw this piece of dog crap.

I drove up Dina's driveway, hopped out, and walked to the door. Mr. EE opened the door, saw the truck, paused a split second, and grunted. "Come on in, Robert. Dina is putting on her face. She'll be right down." He swung the door wide and pointed to a chair. "Sit down."

"Thank you, sir."

Dina's mother, Miss Sally, entered the room, dressed, as always, as if she was about to go to a fancy party. "Hello, Robert," she said. "Yo mama and daddy doing okay?"

"Yes, ma'am, they are. Thank you."

"Sit down. Sit down. Dina will be right out." She paused. "Ollie and Sandra want to come in?"

"No, ma'am. I don't think so."

"Where y'all going tonight?" Mr. EE asked.

"I thought we might ride up to Cuthbert. Maybe get a Coke."

"Don't you be driving fast," Miss Sally admonished.

"He won't," Mr. EE said.

Miss Sally looked at him, a puzzled expression on her face.

Dina glided into the room, her eyes locked on me, that dazzling, full-of-life smile on her face. She was wearing a dress of bold purple and white stripes, a low-cut dress tied over each shoulder with a small knot. Her belt, cinched around her tiny waist, was of the same material as the dress. She was wearing gold earrings. She crossed the room, reached out, and took my hand. Still looking at me but speaking to her parents, she said, "We won't be late." She pulled me gently toward the door.

Mr. EE was looking at her hand holding mine. He didn't like that, but Dina was the princess, so he said nothing.

I could smell the shampoo freshness of her hair and the subtlest hint of perfume. I was stumble-footed and unable to speak.

"Y'all have a good time," Miss Sally said.

"We will," Dina said. "Don't wait up."

Mr. EE grunted. I knew he would be sitting in that same chair when we returned. The light would be on. He would hear the truck coming up the driveway. And ten seconds after I turned off the engine, if we were not coming in the front door, he would be coming out.

Dina paused for a halfsecond as we walked down the steps then turned toward the truck. "Oh," she said.

"Daddy wouldn't let me have the car."

"That's okay."

"You mind getting in on the driver's side?" I opened the door.

"Hey, Sandra. Hey, Ollie," Dina said as she climbed up on the running board, then held on to the steering wheel and slid across the seat.

When I sat behind the wheel, I had to hold my left elbow high in order to shut the door. The four of us were squeezed together so tightly that Ollie was sitting almost sideways, his back to the door. He was bent over and grinning.

"How you doing?" he said laughing, as I backed down the driveway.

We all laughed. But the laughter quickly faded, and by the time we had driven about five miles toward Cuthbert, there was little conversation, only the multitude of sounds being made by the truck: guttural grunts, high-pitched squeaks, clanking, grinding, bumping, and flapping.

Dina turned toward me, her lips brushing against my ear, and whispered, "Why don't we go back to my house?"

I didn't say anything.

"If we go back, Mama and Daddy will go to their room, and we can all sit in the living room. We can play some music, maybe dance. Mama has some cookies in the kitchen. We've got Cokes."

She squeezed my arm. "Please." The smell of shampoo and perfume and girl filled my nostrils, and I wanted to bay at the moon. I nodded.

Dina laughed and turned toward Sandra and Ollie. "Y'all want to go to my house? I've got some new records. Robert says it is okay."

"Okay with me," Sandra said.

"Me, too," Ollie said.

On Fridays I was allowed to stay out until 10 p.m., but that was not long enough for the evening to catch fire. It was barely nine when I dropped Ollie off. And all the way from his house back to Edison, about seven miles, I would suddenly stomp down hard on the brake, bringing the truck to a quick stop, leaving skid marks on the pavement and causing the poles to shift and grind. Then I held my foot on the brake and revved the engine to a high speed, popped the clutch, and caused the tires to squeal as I ground my way up through the gears. Again I braked hard and jerked the wheel to the right, feeling the top-heavy truck shift and go light. I pounded on the steering wheel and cried, "Shit. Shit. Shit." I ground the gears and rode the brake and did everything I could to damage that new, glistening meadow muffin of a truck.

I raced up the driveway at the house, then skidded to a stop and jumped out, smelling the hot brakes and the scuffed tires. I slammed the cab door, knowing Daddy would hear it.

Mother had been in the living room reading, and she opened the door as I walked up the front steps. "Son, you home early. Is everything okay?"

"Yes, ma'am, it is. But I don't think Dina will ever go out with me again."

"Oh, son, yes she will. She is such a nice girl."

Daddy came out of the front bedroom, perpetual scowl in place, and said, "Slam the door of my truck again, and you goan be riding a bicycle on your next date."

SUNDAY after church I killed my daddy. The whole family was there when it happened.

We had finished dinner, and George and I were in our room arguing, when I threatened him with dismemberment. I was talking softly, because Daddy was prone to overreact when I threatened

241

George. My brother glared at me, then turned and walked into the hall, where he leaned over and whispered to Susie. I couldn't hear what he was saying, but I saw him clench his right hand and move it up and down in a piston like motion. Susie was seven years old and had no idea what George was talking about. She nodded and ran into the kitchen.

I closed my eyes, hoping that she would get it wrong or Daddy would either not understand her or not believe her. I was out of Daddy's range of vision but could see Susie as she ran to the table, a big smile on her face, and I heard her say, "George saw Robert doing his wee-wee like this." She repeated the hand movement.

Mother whirled around from the stove, dumbstruck. She could not possibly have heard what she thought she heard.

Daddy was eating his dessert, chocolate cake with chicken gravy poured all over it. He stopped, a piece of dripping cake in midair, and half turned toward Susie, his eyes wide, and his mouth open. He looked as if he had been poleaxed. Then he shook his head as if to regain his senses and, in his parade ground voice, bellowed my name.

I leaned against the door, closed my eyes, and grimaced at what was to come. "Yes, sir."

"Front and center."

"Yes, sir."

I slouched around the corner into the kitchen and found Daddy's eyes, hardened by his steel-rimmed glasses, locked on me. "Stand up straight," he said. He moved the piece of cake to his mouth and chewed a moment, then held up his left hand, clenched it into a fist, and moved it up and down. My eye was trained in these matters, and it seemed he was a bit awkward. For a moment I wondered if he would put down his fork and repeat the movement with his right hand. "You been doing your wee-wee like this?"

Mother snapped out of her trance, spun around, and began working in the sink, rattling plates and humming a hymn from that morning's church service.

I looked at the floor and did not answer. Susie had quoted George, and Daddy believed that whatever George said had ecclesiastical weight. I didn't need a fortune-teller to know an ass whipping was in my immediate future.

On any other topic Daddy would have demanded an answer. But talking about sex made him uncomfortable. "That's bad for you," he said. "Not healthy." He speared another hunk of cake, swabbed it through the puddle of thick gravy, and lifted it to his mouth.

I continued looking at the floor. Why was he so uncomfortable? He had been young once, even though that was a long time ago. Maybe they didn't know about masturbation back then. But he had served thirty years in the Army. Didn't Army guys do this?

"Bad things will happen to you if you keep doing that," Daddy said. "Think about when you are married."

"I don't care." As was my way, I had escalated the argument.

Daddy's eyes widened, his Baptist lips tightened, and I saw the first flicker of his ever-simmering anger.

"What was that?"

"I said I don't care."

"You don't care about what?"

"Nothing's happened so far. And I've been doing it … " I stopped. Mother began humming louder.

"What do you mean? You been doing that before?"

He had that bewildered, owlish look he got when facing a situation not covered in the Army manual for master sergeants. He paused, and I knew he was about to do what he always did: raise his voice and steamroll his way through.

Mother turned around. "Robert, have you had your dessert? Why don't you get a piece of cake and take it outside to eat it?"

Daddy's angry glance caused her to pause. She stared at him for a moment, then looked at me and said, "Robert, Pal is out there barking at the back door. He smells food. Why don't you feed him?"

"Sweetheart," Daddy said in an exasperated voice.

He turned back to me. "Have you been doing it before?" Daddy repeated the motion, this time with his right hand. Now he had the movement down a little better.

Susie skipped blithely out of the room, and I sensed George behind me, grinning, eyes darting about in anticipation. Butch was huddled over his plate, oblivious.

"Yes, sir."

Daddy pushed his glasses up his nose and looked at Mother. Then he turned from the table to face me directly and asked with absolute sincerity, "For what?"

"Sir?" I looked at him in disbelief. I wanted to say, *Because I'm sixteen years old and my dick stays hard most of the time and jerking off feels so good I damn near became anemic four years ago when I first discovered it.*

"Why do you do that? Didn't you have some kind of classes at school? Didn't your biology teacher tell you that was bad for you?"

I almost laughed. Teachers saying jerking off was bad for you? Not in Edison, Georgia, in 1954. The biology teacher stood before the sons and daughters of farmers, kids who for all their lives had seen pigs and cows screwing, and talked of bees pollinating flowers and how the process was so sacred that every bee thought a long time about which flower he wanted to pollinate. Someone at school *should* have talked to us about jerking off. The boys had to take a mandatory class in agriculture, and the girls had to take home economics. There should have been a subset of ag class called ... well, I'm not sure what it should have been called.

"Well, didn't she?" Daddy insisted.

"JB, I'm thinking about going over to Dorie's house," Mother said. "She wanted some advice about her flower garden."

"Okay." Daddy's eyes never left me. Mother, another effort to derail this argument having failed, turned back to the stove.

I ducked my head and shrugged. It pissed Daddy off for me to appear casual about anything.

He looked me up and down. "Those shoes haven't been shined in weeks." Daddy believed a man's shoes revealed all there was to know about his character.

"They ain't dress shoes."

"You sassing me?"

"No, sir."

"Shine those shoes before you wear them out of this house."

"Yes, sir."

"And turn off the light when you leave your room."

"Yes, sir."

Daddy was grinding his false teeth, trying to figure out how to handle the case of the chronic masturbator. Mother was humming hymns and banging dishes. George was grinning and waiting for Daddy to haul out his Army belt and take me to the backyard.

"You ought to know better, Robert. You just ought to know better."

I didn't say anything.

"When are you going to straighten up? You sixteen years old. I'm convinced I got to send you to a military college to straighten you out. They will make a man out of you, teach you some discipline."

"No, sir."

"No, sir, what?"

"No, sir, I don't want to go to military school. I don't care about the military."

Now I had really done it. As Daddy often said, I just couldn't leave well enough alone. Daddy believed the United States Army was the greatest institution on earth. Not only did the Army win wars for America, but it taught young men never to make excuses and to get the job done no matter the cost. The Army taught that there were things worth dying for. The Army personified the highest and best virtues anyone could ever hope to attain. I had just committed sacrilege. Not only that, but my saying I did not care about the military was a slap at Daddy's career. He bowed up and began sputtering.

"What do you mean? I spent thirty years and fifteen days... of my life in the military, and it didn't hurt me. The military... is the only thing that will make you grow up. They... will make a man out of you. They... they will... I think... you..."

I smirked. Daddy was so pissed off he couldn't talk. Then I noticed Mother had turned and was staring at Daddy, half-curious, half-alarmed.

Daddy looked at Mother with a bewildered look in his eyes. "Sweeeeetheaaaart," he said plaintively. The word was long and drawn out.

"JB, are you all right?"

Daddy's mouth was pulled down at the corner. He slumped, and his paper napkin fell to the floor. His hand hit the plate, smearing cake and gravy across the cuff of his white shirt. Silverware clattered to the floor.

"JB?" Mother was alarmed.

I looked from Daddy to Mother, not knowing what was going on.

"JB, what's the matter?"

When Daddy did not answer, she ran for the telephone.

The next day the doctors said that Daddy had suffered a slight stroke but was recovering and would be discharged Tuesday. Mother and Daddy were going down to Panama City for the remainder of the week so Daddy could rest. Rudy and Dorie were letting Mother and Daddy have their house on the beach.

Tuesday morning, an hour or so before he was to be released from the hospital, a massive stroke slammed Daddy into a deep and terrible coma. "We were afraid of that," one of the doctors told Mother. "But we didn't want to alarm you by letting you know that sometimes a major stroke follows the first little stroke."

I was in the hospital room looking at Daddy's twisted face and contorted body. A tube in his nose was sucking out a dark, foul-smelling liquid from somewhere in his body and filling up a big bottle by his bed. Mother and I were in the hospital twenty-four hours a day that week, the only break being when one of us left to go get the younger children for a brief visit. I could not take my eyes off Daddy. I stared at him from the moment I opened the door of his room. And when I left, I backed out slowly, always keeping my eyes on his face. He'd had the first stroke when he was arguing with me. This was all my fault, and I was frightened.

My daddy was an iron man. He had a big voice and was always in control. He and I had never gotten along, and my life up to this point had been spent in fruitless efforts to please him, to have him put his hand on my shoulder and utter a single sentence of affection. He had robbed me of a lot of memories and forced me to put many of my needs on the back burner. Now he was twisted and unconscious, and the stench of the dark fluid filled the room.

No one in the family had ever experienced such a serious sickness. Daddy's breathing was labored, and his face was frozen in a rictus of anguish. He was unconscious but looked as though he was suffering. His suffering made me ashamed of another thought that kept rising to the surface: if he died, my life would be a whole lot better. I kept imagining what it would be like if he were gone, and I saw only good things. I was whipsawed by the fear that he might die and the hope that he would.

At night Mother sometimes went down the hall to a waiting room and stretched out on a sofa to nap for a half hour. But I wanted to stay awake every minute so that when Daddy awakened, I could tell him that I would be a good son, one he could be proud of; that I would go to a military college; that I would stand straighter and keep my shoes shined and my hair trimmed and always turn off the lights when I left the room.

But I never got the chance. Daddy died about 3 a.m. Sunday. I was asleep on the cold tile floor when it happened. I believe he knew I was asleep and Mother was out of the room. I believe he wanted to go when no one was around.

The nurse who had been so warm and solicitous all week awakened me and in a formal, distant tone said, "Yo Daddy is gone." She went down the hall to fetch Mother. I was alone in the room with Daddy. The dark liquid in the bottle by his bed was still.

Mother ran down the hall and stopped at the door. I have never seen such sadness as I saw on her face as she stared at Daddy, remembering the man who once was, the man who was the father of her four children, the man who never called her by name but always, no matter where they were, called her Sweetheart. He was forty-one and she was seventeen when they met. He took her from a family of grinding poverty in the sand hills near Fayetteville, North Carolina, and introduced her to the nomadic life of an Army wife. After he retired, she came with him to the land where he was born, deep in southwest Georgia, and there, far from her own people, she made a new home. Now he was gone. Mother was thirty-five, a young thirty-five, and all she had was a high school education and four children. I was not grown-up enough to be the man of the house. I was not strong like Daddy. I could not fill his shoes. But like it or not, that was now my job.

After a moment the nurse told Mother and me to go down the hall to the waiting room. Mother sat in a big hospital chair, staring at the wall, tears streaking her cheeks. I stood in the door to see what was about to happen. An hour or so later, during the darkest part of the night, just before dawn, I heard funeral home attendants pushing a gurney down the hall, and I watched them enter Daddy's room. When they came out, the sheet draped over Daddy slipped off as the attendant negotiated the door. He saw me and motioned with his head for me to go back into the waiting room. But I stayed where I was. Daddy's eyes stared, unseeing, at the ceiling. His head lolled to the side. His neck was twisted, and one knee was raised. An arm flopped off the gurney. The smell of death filled the hall.

Daddy died on Mother's Day. He died because he had a stroke arguing with me. And he was arguing with me because I had been masturbating.

Yes, I killed my daddy. And the guilt would haunt me for most of my life.

I think half of Edison came to our house that Sunday afternoon or Monday morning after Daddy died. Everyone knew the Sarge, and everyone in Edison enjoyed a funeral. It was a typical post-death pre-funeral affair in that people — mostly women — dressed up and came to the house bearing pear salad, green bean casserole, Jell-o salad, fried chicken, fresh peas, muffins, biscuits, more fried chicken, coconut cake, apple pie … the list was endless. We had enough food to feed one of Daddy's battalions.

What I remember most is sitting in the living room, opening the door and greeting the women, then watching them after they deposited their food on the kitchen table. They rubbed their hands on their hips as if to say their job was over, and then they looked around in mock bewilderment as if wondering what they should do next. But in reality their eyes were raking the rugs and the furniture and the drapes and the china in the cupboard, capturing the room in a glance and then storing it away so that later, when they returned home, they could call one another and say, "Did you see those kitchen curtains? I would not let those things in my house."

Or, "Wouldn't you think she could vacuum that living room rug a little bit better?"

Then the women, still tilting their heads slightly and looking around, made their way back into the living room and sat down. They arranged their dresses and began ever so gently asking questions. Butter wouldn't have melted in their mouths when they said things such as "I know y'all are going to be okay even though JB is gone." Or, "I just hope it doesn't take long for all that government insurance to start coming." Or, "Robert, you planning on going off to college next year?" They never listened to the noncommital response, they just sat there slack-jawed, fingering their fake pearls, nodding, and murmuring, "Ummm."

And that was when I realized that this business about small-town southerners being good and caring people and looking out for one another is hog wash. They are mean and nosy and gossipy. Mostly mean.

DADDY had a Masonic funeral, and the ushers wore their cream-colored sheepskin aprons. An American flag covered his casket, a touch I know he would have liked. People were there whose names I had seen sewn on the inside of Klan robes, but they were some of the most prominent people in the county and showed up at almost every public gathering. I still had no proof daddy had been a member. But I believe he was. After all, he did favor uniforms.

The service was held in the little white wooden Vilulah church. Cardboard fans were scattered up and down the pews, and as soon as a person sat down, he grabbed one of them and began fanning. May is hot in southwest Georgia.

Daddy's Mama and Aunt Grace and Uncle Felix sat in the front row with my immediate family, and one by one everyone in the church stood up and walked by the open casket. I heard half a dozen people whisper the obligatory "My, doesn't he look natural?" Or,

"That undertaker did a good job. Looks just like him." Or, "He looked so real, I thought he was going to sit up and shake my hand." And in this case they were all correct. Daddy's face in death was the same as it was in life: dour and scowling. I never did figure out how the undertaker got those tight lips and frown lines just right. Maybe Daddy's face had just grown that way over the years.

The preacher gave a stem-winder of a sermon, emphasizing Daddy's years in the Army and his service as a telephone lineman and Scoutmaster. Then we all walked across the dirt road to the cemetery. It was only about a hundred yards, but most of us were damp with perspiration when we arrived.

After the preacher said the final prayer, Rudy—on the job personally, which he rarely was—put his foot on a little lever, and Daddy's casket was lowered into the soil only a mile from where he had been born. The red clay dirt that had spawned my daddy was receiving him home.

My classmates and more than a hundred people from Edison slowly walked to their cars and drove off. Finally, the only ones left were Rudy and his crew, the preacher, and my family.

Rudy came over and shook hands with Mother. He held her hand and said, "Miss Gussie, I don't want y'all to worry about a thing. I'm going to stay here and personally make sure my crew does a good job and that we clean up everything just like it should be. Don't y'all worry about anything."

"Thank you," Mother said. She took a last lingering look at Daddy's grave, put her arm through mine, looked over her shoulder at my brothers and sister, and said, "Ah-ite, children. Let's go home."

We walked slowly toward the car, the preacher, Bible in hand, following. I took off my coat and folded it over my arm. At the car the preacher paused, looked at me, nodded slowly, and said, "Robert, now you the man of the family."

I shivered.

17

MOTHER sprawled across the bed, her head hanging over the side, eyes closed as I parted her hair with a large comb and used the end of it to gently loosen the dandruff on her scalp. One of the big band records she and Daddy liked was playing, and the driving, repetitive sounds of "Stomping at the Savoy" filled the room.

I sat on the floor, collecting the dandruff in a pile. When I looked across the room at Mother's dresser, I could see her worried expression reflected in the mirror.

"Robert, if it weren't for Rudy and Dorie, I don't know what I would do."

I made the pile of dandruff a bit neater and continued to scrape gently at her scalp. "Yes, ma'am."

"Rudy took care of all the Social Security stuff, the money from the Army, the insurance, all the paperwork for everything. He got us the money we were owed. And Dorie has been solid as a rock." She paused. "Your daddy did everything when he was alive. He wrote all the checks. He took care of all the bills. I am lost. I don't even know who to call about this stuff."

"I wish there was something I could do."

She reached a hand back over her head, found my face, and patted my cheek gently. "You *are* doing something. This feels so good. It relaxes me." She sighed.

I'm the man of the house, and my job is scraping dandruff.

Mother sighed again. "Robert, I'm going to have to get a job. The government money won't last, and I have to think down the road. I'm worried about how I'm going to support you children. Your daddy up and bought that fancy Chrysler. We don't have much money in the bank, and I have four of you to raise by myself."

"You don't have to raise me. I'm grown."

"Yes, you are. And you're going to have to help me with the others."

"Just tell me what you want me to do."

"Help me look after the children." She raised a hand and pointed. "More to the right. It itches there. I don't know why I have so much dandruff. It must be nerves."

"What kind of job you getting?"

"I called Bill Israel, and he told me I could have a job across the street. I can walk over there and back. It is perfect for me."

I laughed. "At the seat cover factory?"

"Robert, it is a textile mill. They do make step-ins. They will be putting food on our table, so I don't want to hear any of your smart mouth about it."

"Yes, ma'am." I parted and picked and neatened. "What will you be doing?"

"Piecework." She paused. "I can fix breakfast for you children before I go to work in the mornings, but you're going to have to put it on the table, make sure the others are fed, and make sure everybody is ready when the school bus comes."

"I will take care of it."

I was still thinking about that word "piecework." I knew what it meant. It meant leaning over a sewing machine all day long.

It was close work. Hard work. Loud work. I felt a shiver of fear. Piecework. Eight hours a day.

"Robert, I'm by myself now. I don't want any calls from anybody about you misbehaving. You got to help me. You got to behave like your daddy would have wanted you to do."

I didn't say anything. I used the heel of my hand to sweep the dandruff into a neat pile. I parted and scraped and combed, and I thought that no matter what I did or did not do, my days of being ridiculed and humiliated were over. My days of being treated as if I were ten years old were over. Mother would let me have the car more frequently. I could stay out later at night. I missed the idea of having a daddy in my life, but I did not miss my daddy. George and Susie and Butch missed Daddy, but not me, not for one moment. In fact, behind a closed door I did not want to open, I was jumping and shouting and laughing at the thought he was dead. He was dead, dead, dead. He had given me nothing. Taught me nothing. Left me with no good memories. He was dead, and I was glad.

"Rudy and Dorie invited all of us out to supper tonight. We meeting them at the fish camp. You want to drive?"

"Yes, ma'am." I neatened the pile of dandruff.

I sat at the head of the table, the *Atlanta Constitution* before me, pretending to read Ralph McGill's column but with something far more important on my mind. When George and Susie came out for breakfast, I continued reading. As Mother busied herself at the stove, Butch crawled up into a chair and mumbled, "Bouk," his word for milk.

"Susie, fix Butch's bottle," Mother said.

Susie went to the refrigerator, poured Butch's baby bottle full of milk, and placed it in front of him. He tilted his head back and began drinking. The hole in the nipple was so big I could stick my finger through it ... and sometimes did to annoy Butch. It was like a fire hydrant. I don't know why he continued to drink a bottle. He was six years old.

"How long is he going to drink a bottle?" George asked.

"As long as he wants to," Mother said.

"Mother, the Junior-Senior Banquet is three weeks away."

"I know." She turned from the stove. "You invited Dina?"

"Yes, ma'am."

Mother nodded in approval. "She is such a nice girl. Good family."

"Will you let me have the car that night?"

"Of course."

Dina had ridden in the telephone truck. The red-and-white Chrysler would be a big step up.

"Mother, all the other boys in my class and all the seniors will be wearing white dinner jackets."

Mother looked at me as she put plates of food before George and Susie. She looked at the back door where Pal was whining and scratching at the screen. "George, as soon as you finish your breakfast, go feed that dog."

"Something's wrong with him."

"What do you mean?"

"He follows me around all the time. Looking at me and begging."

"Begging for what?"

"Just begging."

Mother shook her head in exasperation. "Just feed him, and he will be okay." She turned back to the stove. Over her shoulder she said, "Robert, we don't have the money to rent you a white dinner jacket."

George looked at me and grinned.

"It's the Junior-Senior," I said.

"Son, I'm sorry. You've got that brown sport coat you wear to church. It will do just fine."

A brown coat at the Junior-Senior? I was going to look like a dog turd among swans.

"I'll be the only person there in a brown coat."

"I doubt if every boy in the junior and senior classes will have money for a white dinner jacket. Some of them will be wearing sport coats like you."

"Mother, I'm going with Dina."

"She will understand. Besides, your brown coat will make her white dress stand out."

George was still grinning, pleased at my distress. I leaned toward him and whispered,

"Stop grinning at me."

George put on his befuddled, owlish expression, eyes big.

"You boys cut out that foolishness and eat your breakfast," Mother said. "Robert, you leave George alone."

Triumphant, George looked at me and said, "You goan be pretty in that brown coat." He paused. "Sugar Britches is goan love it."

DADDY always told me to get a haircut before attending an important event. So a few days before the Junior-Senior, I walked into the barbershop.

"Coram," Judge said, nodding in my direction.

The barbershop was crowded, but it turned out that almost everyone sitting on the pew was there to talk and not to get a haircut. When the man in the chair got down, Judge swept a bit of hair away from his feet, looked down the pew, and said, "Coram, your turn." He clipped and talked, clipped and listened, and the conversation between Judge and the old men was almost soothing.

When he finished my haircut, and I was wondering why he did not unpin the sheet around my neck. Then he was tucking in something behind the sheet, and suddenly he was using his old tatty brush to cover the back of my neck, ear to ear, with hot lather.

He stropped his straight razor, bent my head forward, and began trimming around my hairline, wiping the straight razor on the cloth he had tucked under the sheet, trimming, wiping, trimming, wiping. To the old men on the pew this was nothing. But this was the first time Judge had trimmed my neck with his straight razor, and it meant he thought I was a man.

I climbed down, reached into my pocket, and paid him. "Thank you," I said. And he knew I was not talking about the haircut.

"Yo Daddy was a good man," he said.

I went home and shined my shoes.

I don't know why I even discussed the brown sport coat with Dina. I was a junior, and she was a freshman. But she would be wearing the most expensive dress and the most expensive jewelry at the Junior-Senior. I trusted her judgment and talked about the coat with her and her mother. Miss Sally nodded sympathetically and said the brown coat would be fine; the main thing was to have a good time at the dance.

The night of the banquet, I went to the refrigerator and reverently withdrew a white box with a clear plastic top. Inside was an orchid corsage, the same purple cymbidium that every girl at the dance would be wearing. I carried it to the car as if it were a holy relic.

At Dina's house Mr. EE opened the door, invited me in, and said, "Yo mama doing okay? Yo family okay?"

"Yes, sir."

"Well, everybody in Edison misses yo daddy. You got lot of responsibility now. You ever need anything, you let me know."

"Thank you, sir."

Mr. EE shook his head, looked over my shoulder at the gleaming Chrysler, and said, "I just never did understand why yo daddy went out and bought a Chrysler automobile when a Chevrolet is a perfectly good car. He drove my cars for years, then he up and bought a Chrysler."

"Surprised us, too," I said, fawning over Mr. EE afraid that he might make his daughter stay home that night, concerned that he was afraid to trust her with a philistine who did not drive a car bought from his dealership. "That tail fin they put on Chevrolets makes them look really good."

"Hey, Robert," said Miss Sally from across the room. "Don't you look mighty handsome tonight."

"Thank you."

Mr. EE was still thinking about cars. "Yeah, well," he said, "I just hope you get good gas mileage in that Chrysler." He pointed across the room. "Sit down. She will be here in a minute."

Dina was not one of those girls who made their dates wait. I felt her presence before she swept into the room, leading with that bright smile, and I knew the foundation of the universe had shifted. She was the only child of wealthy parents — what passes for gentry in a small Georgia town- and if she didn't own the world, she thought she did. Underneath the money and the privilege and the clothes and the jewelry, she was vibrant and alive, a good and kind person who did not have a mean bone in her body. I loved her with the all-consuming love that only a sixteen-year-old boy can muster.

I think part of the reason I was attracted to her was because she smelled so good. I keep coming back to how she smelled, of soap and shampoo and a faint hint of some exotic and expensive perfume. I never understood why this was so important to me, but nothing on this earth was more alluring to me than the smell of freshly shampooed hair.

She floated across the room in a dress of pure white and reached out to hold my hand. "You are so pretty," I mumbled as I thrust the white box forward. "I got you a corsage."

Her eyes widened. She knew she would get a corsage. This was not a surprise. Every girl got a corsage for the Junior-Senior. But this was her first Junior-Senior. She would be the only freshman girl at the dance, and the corsage was the first she had ever received.

"I'll be right back," she said.

Her mother rose from her chair and said, "I'll help."

Mr. EE watched them leave and shook his head. "Women get all excited over flowers," he said. He pointed toward a chair. "Sit down. Sit down."

I sat.

From down the hall I heard Dina's voice as she returned. "Robert, I love my corsage. It is beautiful." She entered the room, left hand in the air. "I put it on my wrist rather than on my dress. That way, when we dance and my hand is on your shoulder, it will be right in front of my eyes."

She turned to her parents and said, "We will be a little bit late tonight. People always stay out late after the Junior-Senior."

For a moment they did not answer. Mr. EE and Miss Sally looked at their daughter, their only child, and I sensed they didn't like it that she was growing up so fast.

"Not too late," Mr. EE said flatly.

"Yes, sir."

"And don't you be driving fast. I hear you like to drive fast, but I don't expect I'll be hearing anything like that about tonight."

"No, sir."

Dina pulled at my hand. "We have to go," she said.

"Good night," I said to her parents.

Mr. EE grunted. I knew that he and Miss Sally would be sitting in the living room by the door when we returned.

THE arrival at the Junior-Senior was dictated by unwritten but inviolate rules. Upon driving up to the American Legion Hall on the outskirts of Edison, the couple did not simply alight and walk into the building. They had to sit in the car for a few minutes observing others who were entering. But the sitting in the car could not last more than a few minutes, because then someone might think the couple was making out before the dance — a bit of a no-no — or, worse, that they might be smoking cigarettes.

After two or three minutes in the car, the couple walked slowly toward the front door. Once in the big, wide double doors, protocol dictated that they stand there for at least thirty seconds, maybe a minute, looking around at everyone and letting everyone look at them. At this point the boy was irrelevant. The girls in the room were checking out the dress and corsage and jewelry and hairdo of the girl at the door, and the guys were looking at the girl's boobs, usually pushed up by a daring strapless gown. In the early summer of 1954, the merest hint of a breast rising above an evening dress was about as good as it got.

A girl in an evening dress, with her hair done up for a special occasion, exerts a powerful influence on a farm boy. And when I stood in the door with Dina, some of those boys- the ones who did not have dates — began pawing at the floor like bulls about to charge.

Dina was the youngest girl in the room, but she also had the most poise, the most charm, and that ineffable aura that goes with being the only child in a prominent family. As we stood in the door holding hands, all eyes on us, she gripped my arm with her other hand, leaned close, and whispered, "I want to dance! I want to dance!"

"We will. But it will have to be slow dancing."

I didn't know how to fast dance, and I suspected that fast dancing was what Dina most enjoyed.

"I want to dance!" she repeated.

One of the chaperones handed Dina a piece of blue cardboard folded in half. Inside were lines numbered from one to ten. It was her dance card.

"You won't need that," I said. "We dancing every dance."

"I want it as a souvenir."

We danced the first few slow dances, her temple against mine, the smell of shampoo so fresh and so sweet that I grew addled. As a fast dance began, Dina's eyes sparkled, but I ushered her toward the straightback chairs along the wall. "Let's rest," I said.

"Oh, Robert."

Suddenly, looming over us like a dark cloud, was David, star of basketball and baseball and track, a calculating boy who did not have a date but who did have the ability to see into the future. He tapped me on the shoulder and said, "Robert, if you are not dancing this one, do you mind if I dance with your date?"

I could not say no. I released Dina's hand, and she was swept away, her feet a blur, her eyes sparkling. Whatever David was saying must have been funny because she kept laughing. And when that first fast dance ended, David and Dina stood on the dance floor for a moment, talking, until the next dance began, and then they were off again. David engineered the dance so that when the music ended, he and Dina were at the far end of the dance floor. When a slow dance started, she looked up at him and smiled, and he pulled her close. When she turned her face away from her left hand, away from her corsage, I knew my girlfriend had been snaked.

A few days after the Junior-Senior, Rudy told me he was giving me a raise. During the summer I was working the occasional weekday funeral, and it seemed there were one or two funerals almost every weekend. Rudy said he appreciated my hard work. But when I looked at my first new paycheck, I was astonished. I don't remember the exact amount, but I do remember thinking I wasn't worth that much. All I was doing was driving a truck and digging graves.

"Mr. Rudy, thank you," I said to him. "But that's a lot of money."

He turned on that 200-watt smile and said, "Robert, you worth every penny of it. You take it. You the man of the family now."

Maybe so, but I wasn't being much help, even with my raise. Mother was working so hard and was so productive that the plant manager asked if she wanted to work a double shift. I don't think she wanted to, but she did.

And her sewing did not stop when she left the factory. That summer she worked late into the night on the sewing machine in her bedroom making dresses for Susie and shirts for George and me. The shirts were made from feed sacks that a farmer's wife had given her. Feed sacks came in only two or three easily recognizable patterns, and that summer I was known as "Mr. Purina."

ONE day when I was walking down the sidewalk in Edison, Joe drove by in his pickup truck. He stopped in the middle of the street, rolled down the window, and shouted, "Hey, Coram. I'll rassle you for that shirt."

I didn't think it was funny.

MY senior year was approaching, and I knew that after vomiting over the shoes of the Big Possums and single-handedly losing the biggest track meet of the year, I was no longer a promising young man. I was a pig-killing Mr. Purina. Ahead of me stretched that long and final year of high school, and I knew I would be more isolated than ever before. It was Ollie, beloved of Pal, who unwittingly gave me what I thought would be my redemption, something the Magnificent Ten would look upon with awe.

The nearby town of Morgan had a swimming pool where a number of people from Edison spent their days. One day Ollie picked me up, and we drove to Morgan. When we undressed in the bathhouse, I saw that he had the worst case of the jock itch I had ever seen. The red rash began somewhere around his belt line, covered his butt and groin, and stretched down his legs for several inches. The area where his legs joined his body was a mass of deep, scabbed-over fissures.

How the hell did this happen? Ollie was the only boy in school who had the same athletic ability as I did, which was none. What was he doing with the jock itch? He must have been in a hog wallow and then didn't bathe for a week.

Every boy in the bathhouse stared at Ollie with undisguised admiration as he strutted around the dressing room, going to the urinal, hanging up his clothes, accepting words of sympathy and respect.

"Damn, man," said a boy from Morgan. "How do you stand the pain?"

"What pain?" Ollie said.

"Worst case of the jock itch I ever saw," said another.

Funny thing about the jock itch was, the boys who had it did not want to get rid of it. The angry rash was a badge of honor, the mark of a great athlete. Boys with the jock itch often grimaced when they sat down or squinted in pain if they were jostled. There was some unspoken rule that when this happened, a friend would raise an eyebrow and in a knowing and sympathetic voice ask, "The jock itch?"

Another grimace. A nod of agreement. "Yeah, the jock itch."

I would never be an athlete, but by God I could get jock itch. If Ollie could do it, I could do it.

The coach's words came back to me: "Not getting the jock itch is a simple matter of cleanliness. You got to stay clean down there." So for more than a week, when I took a bath, I did not sit in the tub. I stood up and washed from mid-thigh down and from waist up, careful to let no soap or water encroach on the prime breeding ground. Every day I leaned over and moved my testicles from side to side, studying the seam where my legs joined my body. Nothing. I walked and ran and worked in the yard and worked up a lot of sweat, but there was no redness. I wanted a flaming-red rash but couldn't get even an irritation. I wanted oozing fissures, but all I got was the knowledge that I was probably the dirtiest kid in Edison. Except for digging graves, I rarely left the house.

One Sunday afternoon when I returned from a funeral, Rudy walked out to the truck, and when I climbed down and we shook hands, he backed up a step, wrinkled his nose, and said, "You been working hard."

Mother asked several times, "Robert, did you take a bath today?"

And when I sat down at the breakfast table, George said, "Peee-u."

But nothing. No rash. No fissures. Not even the tinge of pink that signified the early stages of jock itch. I gave up and took a bath. As I soaked in the hot water, I wondered whether Daddy had been right when he said I was sorry. I couldn't even get the jock itch.

18

One Thursday evening at supper, Mother said, "Robert, would you like to take the car out tonight?"

I was sitting at the far end of the table where Daddy used to sit, and she had spoken softly, so softly that I wasn't sure I had heard her correctly. George was sitting to my right and stared at me for a second, then whipped his head around and looked at Mother as if she had taken leave of her senses. I've never seen anyone who could so completely absorb the values and thought patterns of a dead relative.

Susie sat next to Mother, quiet and smiling. Butch sat across from Susie, head propped on his right hand, blowing spit bubbles and mumbling in his private language.

"It's a weeknight," I said in surprise. Usually Mother allowed me to have the car only on Friday or Saturday.

"I know," she said, not looking at me. "But I thought you might want to go out." Then she lifted her head and said, "Just drive slow, Robert. Promise me that."

"Yes, ma'am."

"Why don't you go see Joe or Ollie?"

"It's a weeknight."

I couldn't go visit any boy in my class. If I drove up to their house unannounced, their daddies would think I had lost my mind. Farmers went to bed early during the week, and they didn't take kindly to some scalawag knocking on their door with foolish ideas about riding around.

"Do you want the car?" It was almost as if she was forcing the car on me. She said nothing about what time I should be home. Suddenly aware of a rare chance, I bent to my plate, eating faster, anxious to put that red-and-white Chrysler on the road, maybe drive up to Cuthbert or down to Blakely.

"May I be excused?" I said as I jumped up from the table.

Mother nodded. "You put on nice clothes if you going out."

"Yes, ma'am," I said, pushing in my chair.

"Mother, when will you let me have the car like you do Robert?" George asked.

"George, ask me that after you get a driver's license. You're fifteen years old." She paused. "You better be thinking about that operation up at Duke University in Durham, North Carolina. We going up there in about a week and, I'm worried about it."

"I'm not," George said in his phlegmatic fashion. I believed him. He accepted whatever came his way and rarely fought back or whined. The one thing George could not accept was being number two son now that Daddy was dead. Mother was not as overt in showing her favoritism toward me as Daddy had been in showing his favoritism toward George. But my brothers and sister knew that she favored me, although they probably attributed it to the fact that I was the oldest.

"You let him go out on a weeknight, and you won't let any of us do that," George complained.

"I just told you, you are fifteen years old. Robert is sixteen, about to be seventeen."

"I'm about to be sixteen."

"You are about to do your homework and go to bed. Now finish your dinner."

Five minutes later, radio blaring, I was on the dirt road south of our house, driving fast and pulling a cloud of red dirt far bigger than that pulled by Uncle Felix's rolling store. About ten miles later I came out on the paved road that ran from Edison to Arlington, a road as straight as an arrow for about seven miles. No cars were coming in either direction when I arrived at the paved road, so I barely slowed down as I turned onto the pavement, slipping and slewing and accelerating through seventy and then eighty and then ninety and then one hundred miles an hour, a red flash tear-assing toward God knows where. I held that speed until I saw a car coming north out of Arlington, and then I began to slow down, but I was still doing ninety when we met. I could see the wide eyes of the man who was driving, and as I sped by him, I saw him snap his head toward the woman beside him and I knew he was saying, "That oldest Coram boy is at it again."

I drove for hours that night, racing over dirt roads and paved roads, pushed by something I did not understand. If someone had asked, "Why are you driving so fast?" Or "Where are you going?" I would have said, "I don't know."

I turned into the driveway at home and coasted to a stop. It was almost 1 a.m, the latest I had ever stayed out. I opened the car door and by the faint light of the dome could see a film of dust and dirt along the sides of the car. I knew I would have to wash it the next morning. I shut the door gently, turned toward the house and stopped. There was no light in Mother's bedroom. When I unlocked the front door, she did not come around the corner into the living room, a faint wrinkle of anxiety on her face, to ask if I was okay. I waited in the living room for a moment, expecting her to come out and scold me for being late and causing her to worry. But she did not appear. I waited a moment longer. This was the first night she had not met me at the door.

She must really be tired, I thought. As I went through the hall, I noticed that the door to Susie's room was closed. That was odd. I turned and walked squarely into the closed door of my bedroom and grunted in surprise. I had never known that door to be closed.

I opened the door, left it open, and quietly undressed in the dark. George and Butch were asleep. As I dropped my clothes on the floor, I saw a metallic glint in the moonlight out behind the garage. I leaned closer to the open window and stared hard. It was a car. Why was there a car parked way back there?

I leaned forward until my nose was against the screen. It was a blue-and-white Chevrolet, dark blue on the bottom and white on the top. There was only one car like that around Edison, and it belonged to Rudy. But why was it behind our house in the middle of the night?

I quickly slid my pants on, walked across the hall, and knocked on Mother's door. Usually if we knocked on her door during the night, she opened it in an instant, wondering if one of us was sick or if something terrible had happened. But there was no response. And then I heard a rustling sound and what I thought were frantic whispers.

"Mother?"

A long pause. "What is it?"

"There's something going on. Can I open the door?"

"No, I'll be right there." I put my ear against the door and heard someone walking across the room and then the jangle of coat hangers and knew someone had entered the closet. Mother turned on the record player, and I heard the scratch of the needle and then the sounds of "Stompin' at the Savoy." Why had she turned on the record player in the middle of the night?

Mother opened the door a crack, and I could barely see one eye peeping around the edge of the door.

"What is it?"

"I got home okay."

"Good, son, I'm glad." She was still behind the door.

"Nothing happened. The car is okay."

"Good, son. Now go to bed. It's late."

"Mother, Rudy's car is out behind the garage. Why is his car parked in our backyard?"

"He had to go on a trip and decided to leave it here. He's going to pick it up later."

"Why you whispering?"

"I don't want to wake up your brothers and sister. Now go to bed."

"But why did he park it here? He lives on the other side of town. Why didn't he park at his own house?"

"It was just convenient. You go to bed. Right now."

"Are you okay?"

"I'm fine, son. Just sleepy. Now go to bed." She closed the door.

I stood there a long moment. I couldn't ask my mother to open the door. I couldn't ask her if I could look in her closet. And if she did open the door, and if I did look in the closet, what could I do? I said, "Yes, ma'am," and turned away. I looked back at the closed door and said, "Good night." She did not answer.

I stood by my bed for a long time, looking out through the night at Rudy's car shining in the moonlight, clearly visible to me but hidden from the road. Slowly I sat down on the bed and then leaned back on my pillow, staring up at the ceiling. Rudy was in bed with Mother. He was married and had children. He and his family were our family's closest friends. Daddy had been dead for several months, and now I was the man of the family. And Rudy was in bed with my mother. Around and around my thinking went. What about Dorie, Rudy's wife, and their two children? Surely they did not know about this, and I could never tell them. Was Rudy going to move into our house? How long had Rudy been here tonight? Did he get here while George and Susie were still awake, or did he come after they were in bed?

Rudy was in bed with my mother.

I was bewildered because I didn't know what all this meant. I was scared because everything about my future was now shaky. I was angry because mother had lied to me.

An hour later, maybe two hours later, I was still wide-awake when I heard Mother's bedroom door open. From my pillow I could see across the room and across the hall to Mother's door. She looked toward my bedroom, peering into the darkness. She looked over her shoulder and held her finger to her lips. Then she was walking across the hall to the bathroom, naked, the moonlight streaming through the bathroom window turning her body to marble. Behind her I saw Rudy's smiling face—he was always smiling—and his bald head. He was as naked as a jaybird.

Sometime just before dawn I drifted into a fitful sleep. On the edge of consciousness, I heard Mother and Rudy walk through my bedroom, her quiet "Shhhhhh" hanging in the air. I heard her open the back door and moan as Rudy kissed her. She waited at the door until Rudy cranked up his blue-and-white Chevrolet and eased across the backyard. No lights swept across my room, so I knew he was keeping his lights off until he was on the road. He drove past the end of the house and down the driveway, and the sound disappeared. I knew he was driving east, away from Edison, away from our home, away from his home, toward wherever it was he was going. A moment later Mother tiptoed through my bedroom and across the hall. She went into her room and closed the door.

That closing door was like a great hand squeezing my heart. I had never known such a deep and profound sense of pain. My eyes were wide-open, my body was rigid, and my heart was screaming.

The conversation going on in my head was ragged and jangled, and it made no sense. My earliest memories of Mother were as my protector. She had stood between Daddy and me more times than I could count. She had saved me from countless whippings. She had encouraged me when Daddy had discouraged me. She had praised me when he had diminished me. She had consoled me when Daddy's criticism had flailed me. And many times when Daddy would not let her say or do anything to protect me, she would turn and smile at me. That smile was all I ever needed, because I knew my mother loved me with an unqualified love, and that was enough. She was my hope and my joy during the long, extended boot camp of my childhood.

After Daddy died, Mother and I were partners. We talked often about our family, not so much about George because he was grown, but about Susie and Butch and how they must be pushed toward college and a successful life. Mother did not really ask my advice—I was too immature to offer advice to anyone about anything—but she told me what she was thinking, and I believe just the talking was helpful to her. I was her sounding board, and I took deep pride in being the man of the family. In a practical sense that meant very little, but in the rural South it meant everything. Now it meant nothing.

I had been betrayed by the mother I loved more than anyone else in the world. Of all the burdens I have carried from my childhood, this is the heaviest, the most painful, and the most enduring. This is the one I will take to my grave.

From the moment that bedroom door closed, I knew in the marrow of my bones that all relationships are temporary, that even though other people are around us, we go through life alone. And those we love the most will be unfaithful.

WHEN I knew Rudy was back in town, I drove out to his office and said, "Mr. Rudy, I'm not going to be able to work for you anymore."

He leaned back in his chair and smiled, his eyes probing mine. "What's the matter?"

I shrugged. "Mother has a lot of work for me to do around the house. Next year is my last year of school, and I got to keep my grades up so I can get into college. I need to study more."

He paused, still smiling, eyes still probing. "You sure about this?"

"Yes, sir. I just don't have time to work for you anymore."

"Well, Robert, I got to tell you we will miss you around here. I've gotten to depend on you. You are a good worker. I told your mother that she and JB brought you up right."

For a long moment I didn't say anything. We stared into each other's eyes, and I am sure he knew that I knew. And he didn't care.

"Thank you for the work," I said. And I turned and walked away.

19

THE weeks after Daddy died were the only time in Mother's life she ever did anything for herself. From the first grade on, her life had been about raising her family and helping others. She visited the shut-ins, drove people to Albany on shopping trips or doctor's visits, consoled people in times of grief and trial, and, more than anything else, simply listened when others wanted to talk. She never interrupted anyone. She looked into their eyes, nodded, made noises of agreement and sympathy, and said, "Well, you know I'm here if you need anything." In Edison she was venerated for always being there, and later on, as she aged into her late nineties, she approached a saintly status. "Miss Gussie" was the most beloved person in town.

By then she had buried two husbands, a boyfriend, a son, a daughter, a granddaughter, four brothers, four sisters, and countless friends. During George's last years, Mother's life was devoted to taking care of him. After retirement from the Air Force, and several jobs later, George came back home to Edison, where he had a stroke and could barely walk. Every day Mother drove across town to deliver the newspaper to him because he was too cheap to subscribe. She cooked for him and drove him to the drugstore, where he argued with the pharmacist about how many pills were in his bottles. Once George was scheduled for a doctor's visit in Albany at the same time Mother had an appointment with her doctor in Cuthbert. She canceled her appointment to drive George to his. When George died, she began taking care of a sick neighbor. Miss Gussie just had to take care of people.

Mother was a marvelous and miraculous woman. She was the best mother any boy could ever have. But it took me years for me to understand the pain and stress and anxiety she experienced after Daddy died. She was still young and had four children to raise. When she looked into what she knew would be a hard future, she needed something to make her feel alive. I understand that today.

But at the time I did not, and the pain and confusion I felt are almost impossible to relate. Years later the accumulated pain sent me into a deep depression, years of therapy, and the knowledge that Mother had scarred me forever.

A few days after that terrible night when Rudy was at our house, the whole family drove to North Carolina for George to have his operation. For a day or so before the surgery, we stayed with my grandmother outside Fayetteville.

My maternal grandfather had died about five years before I was born and I knew only two things about him. First, my name comes from him. And second, when he was about thirty-five, he was plowing a field with his mule one day when a fearsome thunderstorm charged out of the west. He pulled his hat down tighter and kept plowing, needing to turn as much dirt as possible before rain made the task impossible. When the storm hit, it spun off a tornado that scooped up him and his mule and set them down about two miles away. Both were unharmed. The mule was still in his traces, and the lines were not even tangled. But when my grandfather began that wild ride, his hair was as black as the night. When it was over, his hair was whiter than white. He and his mule walked back to his house, and there he dropped the reins, picked up a shovel, and began digging. He dug for days. And when he was happy with the size of the hole, he squared it up, covered it with heavy timbers, and pronounced that he had a storm cellar, probably the only one in that part of North Carolina. For the rest of his life, every time he went outside he looked toward the west. And if he saw the merest wisp of a cloud or smelled the faintest hint of rain, he ordered his family into the storm cellar and there they stayed until he deemed it safe to emerge.

I did most of the driving on the twelve-hour trip to Grandmother's house. After a dinner stop we were all walking back to the car when I turned to Mother and said, "Mother, can I ask you something?"

"Of course, son. What is it?"

"Was Daddy a member of the Ku Klux Klan?"

She stopped. "Robert, what in the world makes you ask a question like that?"

I shrugged. "I just wondered."

"Well, he was a Mason and a Shriner."

"I know, but ...."

"Robert, get in the car and drive."

"Yes, ma'am."

I did not say anything for a while. A half-hour later Mother turned to me and said, "Thank you for driving so careful when the children are in the car."

"Yes, ma'am."

She turned back and stared ahead at the road. After a long silence she said, "Robert, your daddy was a good man."

"Yes, ma'am."

A couple of days after we arrived, Mother and George and I drove up to the hospital at Duke University, about a hundred miles north, where a doctor who introduced himself as head of surgery, along with a gaggle of other doctors and medical staff, spent the day getting George ready for surgery. The doctor tried to be solicitous toward Mother, but it was clear he was more interested in the operation than in our family.

"Don't you worry, Mrs. Coram," he said. "I'll be doing the surgery myself. There are very few doctors in the country who can do this sort of exploratory surgery. Your son is in good hands." Mother just nodded, awed and intimidated by this giant medical machine.

The day after the operation the doctor visited us in the waiting room and confirmed what I had long suspect: George was one weird specimen, inside and out. He said that George had a rare condition known as "malrotation of the gut." Everything in his intestinal system was opposite of where it should be. His appendix — long ruptured — was found under his left kidney. The doctor said it was a good thing the doctors in Cuthbert had given George massive doses of antibiotics during his earlier surgery; they had saved his life. He said that other than cutting out a few kinks and resectioning part of George's large intestine, he had done nothing, that it was better to leave things as they were. He told mother that George would be released in a few days.

Mother sighed and grabbed my hand. Over the next few days, while George was recovering in the hospital, Mother and I were either in his room or sleeping in the waiting room. Occasionally she'd look at her watch and leave the room, saying that she had to call friends in Edison to let them know how George was doing. Or, since Grandmother did not have a telephone, she'd say that she had to call one of her sisters to ask if she would go by and check on the children.

"I'm so tired," she said several times as we drove back to Grandmother's house for the last time. George was asleep in the back seat. I was driving, and Mother kept crossing and uncrossing her arms, looking out the window, tapping her feet on the floor, and wringing her hands.

"I know you are," I said. "This has been rough."

"Robert, I need to get away. Maybe drive over to Wilmington to the beach and rest for a few days."

"I'll drive you over. George will be fine. And Grandmother can look after Susie and Butch."

"No, I mean I need to get away by myself. All this coming so soon after your daddy died has really been stressful."

I stared at the road and gripped the steering wheel so hard that my knuckles hurt. At that moment I realized who she had been calling on the telephone. She was going to meet Rudy at the beach.

I didn't speak for a long moment. She turned and looked at me. "Robert, I need to know I can depend on you for this."

I stared straight ahead and mumbled, "Yes, ma'am. It's okay. I can look after George."

She smiled, reached over and squeezed my arm, and said, "Thank you, son."

She did not even wait until the next morning to leave. After we arrived at Grandmother's house and George lay down to sleep, Mother quickly packed a small bag and drove away. "Y'all be good," she said.

Grandmother had no car so we were marooned at the end of a long dirt road where her house backed up to a hedgerow. I had to walk a quarter mile to find a clean piece of dirt to do my business. And I had to hurry, because I always imagined that someone was across the field watching me with a pair of powerful binoculars. I could not, as Uncle Felix would have said, do my bidness in peace.

Grandmother knew all the games and all the tricks that children try with adults, and she had no patience with any of them. She was a ninety-pound dragon who always had a big dip of snuff packed behind her lower lip. Rather than spitting fire, she walked to the door, leaned out, and spit a long, arching stream of brown juice.

After a big dinner that first night, I began collecting the plates. "Sit down, Robert," Grandmother said. "Menfolk don't do that kind of work. I'll do that. You make sure these children get to bed."

George and Butch and I were sleeping in the same bed. About 2 a.m. George began crying and saying his stomach hurt. His crying made Butch cry.

I propped myself up on an elbow and said, "George, what's the matter with you?"

"I don't know. My stomach really hurts. Call Mother."

"We don't have a phone, and I don't know where Mother is."

"Call Grandmother," he wailed. "I hurt bad. Really bad."

I called Grandmother, who came into our room carrying a smoking kerosene lantern. Her head was wrapped in some sort of cloth, and she was wearing a dingy brown chenille robe. She looked at George with the undisturbed air of a mother who has gone through this a thousand times. But the big unknown here was George's recent operation. Did his pain mean this was something serious? The doctors had said that George would be okay, that his days of stomachaches were over. But here he was, curled up in a ball and screaming with pain.

Grandmother turned her wizened face to me and said, "Robert, you think he'd like a Co-Cola?"

Like most southerners, I have always believed that Coca-Cola is good for any ailment short of a broken leg or polio. I nodded sagely and said, "I think that would help."

An hour later George was worse. He was rolling around on the bed holding his stomach and still screaming. Butch would have continued to cry, but one look from Grandmother silenced him. He stuck his thumb in his mouth and, his eyes as big as saucers, stared at all the goings-on.

"Your mother left you in charge of this brood," Grandmother said. "Do what you think is right."

How in the hell was I supposed to know what to do? I was sixteen years old. I had neither the knowledge nor the experience to deal with this kind of medical emergency.

What would Daddy have done? He would have taken charge. He would have made something happen.

"I got to call an ambulance and take him back to Duke. Where is the nearest telephone?"

Grandmother grimaced and shook her head. "There's some folks over on the road to Carver Falls that have a telephone, but I don't know them." She paused. "You're gonna have to walk up to the highway, then turn right on the Raleigh road and go about a halfmile to a gas station that I think is open." She paused again. "What time is it?"

I looked at my watch. "Three thirty."

She pursed her lips. "If they not open now, they will be by the time you get there. If you want to call an ambulance, get dressed and get on up the road. I'll sit here with George. He's not going anywhere."

Five minutes later Grandmother, kerosene lantern in hand and a huge dip of snuff distorting her mouth, opened the front door and ushered me outside into the sandy yard. We could hear George crying and moaning about how badly he was hurting. I was as frightened as I had ever been in my life.

I looked into the darkness. The first mile of my hike took me through fields of white, sandy soil where the road was visible. But then there was a half-mile stretch through Black Bottom, a place where the soil was dark, and trees hung over the road, and thick forests stretched away on both sides. Black Bottom at night was the scariest place on earth.

"Grandmother, you got a flashlight?"

She stared at me, her faced sculpted into harsh lines by the light of the flickering lantern. She turned and spit what looked like a quart of vile juice, wiped her chin with the back of her hand, and said, "Robert, you ever seen a flashlight around this place?"

"No, ma'am."

"Then I ain't got a flashlight. Now get on down the road."

"Yes, ma'am."

I ran through the open fields, but at Black Bottom it was too dark for me to run, so I slowed to a walk, hands stretched out before me. Unlike the dry, crisp smell of the open fields, Black Bottom had a dank odor. Ominous chirps and squeaks and rustles emanated from the darkness. I had walked through the swamp and deep woods and cemetery between Edison and home, however, and now, by shuffling and moving slowly to make sure I stayed in the deep rut, I could walk through Black Bottom. Eventually I came out of the woods and saw the lights of cars on the Raleigh road. I started running toward those lights. I ran as if I was running the hundred-yard dash, flat out, and when I reached the Raleigh road, I turned right, still running, stumbling on the debris that littered the roadside. The gas station was open, and when I lurched through the door, gasping for breath, the attendant looked at me in surprise.

"Boy, you got big eyes. Somebody chasing you?"

A halfhour later the ambulance drove into the parking lot of the gas station. I opened the door to jump into the front seat but stopped when I saw a very pretty young woman there.

"I wanted somebody to ride with me when I came back from Raleigh, so I asked my girlfriend to come along," the driver said. "Hope you don't mind."

Before I could answer, he jerked his thumb over his shoulder and said, "We got a little bench back there next to the gurney. You can sit there and keep an eye on your brother."

As I crawled into the back of the ambulance, he opened the window behind the front seat and said, "Tell me where we going."

I directed the driver back to Grandmother's house, where she ordered us about as we moved George onto the gurney and then into the ambulance. As the driver slid back behind the steering wheel, Grandmother pulled on my arm and said, "Who's that hussy in the front seat?"

"His girlfriend."

"He's bringing his girlfriend while he drives a sick person?" She spit and wiped her chin.

"Get out of here," she said.

Both Grandmother and I knew there was no way for us to let Mother know about George and no way to know when I would be returning. I was on my own.

"You need any money?" she asked.

"I got about five dollars."

"That should do it." She paused. "I'll look after the children."

When we reached the Raleigh road, the driver turned on the red flashing lights atop the ambulance, and as we approached each small town, he turned on the siren. Now it was raining and people turned to watch and to wonder who was in the ambulance and where we were going.

Through the dividing window I could see that the driver's girlfriend had curled up her legs beneath her and her skirt had ridden up, showing off her long legs. The driver rested his right hand on her bare leg. We raced through the early-morning hours, lights flashing and siren screaming, the driver with one hand on the wheel and the other on his girlfriend's bare leg.

As we drove up to the emergency entrance at the hospital, a team of attendants ran out, pulled the gurney out of the ambulance, and pushed it toward the emergency entrance. The driver ran alongside, talking quickly, giving them George's name, telling them that he had recently had an operation, and introducing me as George's brother. George was wailing like a banshee as the attendants pushed him through the door. I was about to follow when the driver said, "You need me anymore?"

"No, thanks."

"Then I'm going back to Fayetteville. Go to the waiting room and have a seat. When there is news they will tell you. Hope your brother is okay."

So there I was, stranded at the hospital with only a few dollars, no car, and a brother who had disappeared into the emergency room. I was surrounded by medicinal smells, but I didn't mind; they were better than the smells of Black Bottom. I went to the empty waiting room, sat down on a plastic-covered couch that gave me a view of the door down the hall from which the doctors would emerge, and waited.

An hour or so later the big double doors at the far end of the hall swung open, and a doctor wearing scrubs emerged. Because I was the only person in the waiting room, I knew he was bringing news of George. I jumped up, had a brief idea that something was terribly wrong, and collapsed.

When I awakened, I was looking into the eyes of the doctor I had seen coming down the hall. A nurse was beside him, waving an ammonia vial under my nose. I was lying on the floor, weak and confused.

"You feel okay?" the doctor said.

"I don't know."

"Did you eat breakfast this morning?"

What the hell was he talking about? I was lying on the floor, and he wanted to know if I had eaten breakfast?

"No, sir."

"Son, you fainted. It happens. No breakfast and the stress of bringing your brother up here. George Coram is your brother?"

"Yes, sir. Is he okay?"

"How old are you?"

"Sixteen. But why . . . ."

"Where do you live?"

"Edison, Georgia. Why?"

He looked at the nurse and said, "He's okay." She grabbed one arm, he grabbed the other, and they lifted me up. "Son, let's put you here on the seat. You feeling okay now?"

I shook my head. "I never fainted before."

"You get a little breakfast, and you'll be fine. Nothing to worry about." They backed up a half step, watching me closely. Then the doctor pulled up a chair and sat facing me.

"Your brother is okay. We gave him something to make him sleep. He told us he had a big meal last night, and we think that was the problem. He ate too much. Too much heavy food too soon after the surgery. The site of the surgery complained. That's all there is to it. But to make sure, we want to watch him for a couple of days."

He paused and looked at me. "Are you taking care of him by yourself?"

I nodded. "My mother went away to rest for a few days."

"Do you know how to get in touch with her?"

I shook my head.

The doctor looked at the nurse. "We've moved him to a room, and you can go in and visit as long as you want. I suggest you get some breakfast first."

"Is it okay if I sleep here tonight?"

"Either here or in the room with your brother. There is a chair in there. People do it all the time."

He stood up and looked at me for a long moment. "Your brother is not going to feel like eating much for the next day or so, but I'm going to order meals sent in anyway."

"Thank you, sir."

In that silent hospital room I realized again that we go through life alone. My doped-up brother was across the room, and occasionally a nurse stuck her head in through the doorway, but I was alone. Alone and frightened. What if George had a serious postoperative problem? This man of the family business was more than a title, and I was not ready for it.

I never knew how it happened, but I think that sometime during that day Mother called one of her sisters to go to Grandmother's to check on George. Grandmother told her what happened and said, "Tell Gussie to get back here and look after her children."

All I know is that late that afternoon, I heard Mother's voice down the hall. I recognized the click of her heels on the white tile floor. George had awakened, and he and I looked at each other, both of us wide-eyed. Then the door suddenly opened, and Mother was walking rapidly across the room. She leaned over George and, holding his hand, asked, "Son, are you okay?"

"My stomach still hurts, but not as much as it did."

Mother adjusted the sheet, caressed George's face, and sighed. She sat down on the edge of the bed and said, "I've been so worried about you. I got up here as fast as I could. I interrupted my vacation to get back here to you."

George smiled weakly. He had no idea what was going on.

I thought mother would congratulate me for taking charge of a bad situation, for taking care of my brother, for sitting by his bed and talking with him. Instead she turned toward me with a stern face and said, "Robert, what in the world were you thinking about when you went out and hired an ambulance? It is going to cost a fortune." She patted George's hand. "I just hope your daddy's insurance will cover all this."

Well, the Sarge always said I was sorry. But, then, maybe she was pissed off because her trip to the beach had been interrupted.

20

I rocketed through my last year of high school. All I wanted was out. Out of school. Out of my family. Out of Edison. Out of southwest Georgia. When this school year was over, I would go to college and then out into the world, probably that big, mythical city of Atlanta, which we in the rural South looked upon as the City of Hope.

My senior year revolved around two things: Sydney and the red-and-white Chrysler.

Dina and David were now going steady and would later marry. Nellie, my girlfriend from back in the seventh grade, was dating Nick, and they also would marry. I had been dumped by my two previous girlfriends, and my mother was sleeping with a married man. In my mind I had already left Edison, so it was natural that I would look beyond my home town for a new girlfriend.

My eye fell on Sydney, the darling of Blakely High School. She was so beautiful that she was worshipped by boys who lived two or three counties away, boys who had seen her only at a basketball game or coming out of church. She was a classic beauty with dark hair and porcelain skin, so stunning as to seem unobtainable. Because she was from Blakely, she was what Edison boys called a "foreigner" and therefore even more unobtainable. Adding to her mythic persona was the fact that her daddy had been the sheriff of Early County for twenty years. A lanky and taciturn man, he was a widower and so protective of his daughter that, so the story went, if he thought you were interested in her and you even slowed down while driving past his house, he would radio a deputy and have you pulled over and ticketed before you got two blocks. Then he would put you in a dark jail cell and you would stay there until you were old enough to draw Social Security.

I met Sydney simply by looking up her phone number, calling, and asking if I could drop by to say hello. When I arrived at her house, the sheriff's car was parked at the curb. In the mid-1950s a rural southern sheriff's official vehicle was more than a little intimidating. The sheriff was the closest thing to God, and his car reflected his status. The sides and trunk sported big, bold lettering spelling out the word "Sheriff." There was a bubble-gum-machine-shaped red light on top and a long whip antenna on the rear bumper. I was a yahoo from Edision, and this was my first visit with the sheriff's daughter. He had taken time off from work so that he could meet me and make sure I understood the rules.

I knocked on the door and heard footsteps. Then I saw Sydney, smiling, and over her shoulder she said, "I got it, Daddy." She invited me in.

In some magical and inexplicable way, Sydney and I were immediately relaxed in each other's company. We had that ineffable chemistry that either happens or does not — it cannot be summoned. As we sat talking on opposite ends of the sofa, her throaty laughter echoed through the house. We grew silent though when we heard footsteps coming down the hall. And then there he was, hand resting casually on the butt of his pistol, oozing the omnipotent musk possessed by southern sheriffs. This was a guy who thought he could hold back the tide, who thought the earth trembled when he walked. And in Early County it did.

He turned his impassive stare on me, I guess expecting me to wilt. But I had grown up as the firstborn son of an Army master sergeant, a man who, in his thirty years and fifteen days in the Army, had kept good order and disciple among thousands of men, a man who had taught young officers most of what they knew about leadership. My daddy had forgotten more about intimidation than Mr. High Sheriff would ever know. I jumped up, walked across the room, stuck out my hand, and said, "Sheriff, my name is Robert Coram. I'm from Edison. I hope you don't mind my visiting your daughter." I looked into his eyes and gave him my firmest hand-shake, just like Daddy had always told me to do.

He blinked, dark eyes almost hidden in his sun-bronzed face, and said, "She don't mind, I don't mind."

"Daddy, I don't mind," Sydney said.

I kept my eyes locked on the sheriff's. "Thank you, sir," I said. "I won't be here much longer. I have to get home and help my mother with some things around the house."

"Uh- huh," the sheriff said. He pursed his lips as if in deep thought. "You the Sarge's boy?"

"Yes, sir. He was my daddy."

"Uh- huh. Thought you was. I saw that red car out front. Only one car like that in these parts." Without another word the sheriff walked out the front door, got in his car, and drove away.

Sydney laughed. "He doesn't know what to make of you."

"What do you mean?"

"You're not afraid of him. Most boys are. And you said you were about to leave. I can't tell you how many times he has come in this living room and chased boys out, told them to go home." She looked away. "Most of the time they don't come back."

"You let me, I'll be back."

She smiled and nodded. "You know my number."

As I walked out the front door, I realized that a southwest Georgia sheriff wasn't shit compared to a retired army sergeant.

THE next week, still feeling spunky, I convinced Joe and Ollie that we should teach David a little humility. David was okay, just a bit superior now that he was going steady with the Princess of Edison. One day after dinner in the school lunchroom, a group of us walked outside into the blazing heat. As David squinted in the bright light, Joe grabbed him from behind and pinned his arms while Ollie took his knees. Then they picked him up, and away we went. We folded David in half at the waist and forced him, butt first, into a fifty-five-gallon barrel behind the ag building. Then we walked away and left him there, face between his knees, sputtering in anger. It was midafternoon before Mr. Dozier found him and turned the barrel over, allowing David to slide out. Hair tousled, shirt out of his dirty pants, and mad as hell, he walked into class late.

"David, where have you been?" the teacher demanded.

"I'm sorry," he said, "but I was unavoidably detained."

That became the catchphrase for the rest of the year. Whenever anyone was late for anything—or whenever we had any other opportunity—we would, "I'm sorry, but I was unavoidably detained." And everyone would howl with laughter. David didn't think this was funny.

OVER the next few weeks I visited Sydney a half dozen times, always in the afternoon. One day while Sydney and I were sitting on the sofa, laughing and talking, the front door suddenly opened, and the sheriff was in the room. I don't know what he expected to find, but I stood up and said, "Good afternoon, sir."

Sydney shook her head, sighed, and said, "Daddy."

He was the sheriff, and he had what for a sheriff was a valuable survival skill: knowing the mood in a room the minute he walked in. When he paid Sydney and me a surprise visit, he knew the moment he opened the door that his daughter and I were doing nothing more than talking and laughing.

He looked at me and said, "At least you ain't racing up and down the road with my daughter in the car. I know about you and how fast you drive. You ever break the speed limit with my daughter in the car, and that's the last time you will see her."

"Sir, I have too much respect for Sydney to drive fast with her in the car."

"Uh-huh." The gauge on his bullshit meter just pegged.

"I like being here in your home. Sydney and I ride around a little bit, but I enjoy just sitting here talking."

That was the last surprise visit the sheriff ever made.

I didn't tell my friends that I was dating Sydney. I figured they would not have believed me. In Edison I was the sum of all my mistakes, but in Blakely I was the out-of-town guy who, as Sydney said, had stood up to her daddy. Eventually the desire to have my friends know we were dating overcame me. One Saturday about noon I called her and said I would be out riding around with some friends. Could we stop in for a visit? "I'd love to meet your friends," she said.

When I asked Mother for the car keys, George puffed up in indignation. "I thought today was my day to drive the car," he said.

"George, you can go to the picture show," Mother said. She turned to me. "Robert will let you have the car in a couple of hours."

"Yes, ma'am."

George's puckered expression said he did not believe me.

I picked up Joe and Ollie, and as we drove west out of town, I turned up the radio. Bill Hayes was singing "Ballad of Davy Crocket," and we were singing along: "Daaaaaavy, Davy Crocket…" When the song was over, I said, "Want to ride over to Blakely?"

"Might as well," Ollie said.

"We can go to the drugstore, maybe get a Coke and look around," Joe said. He paused a moment and added, "They got some good-looking women over there."

"I'll take you to see one of them."

"Who's that?" Ollie asked.

I looked at him, smiled, and said, "Sydney." She was of such legendary beauty that her first name was sufficient. Ollie and Joe whipped their heads around and stared at me in utter disbelief.

"No way in hell you know her," Joe said.

"Sydney, Sydney, Sydney," Ollie said in reverence. "You're shitting us. You can't know her. Man, she is ... she is ... "

I smiled indulgently. "Let's see if she opens the door when we get there."

Twenty minutes later I eased to a stop in front of Sydney's house.

"I don't believe this," Joe said.

"How'd you meet her?" Ollie said. He smoothed his hair. "I should have worn a nicer shirt. Damn, I didn't know I would be meeting somebody like that today."

As we walked onto the porch, Sydney opened the door, reached for my hand, and said, "Hi, Robert." She was wearing red shorts and a summery blouse and had just put on a bit of lipstick.

Both Joe and Ollie stammered as I introduced them. They were awestruck and said little for the next half hour or so. Sydney sat close to me on the sofa, holding my hand, while Joe and Ollie sat in chairs across the room and stared, not believing that some-one from Edison was dating the most beautiful girl in southwest Georgia. Both occasionally shook their heads as if to shake away the cobwebs of disbelief.

We did not stay long, and as we got into the car, Joe slid down in the seat and let out a long sigh. "I can't believe I was in the same room with Sydney."

"Robert," Ollie said, "she likes you. I could tell."

I looked out the window and said, "It's about to rain. Let's get on home."

On the radio Bill Haley and His Comets were hammering out the lyrics to "Rock Around the Clock." We were swinging our shoulders, jerking our heads, snapping our fingers, and singing along: "We're gonna rock...around...the clock tonight."

As we left Blakely, one of those blinding southwest Georgia thunderstorms, unloaded on us. We were racing north on US 27 at about eighty miles an hour.

On a long straight stretch of road, with no warning, the car hydroplaned and began spinning in circles, out of control but some-how staying on the road. We had just passed a big truck, what we called a semi, and now, briefly and terribly visible through the windshield as the car spun around, another semi was headed toward us, coming closer with each terrible spin. The driver blinked his lights rapidly, unable to brake without jackknifing his trailer on the rain-slick road. I could do nothing but hold on to the steering wheel. Ollie reached out and braced himself with both hands on the dashboard, then muttered, "Oh, shit." The semi was getting closer, sheets of water flying from its wheels, and I knew that on the next spin we would collide.

Suddenly the car was off the highway, skidding down the right-of-way as I fought to control the steering wheel. I jammed down hard on the brake a second before we slid down the length of a deep, V-shaped ditch and stopped. No one said anything for a long moment. Joe held up his trembling hands, laughed nervously, and said, "Look at that. I'm shaking."

I pulled on the door handle and said, "Door won't open. We wedged in the ditch."

"What we gonna do?" Ollie said.

"Joe, check on your side," I said. "See if you can open your door."

Joe rolled down the window, looked toward the front of the car and then the back. He tried to open the door but could not. "All I see is grass. Yep, we wedged in here." He examined the side of the car closely. "Car ain't even scratched."

He stiffened as he looked behind us. "That truck stopped. The driver is coming this way."

I watched in the rearview mirror as the driver ambled toward us in the rain. He was wearing jeans and a T-shirt and trying to keep his cigarette dry under the shade of his cap. He leaned over and stuck his head into the window, coming in so far that to get away from him, Joe and Ollie leaned against me. He looked at me in barely controlled anger, then at Joe and Ollie, and asked quietly, "You boys okay?"

"We okay," I said. "But we would appreciate some help getting out of this ditch."

The driver tried to puff on his sodden cigarette, then pulled it out of his mouth, stared at it in disgust, and threw it behind him. He looked at each of us in turn and said, "You boys can stay here until hell freezes over as far as I am concerned."

He backed out of the car, his cigarette breath lingering in the moist air, hitched up his soggy jeans, shook his head, and ambled back to his truck.

The three of us looked at each and laughed nervously. "What's the matter with him?" Ollie said.

"Diaper rash," Joe replied. He looked over his shoulder at the driver, laughed, and said, "Let me out of here. I'm goan tell him that Johnson's Baby Powder can cure that case of the red ass he's got."

"God amighty," Ollie said. "Don't do that. He might come back and kick the shit out of all of us."

"He ain't the daddy rabbit," Joe said.

"Forget about that," Ollie said. He pushed on the door again. "How we goan get out of this car?"

"Climb out the window," I said. "We got to walk down the road until we find somebody with a telephone."

"A tractor would be better," Joe said. He climbed out the window behind Ollie. "You coming?"

"I gotta stay with the car. Y'all go ahead."

"See you when we see you."

"I'm not going anywhere."

I sat there unmoving, staring into the rain, knowing it was a miracle we had not died in a terrible collision with the semi. I was young enough and had been to church enough that I believed our survival was a sign from God. Something special was in store for me in my life. After I left Edison, there would be something I had to do, something I was meant to do. But what?

I was still wondering when Joe and Ollie returned. A nearby farmer had lent them his tractor. Joe pulled the car gently from the ditch. It was covered with grass and goopy mud but otherwise undamaged.

About the time the rain washed away the mud, we drove out of the rain and entered bright sunlight.

"It ain't rained at all here," Joe said as we passed the city limits.

"Dry as a popcorn fart," Ollie said.

"Hot, too," I said, rolling down my window.

Joe rolled down his window and took a deep breath. "Hotter than a fresh-fucked fox in a forest fire."

I was still thinking about how close we had come to being T-boned by that semi. I should have died that day on US 27. But I didn't.

Still jittery as I drove into town, I smiled when I saw Will Lawrence up ahead. He was standing on the street corner trying to loom, but all he could do was slouch.

"Let's fuck with Will Lawrence," I said.

"What you gonna do?" Ollie asked.

"Watch." I pressed down on the accelerator. I was doing seventy miles an hour when I roared down the main street of Edison. It was a reckless and irresponsible thing to do, as the sidewalks were jammed with Saturday shoppers. Dimly I sensed their startled and disapproving faces as I sped through town. I was hauling ass. I was moving like a scalded cat.

Ollie looked over his shoulder and said, "Well, you did it. Will Lawrence is running for his car."

"I'm gonna outrun him," I said.

"Lemme out," Joe said. "Lemme out. I ain't got much sense, but I got enough to know I don't want to be part of this."

"Me neither," Ollie said. "Stop and let us out."

"Candy asses." I whipped into a side street and skidded to a stop. "Get out of here."

They jumped out, and before they could shut the door, I pushed hard on the accelerator, spinning the wheels. The momentum slammed the door closed. As I rounded the next corner, I saw Will Lawrence in the rearview mirror, red light flashing.

The speedometer registered ninety when I crossed Bay Branch and took to a dirt road. On and on I raced, stirring up a cloud of red dust, knowing Will Lawrence was having to drive slower and slower. In that cloud he could not see fifty feet, but he was persistent, and he would follow the cloud. In a moment, however, I was fighting for control of the car as I hit the mud left in the wake of the thunderstorm. I slowed almost to a crawl, but I was so far ahead of Will Lawrence that it did not matter.

A half-hour later I found my way back to the paved road west of Edison, slowed down, and eased back into town. I parked a block off the main street and asked the ticket seller at the theater if I could go inside and give George my car keys.

She nodded and said, "Be sure you come right back out."

"I will."

George was sitting between a couple of his friends and was more than a little surprised when I leaned over and gave him the car keys.

"Really?" he said. Even though I could not see his face clearly in the darkened theater, I knew he was wearing his big-eyed owlish expression.

"Yeah, really. Now get out of here before I change my mind."

He and his friends jumped like rabbits and were out the front door in seconds.

I don't think he got more than two blocks before Will Lawrence, red light flashing, siren screaming, pulled him over. He had not followed the cloud for as long as I thought he would. After a while he had made his way back to town knowing I would have to return.

Dozens of people in Edison stopped to watch. No one could remember the last time Will Lawrence had turned on his siren and stopped a car. And it was clear from his posture, the way he jammed his cap down on his head, and his taut face that he was angry. No one had ever seen Will Lawrence angry.

Had it not been for the ticket seller at the theater, who verified George's story, I think Will Lawrence would have put George and his two friends in jail.

ONE day I read a short piece in the Atlanta paper saying that Frank Yerby had announced he was moving to Spain. He said he was doing so in protest of racial attitudes in his home state.

I read the story again and again, trying to imagine the pain it must have caused him to leave the land where he was born, the courage and the integrity it took in 1955 to publicly describe his home state as racist. The man I would revere all my life as the greatest storyteller ever to come out of the South, the man who first planted in my mind the idea of becoming a writer, was turning his back on all he had ever known and starting anew in a different place.

What Frank Yerby did strengthened my desire to do the same. With Frank Yerby as my model, I would leave Edison, and maybe, just maybe, one day I could become a writer.

I had put aside enough money from my grave-digging career to rent a white dinner jacket for the Junior-Senior Banquet. The picture of Sydney on my arm as we entered the American Legion Hall remained in my desk for the rest of my life.

After the Junior-Senior Banquet I took Sydney home. Her daddy didn't care how late we stayed up talking, but he did not want us riding all over southwest Georgia. As we were sitting at her kitchen table, sipping on Coca-Colas and talking softly because her daddy was half-asleep in the next room, she tilted her head to the side and said, "Robert, I've never asked you this, but what are you going to study when you go off to college? What do you want to do?"

For a long moment I stared into her eyes, not answering. I wanted to tell her that deep in the most hidden part of my heart was a dream I had never mentioned to a living soul, not even my mother. It was a dimly formed dream, probably because it was so scary and improbable. I wanted to tell her about Ralph McGill, who could summon the thunder and whose prose was muscular and visceral and lyrical. I wanted to tell her about Georgia-born and Georgia-haunted Frank Yerby. I yearned to tell her that my dream was to become a writer. With Ralph McGill and Frank Yerby before me, I believed I could do that.

But the very idea of a yahoo from rural southwest Georgia becoming a writer was too ludicrous to talk about. No one from Edison had ever been a writer. As far as I knew, no one from southwest Georgia had ever been a writer. We were so far back in the woods, so far behind the rest of the world, so inferior in every way to those in the outside world that for me to say that I wanted to be a writer would be like saying I wanted to be president of the United States.

Sydney cared about me, and I think she would have reached across the table and held my hand and encouraged me. But that night I was afraid to put my idealistic and ambitious dream into words. Talking about such a fragile dream might shatter it.

So I shrugged and said the first thing that came to mind. "I'm not sure. But I'm thinking of maybe being an architect."

She did as I had thought she might. She smiled, reached across the table, squeezed my hand, and said, "I've never known anyone who wanted to be an architect. You will be a good one."

WHEN I got back to Edison, I met Joe and Ollie downtown. They parked their cars and jumped into the front seat of the red-and-white Chrysler. It was around 3 a.m., and I knew Will Lawrence was long abed. I accelerated rapidly and was climbing through seventy when, at the edge of town, I swerved across the highway and was on the road to Bluffton.

"Where we going?" Ollie asked.

We would not graduate for several weeks, but the Junior-Senior Banquet signaled the end of my high school career. This was my last chance before leaving Edison to do something for which I would be remembered, my last chance to overcome the ignominy of killing Bertha, puking all over the basketball team and the Big Possums, and losing the track meet in Albany. I wanted the juniors and sophomores to hear about this night and to pass the story along. I wanted to leave one thing of distinction behind when I left Edison.

I pressed harder on the accelerator. "We gonna run the Nelly Hoover curve."

Ollie laughed nervously. "At night?"

"Let's do it," Joe said. "Show us what you got." He leaned and turned up the volume on the radio. Les Baxter's "Unchained Melody" blared through the car.

Joe and Ollie stiffened as we approached the curve. Ollie, who was sitting in the middle, braced himself on the dashboard. Joe gripped the armrest.

"Keep your eyes on the speedometer," I said.

"Eighty," Ollie said. "Whew. Nobody's ever even come close to that."

Ollie lived about a mile away and for years had seen the wrecked cars, splintered telephone poles, deep ruts, uprooted shrubbery, and broken road signs that marked many futile attempts to take the curve. Plus, Miss Nelly was his aunt, and for years he had heard her talk about the squealing tires, skittering gravel, and smashed azalea bushes. So when Ollie said no one had run the Nelly Hoover curve at eighty miles an hour, he knew what he was talking about.

Now we were caught in the belly of a beast that could spit us out into the ditch or Miss Nelly's front yard, I sensed that the secret of a successful high-speed run was twofold. First, I should not indulge in the fruitless effort of looking beyond the headlights to see the road and figure out exactly where I was going. I had to stay focused on the road directly in front of the car. Second, I had to keep tightening my trajectory even when common sense told me I was too tight and too fast.

The curve was so sharp that my headlights shone onto the grass or the ditch. Now the outside tires were on the dirt and scattering clods. I pulled harder on the wheel and was back on the pavement, still pulling hard on the wheel, still forcing myself deeper and deeper into the whirlpool. I was outrunning my headlights and on the ragged edge of losing control. The trajectory got tighter and tighter, until I felt as if I was going in the opposite direction.

"Hold on, boys," Joe shouted. "We either goan set a record or we goan bust our asses."

"Still on eighty," said Ollie.

"We running up our own assholes!" Joe shouted over the last verse of "Unchained Melody."

"Still on eighty," Ollie said.

And then the curve spit us out, and we were on the straight road. We laughed and whooped in exultation.

"Slow down, Coram," Joe said. "I don't want a deer coming through the windshield after we set a record."

Ollie patted the dashboard. "It was this Chrysler that let you do it so fast," he said. "Not another car in Edison, no Chevrolet or Ford, could have done it that fast."

As I drove home that night, I was content in knowing that all of Edison would find out about my record by the next day and that for years to come people would remember me for it.

A year later two brothers from the little pissant crossroads of Carnegie drove down to Edison in their parents' new Ford station wagon and took the curve at ninety miles an hour. There were witnesses.

DURING my last summer in Edison, Mother and I talked often of the day when I would leave for college. This was a big deal, a pivotal shift in my life. I was leaving home and taking my first solo steps into early manhood. But parents are part of this process. They help unpack. They leave a container of cookies. For many parents this is an emotional moment, especially when it is the first child who is leaving for college. When Mother and I talked of that day, she always said, "We," and I thought she meant the two of us.

But then early on the day of my departure, Rudy drove up in his blue-and-white Chevrolet and opened the trunk and said, "I told Dorie I needed to help your mama drive you up to Dahlonega to

North Georgia College and get you settled in at school." He pointed. "Put your bag in here." He paused. "You don't have much luggage."

"It's a military school. I'll be wearing a uniform all the time."

I didn't talk much on that six-hour drive. I sat in the backseat as Rudy talked, saying the things my daddy should have been saying, imparting his ideas about going off to college and becoming a man.

I wasn't listening. I was pissed that he was driving us. This was supposed to have been a trip for mother and me. I also knew I had no more business going to a military college than I did going to seminary. But I had killed my daddy and was fighting a mighty headwind of guilt, and maybe going to a military college would help me make amends. And I sensed somewhere deep in my soul that Daddy was still controlling me.

We drove through Columbus, Atlanta, and Gainesville, then on into the mountains, and I simmered in quiet anger the entire trip.

As we drove onto the stately and imposing campus, it was like driving onto a military base. Everywhere there were young men in uniforms. At the center of the grounds was an enormous parade ground.

Daddy always said I would get straightened out if I went to North Georgia College and trained to become an Army officer. I didn't know if I would get straightened out, whatever that meant, but I would try.

As Rudy pulled into a parking space, I realized that I had put aside my dream of becoming a writer. Whoever heard of a writer coming out of a place like Edison, Georgia?

Rudy opened the door and walked to the rear of the car. Mother sat in the front seat, not moving. Over her shoulder, she said, "Be a good boy. And call me if you need me."

Rudy pulled by suitcase from the trunk and slammed the lid. He reached out to shake my hand but I ignored him as I looked toward mother, waiting for her to turn around, waiting for her to get out of the car and give me a hug, waiting for her to say to me the things that a mother says to her son on a day like this. But she never turned around.

Rudy said, "We got to get on back to Edison. It's a long drive." He crawled back into the driver's seat and the car pulled away. I didn't think they were going straight back to Edison.

During the convoluted process of checking in and signing up for classes, I told myself I had done the right thing in choosing North Georgia College. As the son of a dead career Army master sergeant, I received benefits that made college affordable, especially since as I was taking ROTC. Mother had only to pay for a few incidentals. Daddy would appreciate it that I chose a school that not only would straighten me out but also would not burden Mother financially.

At the desk in the bookstore the frazzled clerk was trying unsuccessfully to find a book I needed. I could see it on the shelf and was directing her to it. She put her hand on a big book, and I said, "No, it's the little bitty one next to it." The freshman behind me snorted in derision. "You from southwest Georgia," he said, in the same tone that he would have used for, "You just crawled out of a sewer."

I turned. "How did you know?"

"Cause you said 'little bitty.' Nobody else talks like that except you people from southwest Georgia."

My new life was teetering even as it was beginning. Rural southwest Georgia had regurgitated me into a world where I was an oddity: crude, crass, uninformed about the basics of civility, defensive, and angry. I had no record of success to build on. In a land of low achievers, I was not even on the chart. I had failed in everything I ever tried. Now I was enrolled in a military college, and ahead of me stretched a midnight road with no white line.

I knew that the south was different from other parts of America. Our people were different, and there was much that could not be explained, only endured. I would always be from Edison, from that cruel, God-struck, sun-blasted corner of southwest Georgia. Even though I was a stranger in the land of my birth, I knew that the South did not release its children. My roots were there. My soul was nourished there. I would never get the red clay out of my shoes.

God damn it all to hell.

CPSIA information can be obtained
at www.ICGtesting.com
Printed in the USA
LVOW11s0956140317
527099LV00006BA/375/P